Being Christian

A Novel

Being Christian

A Novel

K. C. Boyd

Rebel Island Press

Being Christian - A Novel

ISBN (paperback): 9781662942013
eISBN: 9781662942235

For all who work to shine light on those who pervert religion for personal enrichment and fame; and especially to everyone who helped guide my research into Dominionism, Christian Zionism, and the personalities who are behind this dangerous element of American culture today.

Jesus said to his disciples: "Beware of false prophets, who come to you in sheep's clothing, but underneath are ravenous wolves."

Matthew 7:15

PART 1

Back to the Future

1

Temptation

June, 1984

CHRISTIAN SLIPPED THROUGH the back door of Ina's Beauty Nook. He closed his eyes to inhale the now familiar smell of gardenia laced with ammonia. Breathing in the heady mix, he reveled in the femininity of the shop.

"Ina! Anyone home?"

His exuberance was met with silence, save for the faint murmur of female jabberwocky that drifted back from the washroom.

"I-I-I-I-I-NA?"

"Pastor C? I kin hear ya. I ain't deaf yet, dagnammit!" Almost instantly, she was at his side, favoring his baby soft cheek with a kiss.

"Ain't you the early bird? How's about you keep your pants on while I finish Deena on up? Thar's a plate a ham an' pineapple samwiches an' a bowl a ambrosia settin' up in my office what's got your name on it. You ain't no stranger, so hep yourself." With feigned annoyance but an adoring smile, she muttered, "Comin' in early knowin' I won't be ready. I swear, he's a child what thinks the whole world revolves 'round him."

A weekly patron these past months—he had a standing appointment Wednesdays at two—Christian looked forward to these grooming sessions more than he probably should. Ina was right. He knew he'd be early today just like he knew Deena would be sprawled out up front in Ina's crackled vinyl chair, her head stretched back into the crook of a yellowing washstand, all the while her mouth flapped mindlessly away. He didn't mind that he had to wait. It was enough just to be here.

Christian was rarely in the mood for Deena's prattle, though, and today was no exception. He tiptoed past the adjoining doorway and crept quietly into Ina's office, unable to keep himself from directing a brief glance Deena's way. Simultaneously drawn to and repelled by her open thighs, he gave an involuntary shudder. Seems fat did that to a woman. No matter where, no matter when, the moment one of those doublewide bottoms made contact with a chair, the pearly gates would open wide. Despite Deena's age and homeliness, the allure of her netherland had an irresistible pull on Christian. Even now, with her neck so taut the veins looked fit to burst, the desire elicited by the unintended show made him do a double take, only to recoil ever more violently. It wasn't that he disliked her. After all, she was running back Fetch Brolly's mama, as well as a founding member of Christian's pulpit, Grace Be Thine Baptist Church. Still and all, everything about her upset his idea of womanhood, particularly in her current position.

Relieved to evade her notice, he turned his attention to the feast before him. As always, the mere sight of food triggered a powerful Pavlovian response in him, trumping all else.

Generously salivating, he heaped high his plate and quietly scurried back to the manicure station and his perch.

Christian had the bearing of a man much older than his twenty-three years. It might have been his imposing build, or maybe the way he commanded a room, but more than likely it was because life had been hard. Never having had reason to expect anything good, he had surprised himself and most everyone else in the small Texas town of Pearsall when, four years earlier, he made an abrupt right turn away from amorality and crime to morph into the revered pastor he was today. Only in the quieter moments, when he was alone with his thoughts, did he admit to being the religious pretender he knew himself to be. All other times, the communal outpouring of love and admiration directed his way was enough to convince him that his newborn sanctity was genuine.

A religious transformation as dramatic as Christian's might raise questions elsewhere. But come-to-Jesus experiences were common in these parts and, aside from his father, Mason, and his former "business" partner and lifelong nemesis, Luke Farley, no one gave it so much as a second thought. Additionally, a good salvation worked as justification for those whose own behavior caused the occasional religious hiccup. Conversely, a tale of repentance as dramatic as Christian's also had the power to prolong sin in others. The real truth about sinning is that as long as a man stays under the radar, he might as well enjoy himself for as long as possible. Salvation would always be there for the taking, right up to the last breath.

The moment Christian had wiped clean his slate, the night he'd found Jesus and Jesus him, he became part of something bigger than himself, something communal, and it felt good. Born a virtual orphan—his mother, Lynette, had been long out of her mind and his father was father in name only—Christian never knew parental love. As was his way, Mason promptly put bottle to mouth—his own, that is—on the day Lynette gave birth to his only son, and proceeded on out the door. For Mason, the newborn was just another symbol of the helpless hopelessness he knew as life.

As if to emphasize the reality that loss was to be Christian's sole inheritance, Lynette Hillcox departed the Earth by her own hand before he turned four. Of the shadowy memories he retained, none were of a loving mother but, instead, of a bleak withdrawn specter, the ghost of grief incarnate. Her death was sudden and in her passing she left behind the small boy to fend for himself.

And so it was. Father and son moved past death, coexisting in their separate universes. Once, Mason let slip that Christian had a blood sister somewhere in the world. If it were true, the little boy surely could have used her help. But he had no memory of her, though he later learned that the teen had fled the unhappy homestead well before his second birthday, never to be heard from again.

In those days and in that place, no one saw the need or gave a thought to calling in Social Services. After all, the boy had a nominal father, a roof over his head and a bed on which to place it, never mind that food was scarce, cruelty abundant, and affection nonexistent.

When Mason looked at his son, all he saw was the sorry product of one drunken night's ejaculation. Come Lynette's funeral, it took but one look at his wife's withered corpse for him to throw off the shackles of the needy child. Intent upon distancing himself emotionally and physically, he made a grand display of showering what limited paternal time and capital he

possessed onto an older, mean-spirited neighborhood tough—
Luke Farley—leaving Christian with the lesson that life held
pain and loss times two.

But that was in the past and what happened from here on
out belonged to the future. And from where he sat today, the
future looked bright indeed.

❖

Snapping plastic gloves from gnarled hands, Ina pushed damp
curls from her forehead and headed back to the manicure chair
into which Christian had comfortably settled his 210-pound
frame. His fair-skinned, dimpled arm did the job of a napkin
as he took a swipe at his sticky lips.

"Heavens to Betsy. Ina. One bite a your ambrosia an'
I declare, all worldly thoughts fly outta my head."

Like most middle-aged, nearly invisible women, Ina lapped
up praise whenever it came her way, no matter how small or
meaningless it was. And when it came from a pastor who was
two parts holy and one part arousing, she was helpless to stem
the excitement that stirred in places that felt foreign and oh-so-
long ago.

"Pastor C," she stammered, willing the red from her cheeks.
"'Tain't like you don't say the same damn thing—pardon my
French—no matter what 'tis I make an' that's the God's honest
truth."

With feigned but deliberate solemnity, Christian trained his
blue eyes on her and reached out to take her hand, whereupon
Ina's long abandoned heart did a sudden and joyful handspring.

"Ina, Ina, my sweet angel of the Nook. If I praise you, how
can I help myself? I declare, whatever you make, you must be

throwin' in a sprinklin' or two from the heavens above, that's all I can figure." He grinned large and gave her forearm a tender pat. "Promise me—no, swear it," whereupon he reached into his jacket and whisked out the pocket-sized Bible he carried, "Swear on this holy book you won't never change this here ambrosia, not one iota. 'Cause if you do, it'll be in full knowledge you're breakin' this one man's heart." Small flecks of marshmallow and bits of orange danced across his parted lips, detracting from the exaggerated air of dignity, sending her into paroxysms of laughter. She pushed him away with a playful slap, relieved to find her heartbeat returning to calmer territory.

As could be expected from a thirty-plus year career as a beauty operator, Ina had heard her fair share of sexual escapades. Nonetheless she couldn't help but wonder at the effect this slightly overweight and far too young preacher had on her. It was a mystery all right. No question theirs was a warm relationship, but he had that with a lot of his congregants. Truth be told, whenever he shined his charm-light upon her, it was like a swarm of butterflies took flight all at once from a forgotten place deep inside her.

She was a simple woman, leastways when it came to people. If a person treated her with kindness, she looked no deeper. That lack of curiosity was why she, and for that matter, so many in Pearsall, viewed Christian's cloak of outward joviality and religiosity as the measure of the man. The trouble with such blanket acceptance was that it kept people from seeing him for who he really was. Ina, for one, never imagined that this man upon whom she had so recently pinned her divine hopes was nothing more than the shell of a human being, a person utterly incapable of genuine human connection, even as he played the role of Good Pastor to perfection.

Motioning with his hands, he exclaimed, "Let's do it!" and almost simultaneously he let loose a deep, sulfuric belch, mugging "Shucks, a man's got a right to express himself, don't he?"

The burden of having to behave with grace at all times was wearing indeed. At least here at Ina's he could relax. Times like this it was safe to let his thoughts wander into dangerous territory, to ponder how much easier his life might have been had he been born female. But for as long as he could remember, his father had taunted him with slurs on his masculinity, so he quashed the thought as quickly as it appeared.

As Ina puttered about, Christian refocused on his hands— to how much stock he put into them, into his hands and the hands of others. One thing he knew for certain was that the hand of God didn't sport no oily grit underneath His nails the way Christian's used to. If Christian had a corporeal hang-up at all, it wasn't that his hair had begun to thin at an early age or that his waist was beginning to expand, it was with his hands.

Examining his nails before Ina began the work of buffing and shaping, he thought with satisfaction about how these ten pampered fingers were a reflection of his new self. The now soft, overly-tended-to hands that looked up at him were all the confirmation he needed of how far he'd travelled, a symbol of the seemingly overwhelming odds he had overcome.

In his adolescence, Christian's hands were perpetually scored with the black residue that comes from working on cars. Thick grease etched its way into the cracks and crevices of his dried-out palms, leaving him with nail beds so dark that no amount of Lava could ever make them clean. At least not clean enough for him to try his luck with the lovely young things whose supple bodies left him aching with desire. Back then, the pretty ones had nothing to do with him, football captain or not.

If he wanted release, he got by with the occasional dirt-tramp or, far more often, with his own greasy hand.

It had taken five years for Christian to scrabble up from the gutter to where he sat today, and the climb had aged him. Each time Ina performed this ritual soaking, it was with unspeakable wonder that he imagined seeing the sludge of his polluted past swirling round and round in the bowl of water before him. Funny. These same waters in which Christian celebrated the dissolution of his grimy past, Ina saw as sacred. In fact, Wednesdays at two had become the highlight of her week. To think that this newly venerated instrument of God had chosen her, well, it was without a doubt the finest thing to have ever come her way.

As for Christian, there was no question that he had come a long way. But even as he basked in the church's embrace, he had yet to receive so much as a nod from his father. If there was anyone on God's green Earth who knew, truly knew, how badly the deck had been stacked against him, it was Mason. Sadly, on the occasion their paths did cross, it took but a glance at Christian's gleaming, moon-shaped nails to invite the father's age-old vitriol.

"Lordy, Lordy! As I live an' die, if it ain't my son the preacher-lady, right here in the flesh, a-prancin' an' dancin' about with her purty little girlie nails!" Then his voice would darken.

"You shore as fuck better hope you *do* got the Lord on your side, else I know some good ole boys who'd like nothin' more'n ta show you what a *real* man does with his hands. 'N believe you me boy, it ain't got fuck-all to do with nail polish." At these moments, face-to-face with his father's unconcealed loathing, it took the strength of Job to keep from hurling him to the ground and beating the living daylights out of him.

❖

The squeak of rusty hinges sounded as Ina's backdoor swung open, admitting a woman the likes of which he'd never seen. She was nothing like Elena, the filthy tramp he left at home each morning, the sinner who shared his name but not his life. Nosiree, this one, she had it all, the whole package and that package, well, it damn near took his breath away.

She was all of five feet tall with every inch of her a carnal delight. Big blonde hair teased to the skies framed sultry eyes of dancing green. Full, lush lips held his gaze for a moment but it was her body that assaulted him with an inescapable force. He had never seen a woman more perfectly built to pleasure a man. Raw animalism oozed from her every pore and that animalism would have knocked him over were he not already seated. It was hard, sensual, and unapologetic.

Ina stepped in to break the spell, a spell she'd seen this woman weave far too many times before.

"Well, you *don't* say. As I live an' breathe, it's Darlene Steeger. Pray tell Missy, where in tarnation you been? I hain't seen hide nor hair of you in a month a Sundays an' you hadta know I'd be low on supplies."

Christian struggled for some kind of equilibrium, a nearly impossible task considering the thoughts that streamed live across his mind in throbbing, pulsing Technicolor. He hoisted himself from the chair, unconsciously releasing a slow, deep whistle whose libidinous message sounded out loud and clear. Extending a moist and creamy hand, he cut Ina off, summoning up what meager pastoral grace he could muster. Darlene placed her two sample cases at her feet and accepted his hand.

"John Christian Hillcox, Ma'am. *Pastor* Hillcox that is. I don't believe we've ever had the good fortune to meet. Folks who know me call me Christian or JC for short."

He was not a typically good-looking man but he had an air about him of late that very much seemed to appeal to women. Standing at six-foot-two, broad football shoulders led the eye away from a girth that was only just beginning to thicken. Delicate features were chiseled onto a smooth, porcelain-colored face that, despite a hint of pending roundness, gave off the unlikely combination of strength and kindness, a combination that was both unusual and compelling. A thick head of slicked-back hair, the color of wheat, and the wired spectacles he wore lent him the air of a learned man and its attendant respectability.

JoAnne Cayton, the bosomy salesgirl from Hazard's Big and Tall Shop, one town over, had done yeoman's work turning Christian into something of a pastoral clotheshorse. On his own he didn't know mauve from taupe much less silk from polyester, but that's where JoAnne came in. She'd chosen carefully, always steering him toward what flattered and, surprisingly, the fabrics and styles she selected had an almost mystical way of draping over his large frame, evoking a sense of solidity and grace. Although his new wardrobe had cost him upwards of three months' salary, the payoff had been enormous. JoAnne's unmitigated success in changing what was once a common looking man into one of substance, at least by South Texas standards, had imbued in him a credibility and sense of confidence he'd previously lacked.

"It's positively thrillin' to meet you, Pastor. My name's Darlene. Darlene Steeger. I been hearing a lot about you lately, seems wherever I go. There are some what call you the finest-talking man west a the Mississippi. Say you got magic where others only got words. As for me, I'm hardly what you'd call a church lady but I venture to say, lookin' at you, you might could turn me into one."

He eyed her with the kind of predatory delight that used to rule him before he turned to Jesus.

With her hand on one hip, Darlene leaned in to graze his arm with the other, sending a shockwave of want to his lower regions. An ache like he'd never experienced; it was powerful, all-consuming, and unavoidable. Peering up at him from beneath heavily lashed eyes, Darlene parted her glistening lips. With that, Ina saw Christian tremble and she knew where this would all end. As much as she might harbor her own private fantasies, she knew them to be just that—fantasies that would never bear fruit. When it came down to it, all she really cared about was Christian's well-being. Like most folks in town, she knew how unhappy he was trapped in a marriage he'd never wanted, and prayed that one day, somehow, he'd find happiness. She just wished it didn't have to have anything to do with Darlene.

"Darlene, if I was you, I'd watch out for this one." Ina issued a guttural snicker. "He might be a man a God but he's a man what could sweet talk a mama's nipple clear outta her baby's mouth."

So much for grace.

"Ina Mae. If only your talk was half as pretty as the resta you," he chuckled, tossing the insignificant bone her way.

"Y'see what I mean? Charms you the same time he's stickin' in the knife."

But Christian no longer heard Ina, so completely were his senses trained on Darlene. Self-consciously, he cleared his throat.

"Miss Steeger. What brings a fine lady like yourself through Ina's back door? Seems to me, you're a front door kinda woman if ever there was one. Classy, if you know what I mean." Darlene picked up one of her two ungainly sample cases, indicating her business with Ina, and Christian reached out to relieve her of it with a grand and sweeping gesture. He had business to conduct with her all right, and it didn't have anything to do with these here cases.

"Let me ease your burden, dear lady. Perhaps 'tis Bibles you carry?" he mugged.

"Bibles! Ain't that a hoot!" she snickered to a sullen-looking Ina. "Sorry to disappoint, Pastor, but alls I got in these here cases is hair dyes and the like. Ain't too much holy goin' on in my depths," she laughed throatily. "A beauty rep, from down San Antone, is all I am."

Ina had known Darlene for six or seven years, ever since Darlene took the job with Loretta's Beauty Supplies straight out of high school. Although she admired the scrabbling, hard-driving Darlene, she'd never been able to get past the stab of jealousy she felt in her presence. When Darlene was around, Ina and every other woman all but disappeared thanks to the bewitching effect she had on men, young or old. Why, even Ina's mangy ole husband Earle nearly wet his pants every time Missy Steeger came within twenty feet. The irony was that when it came to men, Darlene didn't give two hoots for any of them beyond having herself the occasional good time. As a girl, she'd never seen much good come from one; in fact it was always to the contrary. And so, from an early age, she vowed to never let a man control or bring her down: *Let 'em look, let 'em lust, let 'em bed me down every now and then, but no more.* Which was why she was surprised and more than a little disturbed by the discombobulation she felt in the pastor's presence. She fumbled purposefully through the larger of her two cases in an effort to get a grip on herself and, calling up her customary resolve, she turned her attention to Ina.

"Sweetheart, I apologize I hain't been round. Surely you know I meant to," and she bundled Ina up into a warm, effusive hug. "Thing is, Loretta's landed the account of a lifetime a coupla two weeks ago an' I ain't been up for air since. We got us a new product that's flyin' out the door fast as it comes in. I tell you this; when I bring it by, which I promise to do soon's we get s'more back in, I guar-un-tee it'll double your business," she winked, "as well as mine. You're gonna love me from here to next Christmas when you get your hands on what I got."

Simple words addressed to Ina, but Christian felt a stirring. Oh, to get his hands on what she got.

Times like this it wasn't easy to be a man of the cloth. One thing was certain. His pappy wouldn't think him light in the slippers if he knew the kind of thoughts his son was having about this tornado of a woman who'd just blown in the door. It was a sad commentary indeed that he would even think about Mason at a time like this, but Mason's poison was embedded in Christian like a bullet that can't be removed because doing so would kill the patient. It was never far from his mind.

Suddenly he trembled. Like a bolt of lightning, it came to him that his every thought was on full view to the Lord. He had far too much to lose this time around and, momentarily chastened, he squelched his desire. After all, it hadn't been all that long ago when, stripped bare of humanity, he had committed a crime so vile that, by all rights, he should be spending the rest of his life behind bars, if not lit up in the electric chair like a Christmas tree. Back then, in that darkest of hours when he had looked within his soul to find only evil, Christian had given himself to Jesus, vowing there and then that nothing on God's Earth would ever make him lose his way again.

But time passes, temptation resumes its rightful place and here he was, the presumably unassailable Christian, now an esteemed pastor, powerless to fight the lure of the flesh. The truth was that he could no more stop himself from wanting this woman than he could turn night into day. Being no one's fool, he knew this was no innocent conversation in which they were engaged. That quite simply he was playing hunter to Darlene, the irresistible prey, and that there was no blind in the world that could shield his intentions from her. Having come to understand that life would forever present temptation, he couldn't help but plead silently, *Why Jesus, oh why, have you not equipped me with the power to withstand this woman?* With no sign from above, he settled upon the path of the false innocent, telling himself she must have been sent to test him—a test he'd damn well better pass if he hoped to truly leave behind the terror of that haunting, crime-filled night not so long ago.

One more look her way and he knew he was drowning. *Sweet Jesus, where are you now?* he all but cried aloud.

The sound of slippered feet shuffling his way arrested his inner turmoil. Ina placed a small basin of warm, anointing water in front of him, into which Christian instinctively dipped his hands.

"Soak 'em, big man. I'll be back soon's I get Deena under the dryer." For one heart-stopping moment, he looked around and didn't see Darlene. Gripped by panic that she was nothing more than a fantasy, he recovered when she bounded back into the room, plateful of ambrosia and plastic spoon in hand. He felt his breath catch and hitched himself up and then, with his eyes, invited her to sit beside him. With Ina out of earshot and the devil perched on his shoulder, Christian began a dangerous dance with this lady of possibilities.

"My, my if you ain't the finest piece of pulchritude I ever laid eyes on," he crooned when, to his sudden dismay, he spotted a small diamond perched prettily upon her left hand. Jolted from the inevitability of the mating game, he cleared his throat and sat taller yet, hoping to conceal his disappointment.

"Married long?"

"Me? Married?" she snorted. "Hah! I only wear this to keep the ole farts off me."

Air rushed back in, refilling his lungs.

"I tell you Pastor, it's gotten so a gal can hardly leave home these days but for the rivers of testosterone runnin' down the street, that is, if you got any kinda looks at all. Like bees to honey they are, an' it's tiresome as all get out." Relishing the game as much as he, she readjusted her dress to reveal further hints of lushness. "But I don't wanna talk 'bout me. Tell me 'bout yourself," she asked, glancing at the ring on his hand. "Mrs. Hillcox know what kinda man she's got?"

"Does Mrs. Hillcox know what kinda man she's got?" he repeated. Sighing heavily, he answered, "My dear, I have to confess, she does indeed."

Here at Ina's, the vibrancy of this woman brought home the enormity of his entrapment in a way he'd never quite seen before. It wasn't just that his marriage was miserable. It was that, for the first time since turning to Jesus, he felt the tug of war between *his* old ways and *His* Way. Having once stared Hell in the face, Christian couldn't ignore the debt he owed God for giving him a second chance and he suspected he would not get a third. Besides, if he didn't behave honorably today,

Darlene would leave here thinking no better of him than she did of the others of whom she'd spoken with such disdain. Worst of all, he'd have to fear not only for his livelihood, but more importantly, for his very Salvation.

❖

Born into poverty and raised in an emotional vacuum, the only thing Christian had going for him was a golden tongue. Throughout his school years, his salvation came not from God but from his teachers, the only ones who made the effort to look past his noisome exterior. It didn't take long for the faculty at Calvary Elementary to see a boy, emotionally stunted though he was, with a creative and engaging mind, a mind accompanied by a quick and unusual wit. Call it intelligence, call it the art of persuasion or, more cynically, call it the ability to manipulate. Whatever it was, it was a gift whose power Christian was only just learning to appreciate.

When he reached high school, he joined Victory Baptist's football team, the Christian Warriors, and it was there that he saw how easy it was to bring others along to his way of thinking, at least when it came to football. At the time, they were little more than a rag-tag bunch of slackers with the inherent talent to move the ball across the field but not the motivation to do so. That is, until "Preacher Man," as his teammates promptly dubbed him, began to quote from the Bible: "The Lord announces victory, and throngs of women shout the happy news. Psalm 68."

Tell teenage boys high on testosterone that victory will send throngs of women their way, and they'll do whatever it is you ask. Read it from the Bible in as compelling a voice as possible and they'll follow you anywhere.

And so it was. Based on a marginally improved record, Coach Nagel recognized the value of Christian's verbal skills and in the spring of his junior year, he tapped him to become team captain for the coming fall.

The Warriors, much less Victory Baptist, had never experienced a wordsmith of Christian's caliber and, at least on the field, they were completely in his thrall. The team's record continued to improve and sure enough, the Lord's word prevailed, sending willing maidens their way. Having achieved a certain stature, Christian embraced his newfound voice and the powerful way it made him feel. Bible close at hand, he rarely missed an opportunity to bend his peers to his will and each time he succeeded, it was intoxicating. For the first time, he began to contemplate a future far from Pearsall, a future that had nothing to do with the likes of Stamper's Garage, where he toiled afternoons and summers, and even less to do with a life of Mason's rage, a rage he was forced to endure, night after hideous night as he fought to fend off his drunken, vicious father.

❖v

Darlene's sultry voice pulled him back from the darkness of his past.

"PastorMan," she cooed, "I don't usually find myself at a loss for words like I am right now. It's kinda shameful but I may as well come out an' say what I'm thinkin', brazen as it might be."

He quivered in anticipation.

"Y'see, we mighta jest met but I'm feelin' things I don't usually feel. Things I shouldn't let myself feel, what with you bein' a pastor and married to boot. I hope you believe me when I say this ain't my usual way. Somehow though, I find it thrillin' to see a strong man like you willin' to show his feminine side. You know, bein' in a beauty parlor an' all. I wonder, you do this often? Put yourself into a woman's hands, I mean?"

Every word this divine creature uttered seemed to carry a double meaning and it unsettled and titillated him at the same time. It was a kind of verbal jousting so unlike the angry silences of home to which he'd become accustomed.

"PastorMan," he murmured back. "I like how that sounds. 'Specially when you say it." Unable to control his manly reaction, he crossed his legs in an attempt to hide himself.

"Well, uh," he stammered, as he grappled for a semblance of dignity, "to answer your question Miss Steeger, the day I found my way to Jesus, I put myself not unto a woman's hands but unto those of The Almighty." He knew he was taking a big chance here, fully aware his holy talk might well put out the fire on this brief courtship, but the fear of being out there on his own without God momentarily trumped desire once again.

"Aw, that's hardly what I'm askin' and you know it!" she chortled.

"Let me put it another way," and he turned serious. "In the past, when I did put myself into a woman's hands, let's jest say it didn't exactly work out. Which is why when I found Jesus, I found home. Does that make any sense to you?"

"Christian, if I may be so bold as to call you that, did you ever stop to think you might find 'home' with a flesh and blood human being?"

He trembled. Somehow this woman with whom he'd spoken but few words had the capacity to overturn his world and everything in it and, Satan be damned, there wasn't a thing he could do about it. Afraid Ina would return at any moment, temptation overtook reason.

"Could I see you again? To talk is all. I mean, I know—I know that sounds a tired ole line to you but talking *is* what I do best an' you, it seems you were born to listen."

Smokey eyes, seductive and inviting, were all the answer he needed. She rose from her chair and slipped a card into his shirt pocket, the heat from her hand loosing a shockwave down his spine. Just then, Ina reappeared as Darlene bade them both goodbye. Without a backward glance she left, and apart from the two of them no one had witnessed the electricity that had pulsed through the room only moments ago. Just as no one knew of the promise that throbbed inside his pocket.

No one, that is, but God.

For the first time since he'd started coming to Ina's, Christian experienced none of his usual grooming pleasures. He knew where he wanted his hands to be and damn it to hell, it most certainly wasn't here at Ina's Beauty Nook. As primal feelings of abandonment washed over him, he considered the very real possibility that Darlene had been toying with him. For all he knew, the card in his pocket was that of a shampoo company, a ploy to evade him, just as she did the hordes of lecherous others. She could be on her way out of town and out of his life. During these agonizingly long minutes as Ina painted and polished, his hunger for this stranger was balanced by equal parts fear. How could he call himself a Christian, much less a leader of men, with the kinds of thoughts storming him right now?

What had begun as an ordinary day for the reconstituted Christian had suddenly turned into a mid-afternoon straddle across the chasms of Hell, Temptation beckoning from the left, and Submission on the right.

He retreated into himself, searching for the justification to see her again. Once again, the magic of rationalization resurfaced as he told himself that their meeting had not been a random one. That the stronger a man's walk with the Lord, the greater the influence he wields over others, the more determinedly the Devil would fight to bring him down, all of which might mean that Darlene's visit had been a visit from Lucifer himself.

Unwilling to accept her as the Devil in drag, he shook off the image and rather than thinking such a demonic thought, he told himself once again that she'd been sent to him as a test. If that were so, as it had to be, then surely Christian was meant to meet with her again, and this time alone. Only when he demonstrated free will in resisting Darlene without the benefit of Ina's or anyone's supervision, could he prove himself. And you never could tell. Perhaps the next time he would find the words to save Darlene from her liberated, un-Christian self that, if left unchallenged, would lead to her certain eternal damnation. And since he had been put on Earth to harvest as many lost lambs as possible before the ultimate day of reckoning, it was clear there was no soul in the world more worth saving than that of Miss Darlene Steeger, provided she had not played the cruelest joke of all and vanished from his life forever.

With the final coat of polish complete and a small heave up out of the chair, juices flowing and heart pounding, Christian doffed an imaginary hat to Ina.

"Thanks ol' girl. That'll do for today. I'll look out for you 'n Earle on Sunday. Blessings to you both." Then he quickly bee-lined out the door. Once there, he thrust a hand into his pocket, sending ripples of destruction across his newly gleaming nails—a sacrilege of its own—to retrieve the blessed business card from his pocket. Praise Jesus, it was no shampoo handout after all but that of

Darlene Steeger, Beauty Consultant
Loretta's Beauty Supplies
Lubbock, Texas
806-444-6666
"Dyeing to be Beautiful — That's Loretta's!"

2

Heaven in the Backseat

September 10, 1976

OFF THE FIELD AND AWAY from the locker room, Christian remained a social outcast, particularly when it came to the opposite sex. He might be today's team captain but high school girls with marriage on the brain saw a boy with no future, destined to follow in the drunken footsteps of his mean-spirited, abusive, raging father.

Christian's teammates, the same boys who feted him on the field, had little to do with him when the games were over. At the same time that he yearned for their approval he understood why he'd never fully have it. At the end of the day, he was alone, lonely, and, in his mind, deservedly undesirable.

Elena Escamilla, a Mexican illegal and Luke Farley's cousin—the same Luke his father had anointed surrogate son many years before—had arrived in Pearsall several months earlier to stay with the Farleys. Like so many, she came with hopes of finding permanent refuge in America. Not exactly fair of face, she knew how to use her sexuality—and use it she did. Given time, she felt certain she'd seduce some boy or other into marriage, and thus gain her citizenship, but to date there had been no takers. With the clock ticking, she held her nose one Friday night and strutted slowly and intentionally past the night's postgame huddle. She had already tasted most of their wares. Time was running out.

"Preeeecher Man, usted desea cogerme?" she beckoned. He didn't have a clue what she'd said but lustily realized it was directed at him. The obscene gestures she telegraphed with her pelvis accomplished their intended effect and, tail tucked not quite between his legs, though most definitely wagging, he scurried to her and then the parking lot, eagerly heading to his car.

Holding open the door in what could only be construed as a courtly manner, Christian perceived Elena looking at him with what seemed to be desire. Of course, Christian couldn't know that the longing he saw in the dark flash of her eyes was attributable not to the promise he carried between his legs but to her recently expired green card and the announcement that Luke's family would soon send her packing. Need clouded vision, leaving him to see what he wanted to see: a fiery young woman who would have him, background and all. Una nina traviesa willing to overlook his grease-stained hands, work-roughened skin, and impoverished circumstances, if only for a night of pleasure.

Once they settled in the front seat, Christian held up a bottle of cheap tequila he'd purchased earlier that day. "May I offer you some liquid refreshment?" She raised a jet-black eyebrow and, grazing his hand, wordlessly took the bottle. Throwing back her head, she took a long, deep drink. Damn, this was his kind of woman! No talk, at least not in English, and he could ignore the Spanish. *Fuck yeah*, he thought. *This here's the time for the international language of love if ever there was.* They took turns swigging from the bottle when, in a sudden burst of sexual energy, he revved the engine and took off, headed straight for the highway, the car's speedometer rocketing skyward the instant he hit the on-ramp. Times he was excited or pent up, fast driving served as a potent release.

Elena muttered in a tequila-thickened voice, "Donde estamos que van?"

Taking a stab at what she said, he whooped, "We're on the highway to love, my little chihuahua."

"Preecher Man, tambien rápido! Me asustan! Podemos ir mi casa? Mi tio ees un hombre malo," She pointed frantically back toward the direction they had come.

"Calm yourself Chiquitita. Only thing I unnerstand a what you said is 'mi casa.'" He continued to drink and by now, his words were muddling together.

"You wanna go mi casa? Okay. We go yore casa." Excited laughter punctuated the air. "It don't make me no never mind where we do it just so long as we do it, lonnnnng and dirty." He sniggered, knowing full well that she didn't understand a word he'd said. A few minutes later, the Chevy screeched to a halt on the curb opposite her uncle's—and Luke's—house.

These days, he seldom came face-to-face with the delinquent but he was reminded far too often of the bond that remained between Luke and his own father. Tonight though, he determined to empty his mind of all thoughts Luke-ian so as to revel in the all-over boozy want that overwhelmed him. Sliding across the seat, he slapped a scaly hand onto Elena's upper thigh and slowly, he inched his way upward until he found the nirvanic bull's-eye he was after.

The evening's sexual promise carried with it, as well, the bonus of a small but symbolic blow against Luke. However drunk Christian was, he retained enough presence of mind to telegraph a certain revenge Luke's way.

Unbidden, thoughts of Mason appeared to pierce his sexual balloon. Watch me now Paps, he thought. Watch your so-called faggot of a son deliver the goods; goods you ain't never thought I got. So how's 'bout while I'm fuckin' this spic here, you go fuck yourself and that goes for Luke too, motherfucking sons of bitches.

"Vayamos," Elena coaxed, banishing all thoughts of Mason as one after the other, they tumbled onto the blanket-covered backbench of the two-door Malibu. Through a sexual haze, Christian found himself salivating at the sight of her already bared breasts spilling across her chest, two copious melons aglow in the moonlight. She pushed him down onto the seat and climbed atop. He felt hot hands tear at his zipper. Clearly practiced, she reached inside and grabbed onto his manhood and, finding it rock hard, pinned him in place on the torn upholstery. Tearing at his pants, skirt lifted high, she mounted him in one easy motion.

"Praise Jesus!" he yelped as, rocking up and down, she rode him so skillfully that it never occurred to him that he was not the one in control. Far too quickly he erupted, his dazed mind still inside her, wanting more, wanting much, much more. As if reading his mind, she traced her fingers across his skin in easy anticipation of a second round. "Sweet Lord," he whimpered, his eyes squeezed tight as she mounted him once again.

So steeped in pleasure was he that he didn't hear the crunch of footsteps on gravel. Only when the car door burst open and he felt the hard, cold press of steel against his forehead, did they stop.

"What the fuck!" Christian exploded.

The night was devil black and, for one last moment, the only thing Christian comprehended was Elena's warmth. It took a further prod of the shotgun for him to understand the seriousness of the situation. Throwing her off, he struggled to an upright position to find himself face-to-face with none other than Buck Farley, Luke's blood father. When Farley-the-Elder began to speak, the fog of drink melted away as quickly as Christian's erection.

"Well, well, well. What *do* we got here?" Buck-o sneered. "Looks like it's ol' Mason's boy doin' the dirty right cheer on my sister's only-born. Mm-mmm. If I was a bettin' man, I'd put dollars to dimes Elena's padre ain't gonna take kindly when I tell 'im that a piece a white trash had his way with his baby girl. An' I will. Tell 'im, that is. An' m'boy, you best trust when I say you don't wanna make Miguel angry cause believe you me, you *don't* wanna make Miguel angry. Ain't that right, Elena?"

On cue, a teary Elena spoke as if from a pre-written script, "No diga mi padre, por favor."

Sniggering, Buck pushed the tip of his gun into the boy's forearm. "My lil niece here, she agrees. Says we best not tell her pappy." Dramatically, he pushed back his hat to expose a scar that began at the hairline, extended across the left side of his face until taking a ninety-degree dive downward, ending clear at the bottom of his jaw.

"What're ya lookin' at, boy? Y'ain't never seen my beauty mark afore? S'a present from my purty little niece's padre. Which is why I'm thinkin' we best put our heads together an' find ourselves a way outta this sitch-e-ation else I don't wanna think what might could happen." As addled as Christian was, Buck's meaning came through loud and clear.

"Sir, we was havin' some fun is all. I didn't hurt her or nothin'," when again, as if pre-scripted, Elena started to cry. She rubbed her arm as if to suggest pain even though she purportedly didn't comprehend a word of what Buck was saying. Christian heard the panic rise in his voice. "I promise Mr. Farley, I'll do right by her, I swear. Whatever it takes. I promise. In the name of Jesus, I swear it." Beads of fear-scented perspiration glistened off his still naked body. Buck glanced over at Elena, who by now had covered herself with the dirty felt blanket that only moments ago had doubled as their bed linen.

"Damn fuckin' straight you'll do right by her though I don't hardly think Jesus is got fuck-all to do with it," he sneered. He let the gun drift south of Christian's navel, then slowly, deliberately, he brought the barrel back up to the boy's skull.

"Fer now, how 'bout we wait-see if'n the rabbit dies? In the meantime, you best be sayin' them prayers boy."

Buck withdrew the gun and ran his hand across its rim until he located the jagged edge he'd been meaning to file down. Drawing his thumb across the sharp metal, he watched a thin trickle of blood run down his finger. He reached into the car and seized Christian's hand, slicing into the boy's thumb with the gun's edge. Then grasping the boy's bloody digit, he pressed his own to Christian's in something resembling a blood ritual.

"Let's call what we got goin' here a blood oath, boy. Meanin' there ain't no way outta marryin' my niece if you gone 'n knocked her up." He stood upright, and a sliver of moonlight cast his scar in partial shadow, rendering him ever more sinister.

Buck let loose a piercing, demonic howl. "Ahhhh-ooooooh." The chill silence that echoed back at them filled the night air with an ominous sense of dread.

"Ain't this somethin'?" he added glibly. "To think we might could be kin, an' soon. Shit happens, I declare." With an exaggerated stage-shudder, he stalked off and, wiping his hand on the side of his pants, muttered loudly enough for Christian to hear.

"Fuck me sideways if I don't know where that hand jest was."

What the naïve Christian couldn't know was that his hot Mexican cowgirl was already two months with child when she took him for the ride of his life. Or that those few brief moments of nirvana were to cost him the next nine years of his life. It was a journey from heaven to hell in the flash of an eye.

❖

The next morning, Christian awakened to a real-life nightmare. There was Buck Farley outside his bedroom window, a'chawin' an' spittin' away as he leaned flat back against a half-dead oak, Elena slumped lazily at his side. Christian jumped from bed and hurried on out in the hope of heading off an encounter between Mason and Buck, on the off chance that Mason was at home and conscious.

This time, Buck had come bearing news and no shotgun. There was no need.

"Howdy nephew!"

The two poison-arrow-words arced through the air, ugly in their intent and meant to destroy. Poison-arrow-words that struck with life-altering accuracy.

"Yessiree Chester. Yore rabbit gone done an' died! Jest like I 'spected 'twould. Fertile Myrtle here's gonna make you a pappy. Imagine that. The Farley's an' the Hillcoxes is goin' to be kin. Ain't that sumpin'?"

Christian's stomach dropped out from under when, feeling himself to be outside his own body, he saw the future disappear and his heart turned to stone. Ignorant in the ways of procreation and too naïve to see the duplicity in it all, he didn't know that no "rabbit" could live or die in the space of twelve hours. What he did know was that he was trapped, plain and simple, and that somewhere in his deepest parts, he'd expected nothing more. A lifetime of disappointment and loss left him with no fight.

Farley, for his part, savored the moment. He never cared much for the Hillcoxes, had always scorned the relationship between Mason and his son and, quite frankly, didn't give a goddamn about his niece, that is as long as she got the hell out of his house. Still and all, it was amusing that these two feuding families were soon to be joined in wedlock.

He chuckled. "Aw now, don't go frettin' yourself none. You might could look on this as a good thing. After all, yer gonna be a pappy! What d'ya say to us settin' the happy day right here and now? We wouldn't want Miguel's baby girl showin' the world she's got a bun in the oven when she takes her walk down the aisle, would we? *That* would hardly be Christian."

Utterly defeated, the ghost of Christian Hillcox nodded in assent.

"It'd pleasure me greatly to take on the weddin' arrangements, yore not havin' a mama an' all. Give me the warm fuzzies knowin' I'm the one what keeps the worry from you. After all, this here's a special time in a man's life an' I figger it's my time to step up to the plate. Call me a scout leader lookin' out for the newest member of his troop, s'all," his ugly sarcasm bleeding through.

"How's 'bout we make your backseat romp official, what d'ya say, two weeks from t'morrow? That way, you lovebirds kin git settled afore the baby comes. Boy, you take care a the license an' the blood tests an' I'll do the rest. Hell, ya never know. I might even spring for a cake."

With no need for an answer, he tut-tutted away sounding more like someone's old Victorian aunt than the backwater Texas hillbilly that he was. As if in afterthought he turned back, "Feel free to ask your pappy to join the festivities now, y'hear? T'ain't every day a man gets to watch his son strap on the ol' ball an' chain."

With that, he was gone, the tune of La Cucaracha trailing in his wake.

3

Do You Take This Woman?

September 25, 1976

ON THE LAST SATURDAY in September, John Christian Hillcox and Elena Maria Escamilla stood across from each other inside a small, dilapidated chapel at the New Bethlehem Baptist Church, a gnomish, pallid man with overlong-yellowed fingernails officiating. Three witnesses were in attendance: Buck, Luke, and Christian's sole friend, Cal. Luke had come for the laughs; Mason hadn't, having declined the invitation with a great yelp of laughter. Ashamed for Coach to witness his shame, Christian had left him off the list.

Despite the ill-fated significance of the day, Christian arrived at the chapel looking very much the groom. Owning nothing proper to wear, he was spared nuptial humiliation when Cal graciously stepped in to loan him a suit for the occasion. Cal, who still had plans to leave Pearsall upon graduation.

Westward-ho, oh Christian groom. Today's ensemble was of deep chocolate brown, save for a butterscotch colored, faux-suede placket and three rows of white chain-stitching that traveled the length of the jacket, ending in arrow points. Wide lapels and a pointed collar bespoke the fashion of the day, as did the smart, silver snap closures. The costume would have been an ordinary Texas call-to-church suit but for the leather and sterling silver bolo tie that hung from his neck. In the bleakest of hours, this beautiful icon was his only connection to anything good.

Elena didn't look half bad either—Christian gave her that. Her dress was a wink at virginal white save for the few brightly colored embroidered flowers that danced across the hem. Not intended to reveal, it very much did, her lush breasts impossible to contain. Even the memory of shotgun-to-head couldn't quash his desire to reach out and grab the two ripe fruits set to explode from her gown. Atop her head rested a veil of coarse white lace, Elena's black hair tumbling out from underneath. A fan held deliberately in front of her mouth concealed cigarette-stained teeth, rendering her momentarily alluring. With God as his witness, Christian was helpless to control the animal down below.

❖

The day he went in to tell Coach Nagel he was leaving school, Coach looked at him with deep sadness. There was nothing he could say to redirect the needle on this overplayed record, a tune he had heard far too often and always to ruinous outcome. In a halfhearted effort to conceal his despair, he spoke.

"Christian, that you of all boys let this happen makes me sorrier than you can know. I have come to care for you, son, I really have. Funny thing—I thought you'd be one a the few to make it outta here, but now— Do me a favor, will ya? Before you leave tomorrow, come by my office. There's something I want to give you."

The next morning, Christian stood outside the athletics office for much longer than he realized, delaying the irrevocable severance. Finally, he knocked on the door and entered to find Coach sitting at his desk, a far-away look on his face. Neither coach nor captain had gotten much sleep the night before.

Coach rose. "Christian, you haven't been outta my thoughts since yesterday." To think that Christian would occupy anyone's thoughts, much less those of a man he admired as much as he did Coach, seemed a good deal more than he deserved.

"Much as the situation saddens me, I want you to know that I respect your doin' what's right and proper by the girl. I wish it didn't have to be this way, I really do. Wish you'd a thought to protect yourself, but what's done is done an' now, there's a life at stake. A life what'll need a father as well as a mother. As I'd have expected of one of your character, you've stepped up to the plate and shown your colors as a true Christian. An' that, my boy, is no small thing.

"I'm gonna say somethin' now that might surprise you. To some degree, it even surprises me. Y'see, I've come to care for you a great deal more than I have most other students. So much so that, in many ways, I've come to see you as the son I never had. That said, I hope you choose to stay in my life but I'm no fool. I know how things go. People get busy and then—"

Christian stood silent. No one had ever spoken this kindly to him before.

"Christian, no matter whether or not we stay in touch, I want you to promise yourself you'll find a way to finish your schoolin'. Or at the very least, get your G.E.D. If you see your way to doin' that, things can still turn out for you. Get yourself a night job an' use the days mindin' the baby while your wife works. Or vice versa. Jest do whatever it takes. There's so much promise in you, it near ta kills me see it go up in smoke all because a one night you didn't keep your dick in your pants. Y'see, I believe in you. Always have. From the first day we met."

Unashamedly and with unbridled emotion, Coach rifled through the clutter on his desk and, with a sense of ceremony, picked up a long, slim box.

"This here's something I want you ta have. It's been in my family for generations an' I always thought I'd give it to my own son one day. But since Esme and me faced up to the fact she'll never bear us any babies, I haven't known what ta do with it. That is till yesterday." He stopped to wipe his eyes with a dirty handkerchief retrieved from his pocket.

"Christian, it'd mean the world to me if you'd accept this gift as a token of what I feel for you. Maybe you'd even consider wearin' it on your wedding day. Then one day, when you have a son a your own, you can continue my family's tradition and pass it on down to him."

Christian was staggered as much by Coach's words as he was by the tears that flowed openly down the man's cheeks. He'd hardly seen a man cry before, much less from emotion, and he didn't quite know what to do so he remained silent.

"One more thing," Coach added. "It's important you know I'll always be prayin' for you. Prayin' like any man would pray for his son. I'll be prayin' that the times you think of me, you'll remember the love an' respect I have for you no matter where you are. Most important, I'll be prayin' you leave your heart open to Jesus because, in the end, He's all we got. Don't you go believin' if anyone tells you otherwise."

The truth was, it was precisely for young men like Christian that Coach had chosen to dedicate his life to working with disenfranchised youth, and to do so through sports. At best, he might have rescued a handful of throwaways—boys who, through the randomness of birth, had entered the world with no chance for success. For a troubled teen to know that Coach Nagel was there for him, be it with a firm if not always welcome sense of discipline, a warm shoulder or a small kindness not found at home; those times affirmed the path Coach had chosen in life. A native of Pearsall himself, he knew most of the families in town, knew who had trouble at home and usually how bad the trouble was. Instinctively, he also knew when to intervene and when not to. It didn't always work out the way he planned, but when it did, the salvation was as dear to him as the lifeblood that was his faith. When it went bad, like it had now, it was impossible not to see it as a personal failure.

At eighteen, Christian found himself to be the recipient of the first act of unconditional love in his life, and rather than deal with its emotional aspect, he focused exclusively on the gift. When Coach held the box out to him, he momentarily forgot about the downward plunge his life had taken as he surrendered to the wonder of what was inside the box. Gingerly cradling it, he shook it back and forth, up and down, puzzled by its near-weightlessness, wondering what could possibly mean so much to Coach.

When he could hold off no longer, he lifted the lid. Inside, nestled on a bed of soft cotton, sat a bolo tie. Not just any bolo tie. It was, without question, the most beautiful thing Christian had ever seen. He fingered its two braided cords, each one tipped with a point of gleaming sterling. Midway up, the cords were drawn together by an intricately designed silver slide; an ornately worked medallion in the image of Christ rising up from the water. Monetary value aside, the gift was the closest thing to a fatherly gesture he'd ever experienced. The history in this box was one in which Christian played no part. Even with what Coach had said, it made no sense. No sense at all. But here it was. Unable to put a stopper on his feelings, he threw his arms around the good man, wishing only that he'd never have to let go.

❖v

In his early years, school was Christian's refuge. When, in the second grade at East Baptist Elementary, he learned about Redemption and Salvation, he found both ideas to be exhilarating and magical. The catch was that, before he could be saved, he had to first know Jesus. Because wishing doesn't make things so, try as he might, he could never quite convince himself that he felt the spirit. By the sixth grade, he was so desperate to join the club of believers that he abandoned truth and announced to one and all that, at long last, he'd finally received the Holy One. Even though this was patently false, Christian made the decision to proclaim it into being. Unfortunately, where the psyche is concerned, truth *does* matter.

To the naked eye, Christian was but another child of poverty and neglect, but when his teachers got to know him they no longer saw him that way. In fact, it was at East Baptist that his extraordinary talent with the spoken word was first noticed. Together with his surprisingly quick mind, he earned the respect of his teachers, if not his peers, enough so that, by fourteen, he walked through the front door of Victory Baptist High School with a fragile air of confidence.

By now, he had come to see that oftentimes, when he spoke, people listened—and that they listened even more closely if he used a verse or two of Scripture to emphasize a point, something he'd begun to do with increasing frequency. Although he'd never experienced a genuine religious feeling in his life, he had a good memory and enough Baptist training to easily call up a verse or two when the circumstances were right. Before long, he found himself purposefully twisting things so that Scripture was precisely what was called for. Pimply-faced Baptist football players, spellbound by a seemingly bottomless font of biblical and often carnal knowledge, were easily taken in by the teen's natural and convincing delivery. On the field and in the locker room, Christian was the man of the hour, the pride of Victory Baptist. Socially though, he remained off a beat, the reality of intimacy as elusive as ever.

When in the summer before his senior year, Coach Nagel tapped Christian as captain for the upcoming season, the possibility of winning an athletic scholarship and a way out of Pearsall loomed large. As exhilarating as this was, even more satisfying was the grudging, if short-lived, respect the appointment evoked from his father.

Mason was flat on his back underneath Wayne Deters' tractor, his hands deep inside the vehicle's inner workings. His mind registered the ringing of a telephone but, puttering mindlessly along, he paid it no notice, at least until Rory Stamper burst out of his office cubbyhole, whooping and hollering.

"Son-of-a-bitch Hillcox! Git yoreself up from under that there vee-hicle! Wait'll you hear this. Nagel jest named yore son Cap'n a the Warriors. Ain't that the fuck-all?"

Mason stood stock still but for his jaw, which opened wide in astonishment.

"Tell you what we're gonna do," Rory exclaimed, "You an' me, we're gonna have ourselves a cel-e-bra-tion, that's what we're gonna do!" With that he pulled a bottle of amber-colored liquid out from behind his back. "Wadda you say to our knockin' off the rest a the day and havin' ourselves some a this? Deters' tractor kin wait!"

Unaccustomed as Mason was to praise, all the more if it had to do with his son, he tried to wrap his mind around the news. Fuck, he scarcely knew the boy, but Cap'n of the football team? That *was* something. *On the other hand*, he thought, *if Christian got* any *athletic ability, it sure as fuck came from me* when, all at once, a false bravado rushed in to fill the void that, in other fathers, would have been a sense of pride.

"Yeah. Don't surprise me none," Mason offered with feigned nonchalance, rising from up underneath the tractor. "My boy, he's a Hillcox after all. Like father, like son, I say. An' if'n yore offerin' up drink in the middle a the day, you ain't gotta ask me but once an' that's the far-fuckin' truth."

A man of no conscience, not even subliminal, Mason suffered no qualms in stepping up to take credit for Christian's surprising achievement. With boundless emotional dishonesty, it wasn't even a stretch for him to don the mantle of genetic donorship now that it enlarged him. Still, he couldn't help but think they'd named his boy captain on account of his preachy talk and not for his athletic prowess. It had to be. His son was a faggot of an athlete if he was anything, but he and his fancy Bible bullshit could sweet-talk the scent out of a skunk, need be.

Rory grabbed a couple of half empty coffee tins and poured the remaining dregs down the floor drain. As one, they looked with fevered desire at the stream of liquid gold filling their cups. Mason's feeble brain continued to wonder at his son's ability but only until the magic of drink took over, letting him roll first into the bourbon and second into the illegitimate role of proud Papa.

"Like I always say," he boasted, "It don't surprise me none. A chip off the ol' block that's m'boy. Ya know, I was quite the athlete myself in my day. So fuck no, 'tain't no surprise t'me." Rory raised an eyebrow in answer, knowing full well that Mason had never spoken highly about his son before, much less about any athletic prowess in the family.

In no time, they put the first bottle of Black Jack to bed and midway through the second, Mason muttered, "I'm outta here. Mebbe go out carousin' with the Cap'n t'night. Fuck yeah. That's what I'll do. We two ain't never done a night out an' it's time I see what he's made of when it comes ta the womenfolk. Always seemed kinda fruity ta me, but hey, now he's Cap'n—" He let the thought go unfinished and, with a swipe of oil-stained hands onto grime-stiffened pants, he lumbered across the transom of the open garage door.

"Prreeeeeciate the drink." A groan from the besotted Rory was his only farewell.

Christian and Cal were sprawled across the front steps when Mason slammed his car into the curb. Climbing out, he whooped, "Cap'n a the Warriors! Fuck yeah! I declare, you take after yore pappy," winking at Cal. Christian recognized the drink, but not the pride, in his father's voice. When Mason reached the steps he extended a hand to his son, who instinctively pulled back, conditioned as he was for abuse rather than for anything remotely congratulatory.

"Think you might could gander to a night out tonight, jest the two a us, son?" To hear this man call him "son" was miracle enough to rival the Second Coming. But coming late as it did, satisfying though it was, it meant little. There was a time he would have jumped at an invitation from his father, but no more. The truth was, he couldn't stomach the thought of a night of boozing with the old bastard and so for once, he was the one to decline.

"Sorry Paps, but I'm hangin' with Cal tonight. Some other time."

Mason shrugged, his embryonic paternal feelings all but gone. "Have it your way—whatever way you like it, that is," a hint of nasty innuendo bleeding through. He trundled indoors to heat up a TV dinner before heading out for another round of whatever he could get.

❖v

Two months later, when Buck Farley's rabbit put an end to hope, Christian told his father to retire his false pride and in that instant, he saw the flash of cruel pleasure dance across Mason's face. Truth be told, disdain was the only emotion Christian was comfortable with anyhow.

"Whoop-de-do," Mason laughed. "What a surprise. You gone an' fucked up again, you low-life piece a shit. Shoulda known better than ta think you could do somethin' in your sorry-ass life ta make a man proud. They let yer girly ass be Cap'n—give a piece a white trash like you somethin' ta make a man proud, an' you cain't hold to it fer life. Yer one sorry fuck is what you are. Tell the truth, I never did figger why they picked you in the first place. Knew all along it hadda be on account a yer faggoty bible talk what sucked 'em in. So tell me this, Chris*tine*. Where's your holiness got ya now, ya fruitcake bible thumper? Like I say, there's an asshole born every minute. Too bad this one shares my name.

"Gotta say, you're throwin' me a real curve ball here. Never woulda thought you had the stones to knock a girl up, wetback or not. I tell you this Chris*tine*, if you come here today lookin' for hep, all I got ta say is fuck off."

In his failure, Christian had given his father something far more precious than his short-lived success ever had. Mason didn't care a whit that his son had impregnated a girl. It didn't matter that he was no longer captain of the Warriors or that he wouldn't finish school. Unlike most fathers, Mason didn't possess the instinct to wish for a better life for his son. If what Christian had to look forward to was a lifetime of drink and despair, then so be it. Maybe then he'd understand how hard life was meant to be.

4

Good vs. Evil

February 1977

CHRISTIAN AWOKE MOST mornings with two colossal appetites. With open disgust, Elena dealt with the first, and Reba's Down Home Cooking tended to the other. A man could die satisfied once he'd tasted Reba's biscuits. Split down the middle, the flaky wonders were doused with her family recipe, red-eye gravy. Two eggs fried up in salty butter, their runny yolks trailing dangerously close to a side of home fries, completed a breakfast that was sure to get any man through his morning. In an otherwise joyless life, he took his pleasures where and when he could.

In a Freudian irony characteristic of small, inbred towns, Christian found work at Mason's former place of employment, Stamper's Garage. Christian ran into Rory late one night at the pool hall, where Rory explained that he'd finally tired of Mason for good, on account of his showing up so hung over one morning he'd stripped clean the gearbox on Nip Wilson's truck cab, costing Rory upwards of two thousand dollars. Rory would've gone after Mason for the money if he thought he had a chance in hell of recouping it. Grudgingly, he accepted the loss, satisfied to send the drunkard packing.

Over the years, days when Mason was sleeping off a bender, Christian took his place at Stamper's Garage after school and in the summers. Rory had always liked the boy and, believing father and son to be cut from different cloth, he offered Christian his father's job right there on the spot. Already two months behind on rent, Christian jumped at the offer, as much for the desperately needed income as for the sucker-punch it was sure to deliver his father.

Days now found Christian mired in the greasy gloom of his past, eking out a living, painfully aware that destiny was leading him down the only path ever really open to him. Genetically based or not, nights saw him turning to the bottle and frequenting whorehouses in nearby towns where he would eagerly spend his wages on flesh far more willing than Elena's. While life wasn't near as bad as it had been in his youth, money was scarce and happiness nonexistent.

Christian lived with Elena in a rented shack on the wrong side of the tracks—the side he'd been accustomed to all his life. By this time, she was six months pregnant and, the promise of citizenship pocketed, openly hostile to her new groom. She had a hot meal on the table most nights, his clothes were clean and he benefited from the obligatory morning tune-ups, but otherwise there was nothing to recommend his life. Husband and wife shared only their dislike of each other and of the fetus growing ever bigger in her expanding belly. Aside from their animal couplings, Christian was more alone than ever.

Things improved marginally the night he brought home the television. One morning on his way in to work, he chanced to spot a beat-up Motorola junked by the side of the road. Growing up poor, it was natural for him to pull over and retrieve it, if only for its parts. At the garage he used his break-time and innate skills to perform successful mechanical surgery. When he finally flipped the switch and a clear picture materialized he couldn't help but to take pride in his success and began to anticipate Elena's reaction when he hauled it into the house after work.

Aside from two tightly wrapped, aluminum-foil-tipped antennae, the TV was as good as new when he presented it to Elena that night. You'd have thought he'd handed over the keys to a brand new Cadillac, the way she carried on, all the more curious since she still spoke but a smattering of English. Yet from the moment the television entered the house, the set was switched on, its incessant drone lending the house an illusion of life—an illusion that vanished the night he returned home to find her in a pool of blood.

The pallor of her skin and shallowness of breath telegraphed the seriousness of the situation and he knew that if he were to save her, decisive and immediate action was called for. No matter that he despised her with every breath of his being—here he was, on the short side of nineteen, forced to choose whether a human being would live or die.

Overwhelmed by the divine role thrust so suddenly upon him, he was at the same time excited by the feeling of power that surged from within. This moment, he knew, might be the only opportunity he would ever have to free himself of Elena—and he threw it away. Calling up what would prove to be the end of conscience for him, he reached for the phone and called for an ambulance. While he waited for what seemed an eternity but was in reality only minutes, he trained his eyes on the rise and fall of her chest, each tortured breath coming further and further apart. In a last act of decency, he jumped up, fetched a tarp from out back of the house and threw it, along with her limp, bloodied body, onto the backseat of the car. With reckless abandon, he tore a scar across the narrow country roads, the devil at his back, reaching the hospital in minutes.

Upon their arrival, the impersonal medical machine kicked in, delegating him to a waiting room where worried families huddled, each one seemingly more distraught than the others. Feigning a look of concern, Christian settled in for the siege.

Day after day, night upon night, he stayed at the hospital, first in the hospitality room, ultimately at Elena's bedside, where he bore witness to the grotesque battle her body waged with itself, all the while his emotions raced up and down like a roller coaster out of control. The times he sensed the imminence of her demise corresponded directly with an unspoken fantasy of escape, just as the moments when she rallied would strangle him with an anxiety so intense the nurses would come running to soothe what they took to be the grieving husband.

Not once did he think of the baby who struggled inside her, and so he was genuinely surprised when, on the third day, a pretty young nurse came to him, the look of the Grim Reaper darkening her lovely features.

"Mr. Hillcox, Ah'm so terribly sorry to have to tell you this, but your wife lost the baby."

It took a moment for Christian to digest her words, and when he did it was all he could do not to get up and dance for joy. Up till now, he hadn't considered the various possibilities, but with the confirmed death of his child—the very origin of his misery—he spied a faint glimmer of liberation out there in the universe. There was to be no baby. For the first time since they'd arrived at the hospital, he let himself entertain the hope of a similar release from Elena—that she too might leave this world, and not by his hand. Held back by these thoughts too ugly to consider, he made a last-ditch effort to turn away from wishing her dead, only to find the idea too irresistible to deny. Unbidden, it slithered into his brain, seeped into the cracks and crevices of his soul, finally settling inside the very marrow of his bones.

The baby had died and so might she. It could be that easy. And if that came to pass, then glory hallelujah, his conscience would be free and clear. After all, hadn't he saved her life when he could have just as easily let her die with no one the wiser? Even now, it wasn't that he wished her dead. To the contrary, he merely wished himself free.

Days passed and Elena continued to cling to life, the sounds of fluids pumping life through her motionless body, while one dedicated small-town doctor battled valiantly to staunch the internal hemorrhaging and quell the infection that ravaged her system.

It was then that the whisper of an idea crept into his mind, a notion so fragile and unexpected that at first, he pushed it away. But once there, there was no shaking it.

What if everything to date had happened for a reason? That he had been led to this cold and sterile place for Such a Time as This? That the death of their unborn child was nothing short of a blood sacrifice, a sacrifice sent their way as a sign—*the* sign in fact—the one he had yearned for with desperation so long ago, the sign that would finally bring him to Jesus, and in this place where life meets death?

Almost as if reading his mind, Elena began to improve, abruptly cutting short his momentary two-step with Jesus and leaving, in its wake, utter despair. When it became clear Elena would live, the same pretty nurse slammed shut the cell door on his life, the door she had all too briefly cracked open with her earlier announcement. Making it all the worse was the realization that, in saving her, he himself had thrown away his prison key. Downward he spiraled—down, down, down. Down into the infernal abyss that must be Hell itself. Gone was the bright hope of redemption. Gone, too, was the fleeting dream of freedom.

It was then that Satan spoke to him through the hushed murmurs of the nurses.

"Paramedics arrived after the mister had already left with her. Found a coat hanger dripping with blood right there on the floor next to where the body had been. Can you even imagine? The woman murdered her own child in cold blood. She's got the devil in her, that one does."

They continued to whisper, their faces filled with the implied accusation of his complicity. Their words slammed into him, threw him back against the wall, stunning his senses. If what the nurses were saying was true, there was indeed no God. It was all but a tale, a lark, a myth, and had never been anything but. Because if Christian knew one thing, it was that the Jesus he'd learned about would never stand by while Elena heartlessly murdered the child inside her. That is, not if He really existed. Instead of Christian's long-desired encounter with his Savior, he found himself face-to-face with the Prince of Darkness.

Trembling, he rose and exited the hospital.

❖

It had been two weeks since Elena had come home from the hospital and the tension in the house was palpable. Christian took to staying out after work to avoid being around her. Only when he knew she'd be asleep would he return home for a few hours of fitful sleep on the worn-out sofa, its exposed springs jutting into his fleshy torso, denying him any real rest. Never again would he share a bed with that she-devil, just as no longer would he harbor fantasies of good will toward man, and that included himself. It had been made abundantly clear back in the hospital that life consisted of nothing more than a series of unconnected acts of selfishness. He had finally grown into the only birthright he would ever own—bitterness, disappointment, and the sheer joylessness of life.

Then, one night things changed. Luke Farley showed up on their doorstep on the pretense of looking in on his cousin and Christian surprised himself by letting him inside. He found he no longer gave a damn about Luke or his father because he didn't give a damn about anything. At this point, he'd have let anyone in, provided he offered diversion. Oddly, Luke seemed changed—respectful even—never once so much as mentioning Mason's name.

His visits became regular. One shotgun marriage and aborted child later, Christian was so depleted he found himself welcoming in the person he'd spent his youth despising. Whether it was loneliness or because Luke served as a sort of proxy for Mason, it didn't much matter. Nor did it matter that Cal, who shortly after Christian's marriage made it evident that he wanted nothing more to do with the seamy, going-nowhere Christian, Cal had dropped him, creating an opening for Luke to become the next best thing. Christian let Luke in, willing to leave the hard questions for another day.

Before long, the two men struck up a routine. Bejeweled and looking the western pimp himself, Luke bought Christian suitable attire for their nightly outings. He'd call for him and off they'd go, crisscrossing the county, stopping in wherever they thought there might be action. Somehow, Luke had an endless supply of money that he was always ready to share, be it for drink, gambling, or women. Christian didn't begin to comprehend his generosity, but neither did he question it. Unthinkingly though, one night, bleary with drink, Christian crossed an unspoken line.

"Luke, how is it you got so much money, yer not workin' an' all?"

For the first time since they'd taken up, Luke turned on him with the more familiar fury of old.

"Tell me you didn't jest say that. You realize, if I want, I can lay you out flat here an' now, you skeevin' piece a shit. I don't gotta answer ta no one, 'specially you, Chris*tine*. I got my ways is the only thing you gotta know. Mebbe I'll tell you someday. Mebbe I won't. Till then, you'd be wise ta stop askin' what ain't none a yer fuckin' business, that is, if you know what's good fer ya."

His voice brimmed with a darkness the likes of which Christian hadn't known, even after a childhood of living with Mason, and his spine went rigid with fear. Alarmed by the swiftness of Luke's metamorphosis, the two men rode home in silence, Christian aware their relationship had just taken an important turn, and all because he couldn't keep his mouth shut.

He didn't hear from Luke for over a week. Then one day, Luke showed up at the garage acting as if nothing had happened.

"Hey fuck-face. What time you off today?"

"Five. Same as always. Got somethin' in mind?" Christian felt the tension of Luke's absence drain away, having greatly missed him and the escape from the vast bleakness that Luke provided.

"Whaddaya say we head on over to Pleasanton t'night? Catch us some cockfights."

Stunned by the explicit homoerotic implication of the invitation, he was uncertain how to answer what well could be a trap. He'd heard of cockfights and to his knowledge, they were some kind of perverted man-on-man wrestling, something he wanted no truck with.

"Y'ever been?" Luke quizzed.

"Nah. You know I ain't got the dough to be gamblin' with," he equivocated.

"Well then, tonight'll be your first, an' it's on me."

Christian squirmed.

"Ain't no need ta act so spooked, JC. It'll be a hoot."

As fraught with risk as the offer seemed, Christian looked hard at Luke but didn't see any of the old meanness or sarcasm. He realized he *wanted* to go, even if the invitation was riddled with risk.

"C'mon. It'll be the shit. An' fuck, who knows? You might could win somethin'."

Christian hesitated but, when it came to Luke these days, he was in no position to say no. He nodded in agreement, his father's and Luke's ridicule hovering not far in the background.

"I'll be 'round for ya 'bout six, that is, if yer shore you ain't afraid ta go."

"Fuck that. Six it is."

Satisfied, Luke slapped him on the back and left.

Christian went back to fiddling with the aging suspension of a sixteen-year-old Ford. While he worked, he pondered their so-called friendship—how it was as rife with danger as it was with promise—a friendship on which he'd become increasingly dependent. Had he possessed the slightest curiosity about the subconscious, he might also have questioned the small thrill he felt about the night ahead. Instead, all he felt was gratitude to have Luke back in his life. Anyhow, if manly Luke was secure enough to watch a couple of men an' their dicks roll around on a mat, who was he to object?

❖

That night, while Luke steered across the dark Texas back roads, two six-packs of Lone Star wedged firmly between them, he set to explaining the sport of cockfighting. Christian cracked open a beer, anxious about what lay ahead. With the first sip, his head filled with white noise, drowning out Luke's chatter while, try as he might, he was helpless to stop the vision of "Rasslin' with the Homos" that played in his mind's eye. Luke nattered on and Christian nodded, hoping desperately not to let on how terrified he was. Not willing to name his fear, a vague feeling of excitement persisted.

When Luke noticed he wasn't listening, he gave him a poke.

"When we git there, if the fight's started, which I 'spect it will, don't worry 'bout bein' po-lite—you jest push your way up to the front. If you don't, you won't see none a the good stuff."

"Good stuff." Christian gulped.

"First thing you'll see'll be two roosters, dead center, goin' at it."

Christian determined then that "rooster" must be slang for "faggot."

"Them birds, they been trained for blood-lust, nothin' else. It's what they fuckin' live for. Fact is, they practic'ly stroke out on it," Luke said, his excitement evident. "You'll see. Fuck, ta make 'em even hotter, they git 'em all stoked up on drugs, make 'em mean as possible." Christian shuddered. "Even better, they got razor blades attached to their legs. Sharp fuckers, too."

Razor blades? Christian re-tasted his dinner on its way back up and wondered if it was too late to claim sickness. Luke took no notice.

"So you got these two cocks slicin' and dicin' away till one of 'em croaks or falls to the ground from exhaustion." An all-too-vivid picture of two faggots fighting to the death, dicks raised high, flashed across Christian's mind's eye.

"An' that's that. The handler holds up the winner, an' them that's been shrewd walks away with the pot."

A small bell went off inside Christian's head. At least this explained where Luke got his money.

On the verge of confessing that he couldn't go through with it, an abandoned barn appeared as if out of nowhere. Too late. Luke's truck screeched to a halt, throwing up a thick screen of dust and gravel. When the air cleared, Christian was astonished to see upwards of a hundred vehicles parked every which way. Where they'd come from was anyone's guess. All out for a night of blood, homos, and money, he figured. Luke leapt from the truck and Christian, having missed his chance to beg off, followed anxiously behind, coughing up the dust that had settled in his lungs.

"Luke? I got a question. What happens to the rooster what loses—that is if he ain't already dead?"

"What you think happens, ass-wipe? It's sayonara cock-a-doodle-doo, that's what happens. Into the dump he goes, dead or alive. We're talkin' survival of the fittest here." He sniggered, a hint of his innate evil shining through. He pushed open the door with the queasy, uneasy Christian in tow.

Inside, the barn reeked of sweat, liquor, and puke. Never having been around blood sport, it took Christian a moment to acclimate himself to the rank odor and roar of the crowd, all the while a rabidly blood-loving chorus egged the gay boys on. Pushing their way to the front, Christian was flooded with unspeakable relief when, instead of two turgid gay boys rolling around on the barn floor, he saw two honest-to-God roosters going at each other in full fury. He laughed with rare abandon, throwing a comradely arm around Luke.

In answer, Luke pressed five one hundred dollar bills into Christian's hand and grinned crookedly, "Next one's yours."

"Luke, I would," he protested weakly, "but there ain't no way to pay you back if I lose. S'all I can do to keep my head 'bove water as it is."

"Forget 'bout it. I got a hunch 'bout you an' my hunches ain't usually wrong. Iffen you lose, ain't no biggie. It's time you have youself some fun. After all, who deserves it more'n you, nineteen an' already servin' a life sentence with that dog-faced cousin a mine? Go on. Over yon," he pointed. "Take a look at them two in the cages closest to us. They're up next. Check 'em out good. Usually you can pick out the one what is meanest just by lookin'. If you want, I'd be proud to advise you."

The adrenalin flowed hard as Christian headed for the cages. He'd never felt the high he did at this moment. He didn't have to watch the birds long before he knew which one was the alpha. Shit, this was like takin' candy from a baby. An' why should he give a fuck if some cock died, he thought, chuckling at his earlier misconceptions.

Inside the ring, muscled hands pried apart two birds; the current victor, his claws still clutching at his prey as he continued to make great violent slashes with his beak. Wresting them apart, the gloved handler held the winner high and simultaneously tossed the defeated bird, a bloodied, pulpy mass, into the trash. Gloved hands reached for the next pair of combatants when, spontaneously, Christian threw in the entire bankroll, placing it all on this, his first fight.

The battle was on, and from the start it was vicious.

"You sure as fuck picked a doozie for your first," Luke yelled. The roar of the crowd was replaced by the sound of blood pulsing inside Christian's head. Watching these animals fight to the death, Christian felt he was witness to a struggle between Good and Evil. Christian's rooster, whom he'd privately dubbed Good, looked to have it all over his darker enemy, Evil, when, just as fast, the tables would turn. Throwing back beer after beer, sweat streamed from his face as the seemingly interminable struggle dragged on until, suddenly, Luke was pounding him on the back, his arms raised high as he howled, "Holy mother fuckin' son-of-a-bitch, you won!"

The battle was over and Christian, having lost his cockfight virginity, left the barn two thousand dollars the richer.

Tonight, Good had most definitely prevailed over Evil.

5

Sins of the Father

April 1977

WHEN NOT PLAYING THE cocks, Christian and Luke spent their nights roaming from town to town, hitting up any bar or house of pleasure that looked promising. The late hours began to tell on Christian, who still had to get up for work most days, but what really brought him down were the dizzying swings between fortune and poverty he was experiencing. At the moment, he was down by eleven thousand dollars and for reasons unexplained, Luke didn't press. Christian was sure he could win it back but until he did, everything felt sour. In order to stay in Luke's good graces, the only graces that mattered to him anymore, he had to find a way to pay him back, and as quickly as possible. And so, in no uncertain terms, he ordered Elena to get off her ass and find a job. The reality was that her lack of skills and pidgin English didn't recommend her for anything, particularly in a town with labor options as scarce as Pearsall's.

In what the faithful would surely consider a miracle, the very next day Elena, clad in her post-pregnant but still provocative way, went into town to the local five and ten with plans to ply her charms on Jace Hoople, the dark-skinned and overly muscled clerk. Pretending to be mesmerized by Jace's candy selection, she positioned herself close enough to overhear Dee Anne Duggers—that would be *the* Dee Anne Duggers, as in *the* daughter-in-law of Pearsall's oil scion, Cam Duggers—complaining bitterly about how her current housekeeper, Manuela, had up and quit that very morning. Between Dee Anne's emotional disintegration and what English Elena understood—which had always been more than she'd let on—it was easy to determine that the spoiled woman didn't deal well with her children, a fact brought home when the youngest tugged innocently at her mother's skirts only to have Dee Anne lean down and slap her soundly across the cheek. It was then that Elena stepped in.

"Senora? Quizá podría ayudar? Cocino y limpio." Smiling at the children she added, "Adoro los niños."

Like most southwestern women of means, small-town or not, Dee Anne knew enough Spanish to communicate with the help. Having known Jace since their brief fling in high school, she trusted him enough so that when he gave Elena an enthusiastic thumbs up, it was the only reference Dee Anne needed. She offered Elena the job on the spot, no questions asked. A decision as important as this ought to require more than a clerk's nod at a mini-mart, former lover or not, but Dee Anne couldn't imagine another hour on her own with her four children. And that was how, in the space of five minutes, Elena found herself in the back of the Duggers' station wagon, three sticky, sour-smelling children crowding up against her and the fourth, a sullen adolescent, glaring angrily out the window from the front seat.

Dee Anne worked Elena hard. But the way things were with Christian these days, she didn't mind. In fact, she preferred to stay away from home as much as possible. Christian's drinking had increased of late and the combination of alcohol and money worries had turned his merely offensive behavior into something much more ominous.

Most nights, Elena stayed on late to feed and bathe the children in hopes that Christian would be out or, if he was already home, he'd be passed out cold on the sofa. His days at Stamper's kept his hands busy, but his mind had far too much time to stew about the financial cliff he was headed for. Concerns about how to repay Luke occupied him night and day, with no escape valve. That is where Elena came in. Recent encounters between them, infrequent though they were, had not become physical until after one especially bad night at the cockfights.

Christian had taken a financial beating and had come home early to nurse his wounds with the bottle. Inside the house, with the lights ablaze and TV volume on high, he sat in wait, the drink in him fueling his cowardly fury. A lifetime of repressed anger further fed his sense of hopelessness. Who better to take it out on than Elena?

When she stumbled in the door, he was ready. He dove straight for her, slamming into her with a force that threw her backwards, cracking her head on the kitchen table on her way down. A wave of release mixed with the red of her blood, unleashing the long dormant animal of hatred within him. His crazed eyes darted about the room until they lit upon his old school bible. Snatching it up, he tore through the pages until he landed on the verse he sought:

Wives, submit to your husbands as to the Lord. For the husband is the head of the wife as Christ is the head of the church, his body, of which he is the Savior. Now as the church submits to Christ, so also wives should submit to their husbands in everything. —Ephesians 5:22-24

Looking down at her limp body, at the blood spurting from a surface cut on her scalp, he was heavy with regret for having saved her life only months ago, and he heaved the good book at her empty belly before storming out the door. Like an addict, this initial dance with violence had only temporarily slaked his thirst. By the time he returned to the house, she'd barricaded the bedroom door and physically spent, he let her be. But he had tasted revenge, revenge not only against Elena but against everything in his life that had gone wrong. And the taste had indeed been sweet.

Three days later he came home from work and found a letter addressed in Elena's handwriting to her family back in Mexico. Without compunction, he tore it open to find a blank sheet of paper folded over to conceal three crisp one-hundred-dollar bills.

The filthy bitch. How dare she send money that by all rights belonged to him? To think that he'd saved her lying, murderous life *and* continued to provide her with a home and food. For what? For this treachery? He reached for the bottle and planted himself once again to await her return, this time in the dark. Tonight, he'd show her who was boss, once and for all.

Elena's back ached after the long day's work moving furniture back and forth for the Duggers' "Weekly Cleansing." Her English had continued to improve, thanks to the hours the Duggers children spent in front of the television, but she kept it to herself because incomprehension served her indolence far better. Every Friday, Dee Anne would greet her at the back door, each repetition of the weekly orders reinforcing Dee Anne's belief that Elena was incapable of learning English.

"Buenas dias Elena. Hoy es viernes! You—know—what—that—means! It means, today we cleanse—and—purify!" She'd continue, slow and deliberate: "Cleanliness is next to Godliness, Elena, and we are Godly here—en casa Duggers." Elena had worked there long enough to know what happened on Fridays, but Dee Anne seemed to enjoy repeating the weekly orders. More than the words, though, Elena understood the subtext: it's easy to be godly if you're rich like the Duggers.

As she wended her way home, Elena felt her heart thudding noisily in her chest, even as her head throbbed from the deep gash it had sustained three nights earlier. Greatly relieved to find the house dark, she pushed open the door, kicked off her scuffs and shuffled over to the television. As she passed by the Barcalounger, a leg flew out and sent her flying. Before she could right herself, Christian was on top of her, a searing flashlight beam directed into her eyes, forcing them shut. Stunned silent, she screamed when she heard the sound of his belt coming off and she braced herself for the lashing that was certain to come. And come it did, steadily and earnestly. With each strike he cursed. He cursed the lie of their marriage, her treachery, her thievery, even her godlessness. Screams turned into wails turned into pleas turned into whimpers turned into silence. After a momentary respite, she heard herself beg for forgiveness, promising she'd never again go against his will, swearing she'd never again send money to her family if he'd let her be. But Christian had run so hard and for so long from the brutal and horrific beatings he'd suffered in boyhood, and now he had come full circle. Elena's plaintive moans only served to egg him on as he delivered increasingly harsher blows, just like his father used to do when Christian had been the one to cry out for mercy.

Finally tossing aside the belt, he set to striking her with his bare hands. Fist met bone, and with each blow, he grunted with orgiastic satisfaction. This was no longer a man hitting a woman, but humanity itself flailing helplessly against the wretchedness of life. When finally he stopped, he unzipped his pants and released what remained of his anger in a final act of rage and defilement.

❖

Luke and Christian's relationship had soured. He rarely came by, and his absence left Christian with a sense of foreboding that surpassed his sense of loss. Preoccupied with paying Luke back, he didn't know how to do so. Come payday, every cent he had was already spoken for and, with no friends or family, he had nowhere to turn. He also couldn't figure how Luke continued to thrive—Christian had seen Luke lose on the cocks every bit as often as he himself had. Yet Luke never lacked for cash.

One night after a significant absence, Luke reappeared, this time sporting the familiar cruelty of old. Trying his best to appear unafraid, Christian gave his shoulder a friendly pat. "Where you been, buddy? I been missing our nights out."

"First of all, where I been ain't none a your fuckin' business, dick-wad, and second, you and me, we ain't *buddies*." He grabbed Christian by the nape of his neck. "Only thing *is* your business is payin' me back. Wadda you say ta that, *buddy*?"

"Listen Luke. It's not like I blame you fer bein' upset with me," Christian whined. But ya gotta know how bad I feel. I need more time is all and I'll win it back, I swear it."

"You swearin' means jack shit ta me. I want my money an' I want it now. I've thrown my last cent down the toilet on you, y'hear?"

"Luke, my luck'll turn. You seen it before. I always come back."

Luke pushed a rigid finger into Christian's chest. "Now *you* listen to me, you fuckin' weasel." The air between them turned icy. "I staked you these months, because, well, there was a certain sport in watchin' you lose. But now? Now, it ain't as much fun . 'Sides, I been thinkin'. Maybe all this time, you been usin' me, leachin' offa me. That kinda thought don't sit kindly with me, boy, not at all. But it ain't no matter. What matters is that you're into me for the better of thirteen G's and the time's come ta pay the piper. Meanin', I want my money. Every last penny of it. This ain't no game of tiddlywinks we been playin'."

While he spoke, he pushed ever harder into Christian's chest until finally, he had him backed up against the house.

"Luke, I never used you, I swear. We *are* buddies. It's jest— I'm beggin' you, gimme more time is all. I'll get it back. In the name a frenship, I'm pleadin'."

"*Frenship*? Cut the crap. We ain't frens—never was. An' I'm done with your empty promises. I'll give ya one week to pony up the do-re-me else you'll be one sorry fuck." He took a step back, a dark smirk washing over his face.

"Tell you what," he softened, "fool that I am, I'm gonna throw you one last rope." He flung ten one-hundred-dollar bills at Christian's feet. "You got seven days to parlay this into the now *fourteen* you owe me, an' if you don't, well—we'll have to move up the scale another level." The chill in his voice was matched by the steel in his eyes.

"What d'ya mean move up the scale?" Christian whined, despising himself for the high-pitched female squeak coming out of his mouth.

"Wa-wa, baby girl, stop your mewlin'. Be a man for fuck's sake. You wanna play with the big boys, it's time you pay up like one. One week is all you got."

He started to walk away but turned back. "Ya know what, Chris*tine*? Maybe your pappy an' me, we weren't so wrong about you after all, you freakin' faggot."

❖

True to his word, Luke returned seven days later. Startled awake by a late-night tap on the window, Christian rocketed from his tortured sleep to find Luke's gap-toothed face scowling at him through the mud-encrusted pane. He went outside to meet him, the cold of dread flooding his veins.

"Fork it over Bub. Fourteen G's. *Ahora!*"

Luke's agitation was clear as his eyes darted about and his hands twitched. Christian spotted the sharp tip of a knife peeking out from Luke's boot and he cowered against the doorframe in terror.

"Luke, I don't know what ta say. I tried to win it back, but it ain't workin' no more. You gotta know I never meant for things to go like this." Christian was almost in tears.

Luke took a step forward and slammed his hand against Christian's throat. "Shut the fuck up you snivelin' worm. I tole you last week things'd be different if you didn't come up with the dough. What'd ya think? That I'd forgive fourteen thou?

Say, 'it's ok sweetie. Don't you worry yore purty little head 'bout my money?' Well, fuck that!" With the hand that wasn't holding onto Christian, he reached down toward his boot, his eyes never leaving Christian's.

"Please Luke. I'm beggin' you. Don't hurt me. Tell me what I kin do. Anything. I'll do anything you say. Jest don't hurt me."

A look of victory flashed across Luke's face as he savored the disintegration of the despicable excuse for a man cowering before him.

"All right then. Y' say you'll do anything?" Christian's head willingly bobbed up and down. "Then, buckle your seatbelt cause you're in for the ride a your life. Time's come for you to show me what you're made of."

Without another word, he was gone.

6

Runnin' on Empty

August 1977

LUKE AND CHRISTIAN HAD been running drugs for upwards of four months. Between runs, life played out in a merry-go-round of booze, gambling, and women. If this was Luke's idea of moving up the scale, Christian was happy to go along for the ride. He strutted into Stamper's one day and, without so much as a word of thanks, handed in his notice. He rarely spent time at home these days, and when he did Elena was little more than a nuisance. In a rare gesture of generosity, he graciously let her resume sending her wages back to Mexico.

Before long, Mason joined their nighttime outings. In a primal kind of way, this seemed a natural outgrowth of Christian's burgeoning relationship with Luke. Never having been one to contemplate the psychology of self, he had no idea that what he chose to accept as the long wished-for fatherly approval was merely Mason's desire to leech off his son. Thus, the twosome became a threesome: The Father, The Son, and

The Holy Spirit, the unspoken question being, could Christian ever be more than a spirit, much less holy, to his father?

Now that they were spending time together, Christian felt at long last he was part of Mason's world. Everyone had what they wanted. Elena had her green card, Luke had more money than ever thanks in part to Christian, Mason had all the booze and snatch a man could desire, and Christian, well, he had it all. From the start, he had no moral issues with selling drugs. They dealt primarily in pot and coke, peddling their wares six hours north at East Texas State up in Commerce, where Luke, so to speak, owned the corner. If spoiled-rotten college punks chose to spend their daddies' money getting high, well, Christian certainly had no problem taking it. Anyways, when had their kind even so much as looked his way? They saw him now, that was for sure.

Then one day Luke told him the time had come to expand the business. They would add human trafficking to the list of services they offered. This time around, though, Christian balked. The collapse of the Mexican economy had provided a ready supply of bodies eager to be smuggled into the U.S. and Luke wanted in. Bringing immigrants in, illegal though it was, didn't bother Christian. Not at all. It was the stories he heard about the ones who didn't make it in alive that troubled him, no matter the financial promise. While he believed he'd left religious dogma and its accompanying threat of Hell behind, he held onto enough superstition to worry that if, in the End, Salvation did turn out to be real, he was afraid he couldn't afford another black mark next to his name.

Moral fraud that Christian was, it took less than twenty-four hours for him to throw in, seeing as all he had to do was call up, yet again, the appropriate psychological tool to justify his acts. Like Luke said, if wetbacks wanted a chance to live in these here U-nited States, who was he to stand in the way?

Thus Christian sank deeper into the quagmire of ill-gotten gain derived from the misery of others. They'd do a run every few weeks—sometimes drugs, other times immigrants—occasionally both. The load always included a legitimate product to use as a cover in case they were stopped. It was easy work and, incredibly, they never once saw so much as one Policia Mexicano or U.S. Immigration agent.

Every time they crossed the border and opened wide the container doors, the bleary overheated immigrants would stagger out, squinting into the dark as, one by one, they fell to their knees to kiss the ground. The fact was, he told himself, you can't get much more gratitude than this. The way he saw it, it was a "Christian" thing, what he was doing—giving these poor souls a chance at the American Dream.

To put it another way, he was learning to live with it.

That was until the night everything changed. They had successfully crossed the border. The container of their eighteen-wheeler was loaded with disposable diapers and six illegals heading to a "dealer" in Houston. They approached the abandoned gas station where they were to unload and transfer the illegals for the next leg of their journey, and where Luke and Christian would split up and take separate routes back to Pearsall. But something was wrong—there was no one at the station to receive the delivery. Then, in a flash of the headlights, Christian saw why: an unmarked car was hidden in the brush.

"Fuckin' A! Over there! Move it! *Now!*" They pulled the rig off the road, vaulted from the cab, and sprinted a hundred yards to where Luke had left his pickup. Off they went, Luke at the wheel, a sharp one-eighty slamming shut Christian's door.

Skillful driver that he was, Luke tore across the countryside zigging and zagging, much of the time off-road. Whoever it was in pursuit wasn't nearly as adept a driver and, an hour into the chase, Luke saw the car, in his rearview mirror, flip and roll over three times, its occupants ejected from the open top and thrown into the night. With no feeling for the victims, they deemed it prudent to drive till daylight in case the pursuers had not been working alone.

They didn't stop until six the next morning, low on gas and far from civilization. Worn out but confident they'd given their pursuers the slip, they agreed that to be on the safe side, they'd stay put until nightfall. Luke backed the pickup into a wooded area where they sat out the rest of the day swilling beer, eating what remained of their dwindling stash of beef jerky and fireballs, and nodding off.

When night fell, Luke declared matter-of-factly, "We're goin' back t'night, ya know. Just cuz them fuckers from Houston didn't show, we still gotta finish the delivery. If we don't, there's men you don't wanna know what'll be after our asses."

"Over my dead body I'm goin' back, you motherfucker," Christian snarled. "You ain't gonna catch me within a hundred miles a the border. Fuckin' douchebag, you must be outta your mind. I guarantee the cops are layin' in wait fer us, dickwad. If you're goin' back, this is where I get off. I more'n paid up. Fact is, if I walk away t'day, I got all I need to last me a long while. All a which means, adios amigo. I'm out a here, O-U-T, out." With that, he jumped from the truck.

"It's yer funeral, Ain't like I give a rat's ass," Luke snarled. "I'm thinkin' it'll take you most of a day ta git back to civilization and it can get mighty thirsty out there. I'll say a prayer you make it back." Christian stopped in his tracks. He looked over the arid landscape surrounding them, then glanced at the half-empty jug of water Luke held tight to him. Aside from the copse of trees where they'd spent the day, the landscape held scant promise. There was no chance for survival if Luke left him out there on his own. That was clear. Much as he was afraid to go back to the container, making it back on his own was far riskier. With equal parts dread and fury, he climbed into the pick-up and off they went, an angry silence pinging throughout the cab, Luke's sights trained on the border and who knew what else.

A full day had passed and it had been a scorcher. When Luke and Christian finally made it back to the semi, they were surprised to find the doors still sealed. Surely, whoever had come after them last night would have been long gone, "cargo" in tow. And if it was the law, well then, they ought to be lying in wait for Luke and Christian to return. Yet neither seemed to be the case.

A couple hundred yards from the truck, Luke cut his lights and coasted to within twenty feet of the container. They froze, their ears tuned for the slightest noise while their eyes adjusted to the inky night. Aside from the usual haunting sounds of the desert, all was quiet. Taking the industrial-strength flashlight Luke kept in the cab, they crawled cautiously, across the dry ground to the container. It was then that Christian heard the plaintive wail of a lone coyote, a sound that was to haunt him for the rest of his life.

The padlock on the container remained in place, showing no signs of tampering. They stood silent a few moments longer and only when they felt sure they weren't being watched did Luke dig the key from his pocket and slide the door open, its rusty hinges emitting a shriek so piercing it was a broad announcement to anyone within miles. The wind had picked up, foretelling an approaching storm, and the sound of thunder rumbled ever closer. Christian directed his flashlight toward the darkness inside. He and Luke peered in and simultaneously they screamed. Lying there amongst cartons of disposable diapers, in various positions of rigor mortis, were the bodies of five illegals, huddled together as if in prayer. Luke stifled a scream-whisper, "Jesus-fucking Mary an' Joseph. They're dead. Every freakin' one a them. We gotta get the fuck outta here. They catch us now an' we'll be dancin' our way to the electric chair. Lock this thing up and let's move!"

He hurled the keys at Christian and ran for the pickup. Christian shined his flashlight further into the darkness illuminating the grisly scene. Willing himself to slam shut the doors on this indelible nightmare, the greater part of him was helpless to fight the irresistible pull that drew him up and inside the darkened hot-box, no matter the stench of overheated, rotting flesh. He tasted yesterday's beer and beef jerky and, unable to control himself, he doubled over and vomited his shame and fear onto a corpse whose eyes stared back at him in death.

Then, from a place deep within the container, he heard a noise. The sound was so faint he thought it might be his imagination. It came again, this time declaring itself to be real—to be human—and there was no denying there was life still aboard. Thinking back to when they'd loaded the cargo in Mexico, he cursed himself for not having hidden his face from the immigrants. Now, with the worst having come to pass, he was sure to be identified if any of the travelers survived their eighteen-wheeled coffin.

With the flashlight still lighting up the bizarre scene he ripped open a carton of diapers, pulled several out, and tiptoed back in search of the source of the sound. There, in the back of the truck, he found her. She was young, her ashen mouth gasping for breath. Their eyes locked and the power of her silent plea nearly overwhelmed him. At this moment, a moment between life and death—the second time in his life that he'd been granted divine power—he looked into eyes that begged for mercy, and didn't know what to do. He heard the sound of Luke's pickup idling outside while flashes of nearby lightning illuminated the truck's interior. Without another thought, he ground the wad of diapers onto the girl's face until he'd squeezed the last breath of life from her. Leaping from the container, he pulled the door shut and threw on the padlock just as Luke slammed the pickup door and revved the engine, desperate to get moving again.

They roared away from the container for the second time in twenty-four hours, Luke with the image of himself strapped into the electric chair and Christian, overcome by the fear of Eternal Damnation. In the distance, the lone coyote wailed once more. It was then that John Christian Hillcox felt the spirit of Jesus enter him. While Luke shrieked in terror, JC cried out for forgiveness.

On that horrific yet glory-filled desert night—a night when the old Christian chose death—a shining new Christian was born.

7

Grace Be Thine

November 1978

GRACE BE THINE HAD ITS start in the dank and crumbling garage behind Christian's house with all of twenty-five families and a few dozen foldout chairs. Its modest beginnings didn't prepare him for Pearsall's enthusiastic reception and in almost no time, the church was bursting at the seams. Most of the founding members were former classmates from First Baptist, many of whom had played football with Christian and retained fond memories of Preacher Man's inspirational "sermons."

An ocean of faith separated the diaper-wielding murderer of the Tex-Mex border from the Christian of today. With a fair measure of disgust and a much greater sense of relief, he forever severed his parasitic relationship with Luke that fateful August night. Once committed to Christ, he immersed himself, mind, body, and soul into all there was to know about Redemption, at the same time continuing to perfect the art of rationalization by convincing himself that it had Satan himself who'd forced his hand that terrible desert night. In order to get past the horror of what he'd done, he had to believe that the only reason he'd escaped capture and punishment was that He, Christian, must somehow be vital to God's "Master Plan."

That's not to say he didn't question his worthiness, particularly in the dark of night. Or that Elena's deep black eyes—eyes set against a dark complexion in a face, that too closely recalled the mirror of death—didn't have the power to send him into a cold sweat. Though he was convinced that his come-to-Jesus makeover was genuine and that he had put evil in the past, it still took nearly a year of intensive study—he wore out three copies of the Bible—before his conversion felt complete.

Dramatic religious U-turns might be viewed with suspicion in some places, but this was South Texas, where reborn Baptists are a dime a dozen. To a large extent, folks enjoyed trading gossip about the newly-reborn, there often being a striking correlation between the fervor of the convert and the magnitude of the sin. While it was titillating to speculate on what brought a neighbor to Christ, few dared to judge, thanks to the darkness hidden away in their own closets. All in all, Texans were a forgiving lot and before long there wasn't a soul to be found in Pearsall who questioned the sea change that had taken place in Pastor JC. Many saw, in fact, a satisfying circular logic when they considered his high school talent for biblical speechifying.

Life was full, the bad times repressed ever deeper, and the months flew by. When not preaching, Christian might be found trying to banish the scales from the eyes of the unbelievers. When not sharing the Good News, he could be found offering up counsel on issues ranging from adultery to promiscuity, addiction to personal property disputes, physical abuse or, perhaps worst of all, man-on-man sexual urges. The good people of Pearsall didn't lack for problems, nor Christian for answers.

The certainty that now ruled his life was the polar opposite of all that had been before.

For Christian, never having had a real family, the very idea of it took on a mythic dimension, becoming *his* gospel beginning and ending with marriage. The sixties had rained down every kind of abomination imaginable, all in the name of tolerance. Though Christian liked to think of himself as a tolerant man, his current view of tolerance extended no further than that which was mandated in the Bible. No exceptions. No add-ons. Period. Beyond that, the tolerance preached by the current "me generation" was little different from the free love hippie radicalism of the 1960s. In Christian's enlightened state of mind, today's liberals were closer to pinko Commies than they were to the good, solid Christian Americans by whom this country was founded.

When Taylor Purswell's Pony Keg came on the market, Christian only had to stop in for a quick look-see to know that the time was right for Grace Be Thine to move. Many times the size of his garage, the price was reasonable and it was located close to the center of town. Practically speaking, it was 1982 and mortgage rates were usurious, a fact that should have presented the good pastor with an insurmountable challenge. But God brought fishes and loaves to Christian in the voice of Lloyd Weber, congregant, former teammate, and head teller at First National Savings and Loan in Pearsall.

"Pastor? Lloyd Weber here. I've heard talk you've an interest in the ole Purswell place? Why not stop by my office this afternoon an' we'll see if we cain't help?"

Yea, and so the Lord chased the moneychangers from the temple. Combining the bank's offer with the blood money he'd stashed away in a waterproof pouch under his porch, a deal was struck. Christian rationalized that if it was God's will to put his wages of sin to work for Jesus, then so be it. "And the Lord turneth evil into the foundation for Good," he told himself.

Grace Be Thine had a new home.

Caught up in his newfound righteousness, Christian relegated the nightmare of his past to the trash heap of forgotten transgressions as he reveled in the certainty that all was forgiven, thanks to his personal relationship with He-Who-Died-for-Our-Sins. Each day brought more able-bodied helpers around to scrape and paint, to nail and putty. Pews were ordered, the pulpit put in place and in a few short weeks, Grace Be Thine opened its doors for business.

❖

It is curious to ponder why one performer succeeds where another fails, and pastors are nothing if not performers. As such, Christian was more than the sum of his parts. A winning smile went along with the easy charm he'd recently perfected, and that was all to the good. But it was when he preached to a crowd that the heavens moved. A natural rhythm, the innate sense of precisely when the voice should rise and when it should fall, and the folksy way he could turn a phrase mesmerized all who were lucky enough to be in his presence. Whenever he preached, buckets of perspiration poured from his brow, a musky dampness he mopped up with his trademark black cotton hanky, always at the ready. Christian had the consummate performer's ability to hypnotize, and those blessed to sit through one of his pulsating, throbbing services walked away knowing God just a little better than when they had come in. There wasn't a man, woman, or child who, after witnessing him in action, felt anything but a magnetic pull toward God in general and JC in particular.

Word spread across the county about the new breed of preacher in Pearsall and requests for him to guest-preach poured in. In every town he visited, he enjoyed a welcome grander than in the last, imbuing in him an ever-increasing air of confidence, a confidence he promptly deposited into the bank of his ego for withdrawal at a later date. His ability to inspire grew more passionate with every sermon, as did his command over the spoken word. Demand for Preacher Man grew rapidly. Recognizing that his gift from God was meant to be shared, Christian rarely refused a calling.

❖

No man is perfect in the sight of God, and Christian was no exception. The one irreconcilable area of his life remained the sorry state of his marriage. Elena, brought up Catholic, had turned away from faith in her teen years when, mired in poverty and deprivation, she came to question how there could be a God—at least not one of good intent. Though she was lacking in formal education, she had an inquisitive nature that drove her to consider such topics deeply and thoroughly.

Christian hadn't physically abused her since he'd found religion and for that, she was grateful. Otherwise, she had nothing but contempt for him and what she saw as his false idolatry. The television did little to drown out his constant attempts to witness to her. To his cries of "If thou shalt confess with thy mouth, the Lord Jesus, and shalt believe in thine heart that God hath raised him from the dead, thou shalt be saved," she spat in his face. Her sneers and insolent rejections were becoming increasingly difficult for him to tolerate. And were she not a lazy, faithless harlot—or if he had had the luxury of finding a wife better suited to his position—*then* he would have had the helpmate God surely must want for him to have: a woman who would share in his duties and take on the responsibilities that came with being a pastor's wife. A partner who would do her share in running various church ministries the community so needed. Unless Elena were to wake up, and soon, there would be a reckoning of some kind or other. Until that day, he would busy himself with the growing church.

Circumstances being what they were, he bestowed the honors that should be taken up by a proper pastor's wife upon a dutiful congregant named Dorothy Brae. Dorothy immediately set to work and within a matter of weeks she had established The Women of Valor, The Young Stallions Boys Club, and a club for preteen and teen girls she cleverly named The Ladies in Waiting. Her zeal was unsurpassed, and within no time several other ministries were up and running, each one filling a void in the community. The Women of Valor were already hard at work planning next year's Vacation Bible School and, thanks to Dorothy, Grace Be Thine showed its innovation by becoming the first church in the region to provide free daycare for the young.

But it was Christian, his words and his music, that made Grace soar. JC, a natural baritone, was blessed with a rich and resonant voice. On any given Sunday, his vocal performance brought the congregation to tears. He loved nothing more than to cherry-pick verses from the Bible and set them to a melody of his own composing. Before long, his ditties were heard on lips all over town, all of which resulted in an unforeseen but highly effective marketing tool that served to increase interest and swell church attendance. Grace Be Thine had become the nerve center of Pearsall making other congregations seem dull in comparison. Additionally, the community was more than happy to rally around Christian's frequent reminder that it's not *what* you do in this life, but *who* you accept once you've done it, that counts.

"For it is by grace you have been saved, through faith—and this not from yourselves, it is the gift of God—not by works, so that no one can boast."

A person would have to be a fool not to welcome Jesus into his life with that kind of pass. Talk about effective marketing. Damn but the Bible was good!

8

Lucifer's Return

May 1978

THE CLOCK READ TWO WHEN the howl of a coyote insinuated itself into Christian's sleep, jolting him upright. The night-terrors had returned after having left him at peace for more than a year. Christian threw off the sweat-drenched bed sheets tangled about his fleshy midsection, his nightmares more real than reality. As of late, he'd been visited nightly by images of bodies in various stages of death, some decaying, others alive but barely moving. A storm was approaching. Air thick with ozone crackled with lightning, the night sky offering scant relief from another day of blistering heat. The acrid odor of burning rubber assaulted dream-nostrils as a pickup truck peeled away. Sirens wailing in the distance. Hell.

Awake and trembling, Christian pulled on pants he fished out from under the bed and went outside. A real-life coyote wailed in the distance. Earlier that night, flashes of long-ago had returned at supper over a plate of Elena's greasy tacos. Mid-bite and with calculated relish, she delivered a sucker-punch.

"My cousin Luke, he stop by today. He be lookeen for you."

There it was. While he had been off spinning lust-filled fantasies at Ina's, history was paying a call in the body of Luke Farley. For Christian to have thought he was done with Luke, *that* was the real fantasy.

She sneered. "I know Señor Luke when he ees up to no good, ees easy to see. Maybe you tell me what he want weeth you, Meester Beeg Shot. What thees jailbird, he want weeth the holy one? Thees, I like to hear."

Christian snarled, the ever-present specter of his past overwhelming all feelings of righteousness he'd recently assumed, the terror rising fast from within.

"You're some piece-a work, *puta*," he spat. "You fuckin' tell me *exactly* what he said to you, an' I want it word for word."

"Don't you be talkeen all high an' mighty to me, Meester. Hees comeeng ees tu problemo. Me, I have done notheen."

"Hah! *You! You* have done notheen?" he mocked. "You wanna know the notheen you done? I'll tell you a *leetle* 'bout your notheen. You're the tramp that slept with anything that moved, all so's you'd get knocked up, an' me, I was the sorry fool who fell for your whorin' ways on the unfortunate night your fuckass uncle decides to show up. Next thing I know, I'm servin' a lifetime sentence—with you—you fuckin' baby killer. You call *that* notheen? Top it off, you're the one with a cousin only Satan coulda spawned an' who's come lookin' for me. Ees that notheeng?"

As most people have their public and private faces, so too did Christian. When riled, the age-old rage bubbled to the surface, reminding Elena all too well of what he was capable. One look at him and she softened her voice in hopes of keeping a lid on his rapidly escalating temper.

"Hee's specteen you tonight een Cotulla. A bar called thee Blue Devil. Eight o'clock sharp, he say. The way he look, I theenk you better go."

Luke's unexpected reappearance and its career and reputation threatening potential thrust Christian into a dark and dangerous place. He pushed back from the table, his chair clattering to the floor, all piety driven from mind.

"What the fuck is this shit you always feedin' me anyhow?"

They both knew her answer was of no consequence, so Elena chose silence, leaving Christian to head for the TV. Turning the volume up, he fell into the Barcalounger while she scurried about, cleaning up. He tried to calm down but fear was choking at him. This was bad all right. Really bad. The last he knew, Luke was locked up in prison for the rape of a young girl, giving Christian enough time—or so he thought—to establish his religious bona fides before figuring out a life away from Pearsall and Luke. Expecting he'd have years before that day came, he had pushed Luke out of his mind. But now, it would all come crashing down. Luke was out. And if he got to talking, as surely he would, everything Christian had built would turn to ashes.

Get a grip, he told himself as he looked down at his trembling hands. *I gotta meet the ass-wipe so's ta know where I stand.* One thing was certain. He'd watch him like a hawk. Luke might not have had much in the way of schooling, but he was wily as a hellcat and that alone was reason for concern.

The noise from the television receded as memories of Christian's youth took over. Luke, the smarmy tough who, early on, served as a form of revenge toward Christian, the child Mason had never wanted. Neglected by his own father, Luke asked for nothing and therefore was given what little Mason had to offer. Many were the times that father and surrogate son would disappear for hours, sometimes returning home with a squirrel or a rabbit, just as often with nothing more than liquor-soured breath. Luke's own pappy, while not exactly cottoning to Mason, didn't much care who his son was with nor, for that matter, what he was up to. That another man showed an interest in his boy didn't dent his conscience. And the times Christian asked to join in, he was greeted by their pointed jeers and daggers.

"What d'ya want boy? Think you're man enough to come with us?" his father would sneer.

Ever hopeful, the young Christian would answer solemnly, "Yes sir," offering up the irresistible bait-nugget which his father never failed to bite.

"Hey Luke. D'you hear that? My little girl Christine here thinks she's man enough ta join us. What d'you think a that?" he'd hoot.

Luke, basking in the man's attention, would up the taunting to the next level as the two sliced ferociously at Christian's young heart. But Luke was no innocent; he knew well that the shared taunting served to deepen the bond between him and Mason, a bond that was to last decades.

Conversely there were the times when, home alone with his son, Mason, filthy and reeking of liquor, would force his son into the shower with him, whereupon he proceeded to pleasure himself while Christian looked on.

"Boy, better take a look-here," as he furiously whacked away at himself, fondling the boy's penis at the same time. "Manliness s'all we got, an' you, boy," his breath short and hard, "you got a helluva way to go." At the time, Christian didn't understand what was happening but he knew it was desperately wrong.

With a father like that, Christian was fortunate that he was left mostly on his own. His only sibling, Della, of whom he'd heard mention but once, was fifteen when Christian was born. In those years, she was apparently cunning enough to escape her father's abuse and spent her time running after the local boys, unaware that these were to be her only glory years: the times when a willing body was all a girl needed to get by. Cheap liquor was plentiful and the future of no concern to her. The only rule she lived by was that of staying below Mason's radar. Years of seeing him beat her mother had taught her well. Far too often she sat by as her father used his worn leather belt, its surface punctuated with sharp metal studs, on her mother's weakening frame. For special occasions, he used the buckle.

❖

Eighteen years into Mason's and Lynette's turbulent marriage, one night of animal coupling produced a baby boy. Lynette named the child John Christian Hillcox, his middle name having nothing to do with her being a religious woman. To the contrary, the only God she believed in was the God of Suffering. She chose the name Christian on account of a peculiar obsession with Buddy Ebsen of *The Beverly Hillbillies* fame. Her one remaining real-world pleasure came from the tabloids she'd pick up at the market, and it was in one of them that she learned Buddy's given name was Christian Rudolph Ebsen. Lynette had descended so completely into a world of her own making that she'd convinced herself that Mr. Ebsen was sure to swoop down any day now and whisk her off to the alternate reality that was Beverly Hills. And so it was thanks to a tawdry tabloid that Christian received his prescient name, a name that was to serve him well.

In the occasional lucid moment during her pregnancy, Lynette fantasized that if she gave Mason a son he would magically morph into the kind of man he'd never been. But when she brought the baby home, it took but a glance at the swaddled infant before Mason headed out the door, not to be seen for months. For Lynette, this final rejection was the last time she inhabited the real world. With no capacity for self-reflection, Mason couldn't see that his loathing for the child was the only way he had to conceal his own deep-rooted rot of self-hatred and despair. Then again, these were neither the times nor the social strata for self-analysis. Drink was the only therapy he'd ever know.

Like any child, as Christian grew into awareness he sought out whatever approval there was to be had from his rapidly fading mother, instinctively knowing, young as he was, to avoid his father. But he was small and his attempts were pitiful, considering the speed of his mother's spiraling depression. Worse still, Christian's attempts to bond with his mother served to further fuel Mason's fury. Grand cycles of drink and violence made the rented shack a living hell, while continual debt quashed any hope of change.

As a man, Christian retained only a shadowy memory of his mother. He wasn't quite five when she died, and he remembered thinking at the time that the angels must've wanted her something terrible. Why else would she have slammed her car into a cement wall at ninety miles an hour? A wall built to keep vagrants and teenage boys out of a defunct mine, a mine whose sole legacy was the scar it left behind on the hopeless landscape and people of Pearsall. A wall that absorbed the flesh and bones of the body that had given Christian life.

Most of what he remembered of his mother derived from a faded photograph he took from a box on his father's dresser the day of her death. In the picture, Lynette was a pretty, smiling, and very pregnant teen. Aside from the photo, all he remembered of her was an anxious, fearful woman rocking back and forth, back and forth, always in the same rusted out aluminum porch chair, always staring blankly into space. Emotionally, she had left long before the "accident." After her death, there was no mention of her, her very existence fading away like the sepia in the old photograph.

❖

Whenever Rory Stamper needed a break from Mason's drinking, he'd lay him off. When that happened, finding something to get by on was never easy, and the new jobs never lasted long. The fact that Mason knew cars better than most was the only thing that saved him. When money ran out, he would clean himself up and find work at some garage or other, no matter how far away it was, never giving a thought to leaving his son completely on his own. Young though he was, Christian used his wits to survive. The year after his mother died he started first grade at the nearby Baptist elementary school where many of the teachers, aware of his sorry plight, would invite him home with them for meals. That he was enrolled at a Baptist school was incongruous with the Hillcox way of life, but one kindly teacher who knew about Christian's circumstances had dared to approach Mason about a funded enrollment. Since the school was close enough for Christian to get to on his own, Mason begrudgingly signed the papers. The fact that it was a religious school played no part in Mason's decision. The Hillcoxes had always been a people who lived by their own code, a code that had nothing to do with love and honor and everything to do with sloth and sin.

It was at school that Christian heard for the first time about God, Salvation, and the promise of Eternal Life. To a child as lonely as he, such promises were irresistible and made a powerful impression on him. He began to pray nightly for Jesus to come to him but nothing happened. Desperate, he upped his prayer sessions to twice a day, then three. Still nothing.

One day the principal, Mrs. Stolper, called Christian to her office to ask whether or not he'd seen the face of the Lord. Lying soulfully, he replied, "Yes ma'am, I have." Basking in the purported salvation of this wayward soul, Mrs. Stolper sent home a note asking to set up a water baptism for the newly reborn Christian. Infidel that he was, Mason shredded the note in front of the quaking boy.

Yanking the child by the arm, he raged, "Son of a fuckin' bitch. You think a dip in piss water'll save the likes of you? Fairy tale, my boy, fairy tale, far's I'm concerned an' I'll have no truck with it. Never did, never will. What're you tryin' to do bringin' home a note like this? Shame me? Tryin' to show yer teachers yer better 'n me? Well, 'tain't gonna happen, boy. More likely I'd let 'em fiddle with your diddle than sign this," he laughed, pointing at the scraps of ripped up paper. I'll tell you one thing. If I hear 'nother word a this, I'll pull you outta that school so fast yer head'll spin. Ain't gonna have this horseshit in my house, I promise you that, girly-girl." Out of habit, Christian hardened himself, at least outwardly. Whatever mask he needed to survive was the one he wore, so he shrugged off the baptism, never indicating he cared. If that's what it took to stay in school, then that's what he'd do.

❖

The screen door slammed, jarring Christian back to the present. A flash of Elena's backside whirred past as she ran from the house and he bellowed, "Get yer fuckin' ass back in here, you God-forsaken whore. Damn you to hell! You're my wife as God is my witness!" He gave chase and nearly caught up with her when, with a sudden spurt, she took off, leaving him gasping for air in the middle of the road. Back inside, he glanced at the half-eaten dinner on the table, and in one grand swipe, he knocked it all to the floor. "Let her come back to this!" he howled. "*Then* the spic'll have some real cleanin' ta do." He stomped around, deliberately grinding bits of refried beans into the cracked linoleum. Shattered taco shells oozed their fatty shards of pork, beckoning to the two stray cats fool enough to have made their home with them. The only food the felines ever saw was that which they could beg, borrow, or steal.

Praise the Lord he'd stashed a golden bottle of Wild Turkey, "the kickin' chicken," in the potted plant behind the TV. Had Elena known about it she'd have poured it down the drain long ago. Since finding Jesus, Christian had forsaken all drink. Well, fuck that. If he needed a nip to take the edge off before he met up with Luke tonight, then so be it. He picked his way across the scattered, broken dishes, his bare feet sticky from the orange Hi-C sprayed across the floor, and groped behind the philodendron until he felt the cool bottle that would be his salvation. What the fuck anyhow? The Bible made no bones about spirits. Hadn't Jesus himself turned water into wine? Fuck yeah. It weren't no one's business if he needed a nip to get himself through a time like this. Once he finished with Luke, he'd return to his more Christian ways. And it wasn't as if he was like his father. Christian understood the sin of drink, and unlike Mason, *he* didn't have a drinking problem.

The first long pull from the bottle sent its warmth through his veins, quickly working its magic and driving the fear and tension into the background. It was still only five-thirty, giving him plenty of time to relax before he had to head over to Cotulla.

Christian felt the spirit all right. Only this time, the spirit was that of Bacchus, not Jesus.

9

Games People Play

That Same Night

BLUE NEON LIGHTS FLASHED their come-on in the shape of a long-haired she-devil. It was eight o'clock and the place was jumping. The Wild Turkey had done its job, steadying Christian for what lay ahead. When he slammed the door of his pale blue Lincoln, its vanity plates bearing the acronym JC4ME rattled ominously. The moment he entered the bar, he felt Luke's eyes trained on him. Sure enough, there he was, seated in a darkened corner in the back, two empty shot glasses on the table in front of him, his lips curled into a nasty scowl, making clear his hatred. Christian elbowed his way through the crowd and planted his wide frame on the bench opposite Luke. Without missing a beat, he ordered a double bourbon straight up from a scantily clad waitress, while simultaneously jamming a finger into Luke's chest.

"How the fuck you get out already? If I counted on one thing in my life it was that I'd seen the last of you, you child-rapin' freak. Did ya grease the warden's palm or maybe one a his other parts, huh?"

A bone-penetrating cold washed across the table. Luke, further toughened from his time in prison, snarled, "Shut the fuck up, girlie-girl. I'm here ta talk. It's you gotta do the listenin', y'hear? T'ain't none a yer bizness how I got out. Only thing matters to you is that I know everythin' there is ta know 'bout you. Like how you diapered a woman ta death not all that long ago, eh? I know *everything* you done ta get ta where you are today, you an' your fruity-ass church. If you think fer a minute I won't use said information, you're dumber than I thought, Chris*tine.*"

Christian lunged across the table, grabbing Luke by the throat.

"You fuckin' son-of-a-bitch. You got no right comin' round my house, threatenin' me. It ain't like you was lily-white even a'fore they caught you nailin' the girl. They find out 'bout what else you done an' I wouldn't put odds a your seein' the other side a next year. You mighta gotten sprung early, you freakin' pedophile, but I promise ta take you down if you rat on me. What's in the past stays buried. I ain't proud of what I did, but least I did my penance. More than that, I'm right with God, which is a lot more'n you can say, you shameless fuck."

Luke's size belied his strength. He flew across the table and jumped atop Christian. The Friday night crowd gathered round, eager for a fight. There was nothing like a good brawl on a long Texas night to keep the patrons drinking, thus no one from the bar stepped forward to stop things from getting out of hand. But Luke, having come with bigger plans, pulled back, forcing himself to sit back down. The disappointed crowd dispersed and Christian pulled himself together. Their gamesmanship resembled something of a chess match, with the next move belonging to Luke.

"You listen up an' you listen good. I'm only gonna say this once. I don't give a goddamn if I go down long as I take you with me, so you might as well know that your empty-ass threats don't scare me. Thing is, I ain't about to sit back and watch you git rich while I crawl around shamed and broke, 'specially when I'm the one what made you in the first place. No fuckin' way, Pastor Dick-for-Brains. Sides, I know you. I'd put dimes ta dollars yer stealin' from your flock *already* with no one the wiser 'cept you an' your phony-ass God. But me, I'm broke so I ain't got shit ta lose an' I'd sooner spend the resta my days in prison then watch you live the high life while I'm stuck in the gutter. When you leave here tonight, it'd be wise fer you to give a think on the proposal I'm 'bout to offer you. This is a onetime deal. Don't take it—an' you might could find yerself preaching on Death Row 'fore too long."

Move: Christian.

"Fuck you. Who'd believe anythin' you say? I'm a man of God. I got respectability. You—why you're nothin' more than an ex-con pedophile. You think anyone in their right mind'd take your word over mine?"

Christian spoke with a confidence he didn't feel, and Luke knew it. He reached into his coat pocket and cackled derisively as Christian flinched. Luke slapped a newspaper clipping on the table between them. It was one Christian had read over and over, written the day after they'd fled the scene murder.

> Sheriff's deputies found the bodies of six people early this morning northeast of the Tex-Mex border in an abandoned, unmarked container and semi cab carrying a load of baby diapers. County Coroner Jeff Bingaman ruled that the cause of death was asphyxiation and

heatstroke from prolonged exposure to extreme temperatures and limited oxygen. Judging by a series of small holes in the doors, the victims tried to oxygenate the interior but were unable to let in enough air to survive. Temperatures within the container were estimated to be well over 150 degrees. "As agents of the great state of Texas, we vow to track down and prosecute those involved to the fullest extent of the law," said Bingaman.

With orchestrated cunning, Luke softened his pitch. "You kin keep that if ya want. Just so happens I bought me a pile of newspapers that day."

"Fuck you."

"Tsk-tsk. Christian. Where's yer godly feelin's for an ole fren? Ain't that what you used ta call us? Frens? *Buddies?* I ain't askin' for much. Jest a little brotherly love, s'all. We *are* practically brothers ya know, what with Mason and all."

Christian's knuckles whitened as he gripped the table's edge. Hearing his father's name from this bastard's mouth yet again was more than he could take. Luke saw the steel in Christian's eyes and gentled his pitch even further. "Christian, I like to think a myself as a reasonable man. What do ya say to us maybe sharin' the wealth in exchange for my silence? Call it a down payment on your career. Seems more'n fair ta me."

"Fuck you."

Move: Luke.

"No, it is I who am about to fuck *you*," Luke snarled, dropping the facade. With a broad smirk, he dangled a large manila envelope in front of Christian before slamming it down in front of him. "You think I'm gonna let you get away scot-free with what I got? I got all I need to take you down forever here in this envelope an' there ain't a lot what would make me happier." Christian looked at the ragged envelope on the table, stumped by what could be inside. "Yessiree, it's all here. Everythin' I need to take you outta circulation fer good. Way I see it, you either play it my way or you can kiss yer phony-ass church goodbye on yer way to the eee-lectric chair. INS and the governor of Texas ain't gonna take kindly to the good pastor when they see what I got."

He pushed the envelope Christian's way. Inside were two dark but clearly decipherable photos with the dead Mexicans in the foreground and Christian, the wad of diapers in his hand, reaching toward the desperate face of the still-living woman. "What the fuck? How the fu—?" All bravado went out of him. He turned the photos over to avoid seeing them.

Luke grinned broadly. "I'm what they call a am-uh-ter photogapher, buddy. I like ta take nice pitchers a whores after I shoot my wad. It's a few dollars extry, but worth ev'ry dime. Lucky I keep my Instamatic in the glove box. Come in handy that night." His grin had turned to a menacing sneer.

"Why you doin' this ta me anyhow?" Christian said, trying not to plead. "Can't you see I turned my life around? I been forgiven in the eyes of the Lord. Maybe you might could let me help you find forgiveness a your own. In the End, that's all that matters, an' the End is near, you know. The Lord, He's a'comin' back."

"Cut the crap. I know you don't buy this Jesus shit any more'n I do. It's your game for now, s'all. Scammin' religious wackos outta their money. Personally, I could give a rat's ass who you con. That ain't why I'm here an' I'd appreciate your not insultin' my intelligence. I tole ya this here's a one-time deal. Either share the wealth with me on a reg'lar basis, or your sissified fan club'll pick up their newspapers one day soon ta see your ugly mug shot starin' back at 'em. S'up to you, Christine. I don't give a goddamn what you wanna call the payments. Call 'em a business expense. Call 'em marketing. Jest remember, as your 'business' lives or dies, so does mine. So, as a matter of fact, do you. Oh, an' in the unfortunate event I should reach an untimely demise, be assured that copies of these photographs have been deposited around the state, guar-an-teed to surface should anything happen to me."

Checkmate: Luke.

10

Dance With the Devil

May 1978

NO MATTER HOW MANY times Christian turned things over, it always came back to the fact that Luke had him. The blackmail wasn't particularly ingenious or sophisticated. The fact that Christian had tried so hard to be good, *meant* to be good, and had sworn to himself and to the Lord on high to be good, in the end it didn't amount to a hill of beans.

All that mattered, quite simply, was this: Luke had him.

In forty-eight hours, if Luke wasn't on Christian's payroll, the past would detonate his future. It should be enough to know that, come what may, he was right with the Lord. But Christian had tasted success and he knew he would never walk away from it. There was nothing like the feeling he got when a stranger walked up to him and said, "Howdy Pastor. Lookin' forward to the next time you preach down our way." Or the sense of accomplishment he felt after rummaging through the messy life of a congregant and helping to put him back on track. But most important was the sense of belonging that, for the first time in his life, Christian could now claim for himself.

Christian made certain Luke had pulled out of the parking lot before he ordered himself a bottle of Wild Turkey. Hours later, as he wended his way homeward, he was startled by the piercing wail of a police siren. He spotted the familiar flash of red lights coming fast upon him and, instantly, his drunken mind careened back in time to the border. He considered making a run for it, but knew that in his current state there was no chance of success. He pulled off the side of the rode and instead of Border Police, he was momentarily befuddled to see the face of Officer Chuck Shrote, a police officer two years his junior, appear at his window. Chuck shined a flashlight inside the car and was flummoxed to see Pastor Hillcox at the wheel.

"Uh, Pastor, it's me, Chuck. Everythin' all right?"

Christian's skin was clammy with fear, his mind a dizzy craze of alcohol and dread.

"Chuck? That you?" he stalled, frantic to understand what was happening. "I'm, uh, I think I'm, uh, fine. 'Pologize if my drivin's a little sloppy. S'late, you know, and my mind went wanderin'."

The officer took a step back, the better to ignore the powerful smell of alcohol coming off of Christian. He knew he ought to take him in for his own good. But to arrest your pastor? Not this officer.

"Got it. Pastor, I hafta say though, the way you was drifting all over the road, you worried me plenty. Count yourself lucky this time. Might not always be so. I'd sure hate for anything bad to happen to you even if we do know you're goin' to a better place." The sour smell of whiskey mixed with fear hovered in the air between them.

"Thanks Chuck," he slurred with obvious relief. He was suddenly aware of the manila envelope on the seat beside him—one glance at the news article and Luke's photos and Chuck might see a promotion in his near future. "Glad you stopped me. Tell the truth, I was thinkin' through next Sunday's sermon." He tapped the envelope casually, rendering it, he hoped, inviolable to Chuck the congregant. "Musta lost my concentration. I promise to take your advice to heart an' from now on write my sermons at a desk. Say, how's Doris and the little one—Emberly, right?"

Eyes shining with pride, Shrote pulled out his wallet to share a picture of his wife Doris, a faded young woman, holding their infant child.

"Look-ee there," Christian cooed. "If that ain't the mos' beautiful baby girl I ever did see. You must be one proud papa."

"Yessir, that I am. An' I thank you for bein' so kind as to ask 'bout my Emberly. You know how much that means to me, her bein' Down Syndrome and all." Christian saw tears in Chuck's eyes and he reached out to give his hand a squeeze. Chuck swallowed hard before answering. "Pastor, you go on home now. Just promise that from now on you'll drive more careful. I don't want to be scrapin' my favorite spiritual advisor off the side of the road. I prefer to see you in one piece and on the pulpit Sundays."

"Thanks Chuck. 'Preciate it. Truly I do. Blessings to Doris and a special kiss to little Emberly."

❖

Perspiring like it was high noon on a hot summer day, Christian stayed put on the side of the road, willing himself sober. Seeing

Luke tonight had thrust him back into the mindset of border police and dead bodies and Chuck's police siren had had a profound effect on him. He knew that the only reason Chuck hadn't hauled him in on a DUI was because of his position. A position he would *never* willingly relinquish.

And so, he had his answer. Whatever it took to remain pastor to these fine people, to walk above the fray and to garner their respect, well, that was what he would do. If it meant giving in to extortion, then so be it. As Luke said, it was the cost of doing business. Christian had no doubt that he and Luke were headed separate ways come the Rapture, but in this life it appeared that they were to be inextricably linked together in shared sin.

With a heavy heart, Christian phoned Luke the next day to arrange a second meeting. Luke would get twenty percent of all present and future income in exchange for his silence. He was to be given unfettered access to the books and financial records, unannounced and at any time. Should anyone question the relationship, Christian would say he'd brought Luke on in a marketing role. No papers were signed, no witnesses were present. It was done on a handshake. The way business used to be done. On trust.

❖

From that day forth, Christian focused on nothing but money. Requests to guest preach now went through Marva, the newly hired church administrator, who persuasively explained Christian's newly instituted five-hundred-dollar stipend per engagement. Interestingly, putting a monetary value on his time served to increase demand, and Marva had no difficulty filling his calendar. He set about learning all there was to know about the burgeoning Word of Faith Movement, a branch of Christianity he realized might well hold the keys to *his* kingdom. Almost immediately, he set upon coaching the congregation on the spiritual necessity and benefits of tithing, his exhortations all the more passionate after he spent two days at a Word of Faith Leadership Conference in Newark, Texas where Pastor Strangelove—yes, that was his name— opened Christian's eyes to the benefits of the annuity-like payments his Newark church collected each week. Soon, the good pastor of Pearsall could be heard Sundays, no matter where he was, spreading the gospel of Wealth and Salvation, with promises of earthly and heavenly riches going out to those who generously "sowed their seed." And this time, he didn't mean sexually.

One Sunday morning, having recently learned that parishioner Eula Mae Anders was struggling mightily with lupus, Christian descended from the pulpit at Grace Be Thine to take her arm. "Sister Eula Mae, come on up with me so that, as a congregation, we can do our utmost to work a miracle an' ease your pain an' sufferin'. It's high time our little community had itself a livin' example of what real faith can do."

Together, they made their way up the stairs, whereupon Christian made a show of getting Eula Mae comfortably situated before holding the microphone up to her mouth.

"Eula Mae, before we go any further, I'd like you to answer me somethin'. Tell me, an' the congregation, have you welcomed the abidin' presence and power of the Holy Spirit into your life?"

Eula Mae, unused to attention, coughed uncomfortably and, with eyes looking downward, answered timorously, "Yes, Pastor, I have. Fact is, it was on the day you began ministering to me that I first received His Greatness, praised be."

Christian released her hand to pace the stage in silence, letting the power of her witnessing sink in. "Sister, I brought you up today so as to lay hands on you in hopes that you be cured. We all know that the Lord, in all His mercy, doesn't want you to suffer. You know that, don't you?" Eula Mae nodded.

"Then you must also know He sent His only Son to die so that you wouldn't suffer. Ain't that right?" Eula Mae moved her head up and down again, a somber, mournful nod.

He laid a hand on each of her shoulders and then slowly, softly, Christian sang a melody so hauntingly beautiful that, when he and the organist reached their concomitant crescendo, Eula Mae, forgetting her pain, jumped up from her chair. Incredulous at her momentary agility, tears of joy mixed with those of happiness at this apparent diminishment of her longstanding agony. Christian continued to sing a song of his own composition, its fluid melody repeating over and over the words from Matthew:

Every sickness and disease among the people.
He healed them all.

There wasn't a dry eye to be seen.

With careful, and deliberate pacing, Christian brought the crowd to a fever-pitch, then roared, "People! Jesus is here with us today! Now! In this, *our* sacred space. As he will be forever, Glory to the lamb of God!"

Hands waved frantically while cries of Amen! and Hallelujah! rang out, some shouted in hope, many in desperation. When Christian began to pass out prayer cloths—small squares of pre-cut linen guaranteed to fix whatever ailed you—he called upon his minions to offer up a healing seed for Eula Mae.

"Friends, I ask, in His name, that together we sow the seeds of healin' for our sister in Christ, Eula Mae Anders, so that she may finally be freed from her bodily anguish. If you wonder how much to sow, your answer is in the book each of us holds right now in our hands." He opened his Bible as if to read, but without looking down, he proclaimed, "Second Corinthians Chapter Nine, Verse Six, 'And remember this—if you give little, you will get little. A farmer who plants just a few seeds will only a small crop, but if he plants much, he will reap much.'"

Allowing a few moments of silence, he continued, "As you sow, so shall you reap. Give all you can, for Eula Mae. Give for yourself. Do it in multiples of seven an' you answer to the holiest of numbers. Seven, you ask? Think on the Bible. Why, the world itself was created in *seven* days. An' on the *seventh* day, we rest. Or how 'bout here?" He paged through his book. "'Noah took every clean beast and every bird by *seven*.' Or the fact that Egypt had *seven* years of plenty an' *seven* years of famine. I could go on an' on, but I think you get my drift.

"If seven dollars is all you can give today, well then, make it seven. If you can give seventy, then sow your seed for seventy. An' who can say but that there aren't a few among us who might even have saved up enough to offer up seven hundred? Remember, the more you give, the more comes back to you. Oh, an' if you don't have cash on you, no worries. You can write a check—or fill out the credit card slip in your program. Yes, the Lord takes credit." And he chuckled. "Who will be first to come forward?"

With a flourish, he lowered his Bible, placed his hand atop and closed his eyes. "I stand before you today an' make this pledge. I pledge, my hand upon this sacred book, that whatever you sow, it'll come back to you a thousandfold. If you're strugglin' with money, ask yourselves this, 'Will seven dollars, or seventy, or even seven hundred pay off my debts? Will it buy me a new home? Get me a new job?'

"You *know* the answer. *No! It will not!* But what you might not know is that *your* seven, or seventy, or seven-hundred-dollar seed will, beyond the shadow of a doubt, *guarantee* an eternal place in Heaven. An' guess where that'll be?" He paused. "What if I said, in the seat at the right hand of God? How's that sound to you? An' don't worry none. There's room for everyone." By now he was smiling broadly. "I'd say that's a danged good investment to make on a piece of eternal real estate, wouldn't you?"

The congregants looked around at one another only to see faces as enraptured as they felt. A new spirit was awakening in the church and those present felt privileged to be part of it. When John Dietz stepped up and declared, "Here's my seventy dollars," others began to stream forward, some with checks or credit slips, most with cash. By the end of the service, the basket was overflowing. A grateful and gracious Eula Mae Anders saw the wonder of it all; her friends and neighbors opening not only their hearts but their wallets as well, all in service of the Lord so that He might heal her. Fortunately for her, she would never know how much of the money would line the pockets of her adored and trusted pastor and his extortionist, Luke. Trembling with emotion, her son Wayne humbly gathered her from the stage to take her back to her seat for the closing prayer.

The morning had been a fruitful one, most of all for Christian. The plain truth was this: The simple are easily led.

11

Born That Way

July 2, 1984

THE INTIMACY THAT PASSED between Darlene and Christian at Ina's Beauty Nook hadn't diminished in Darlene's mind even though she had had to push it to the side for another day. From the moment she returned home from Pearsall she was preoccupied with what was certain to be her best quarter since joining Loretta's Beauty Supplies, leaving her with little time to absorb what had happened that day. Now, the long month of June behind her, she was physically exhausted but content—her efforts having paid off in the best of all possible ways.

When Loretta's was chosen as the Southwest Distributor of Dye-It, the most coveted account in the mid-priced national beauty portfolio, it was a sure sign that the beauty supply house was on the rise. To sweeten the pot, Dye-It had themselves recently acquired a small company with a patented innovative color extender named Born That Way. Throughout the month of June, Darlene knocked on every beautician's door in her territory to introduce Born That Way, frequently calling on each salon more than once, and her sales went through the roof. Dye-It's national media blitz and corresponding catchy jingle hadn't hurt either.

> Glow away, don't fade away.
> An' when they ask you, you say,
> Me? I was borrrrn . . . thaaat way.
> The sun's no foe
> Outside you'll go
> Cause you were borrrrn . . . thaaat . . . way.
> Born That Way—The Answer to The Fade-Out Blues.

Sparing no expense, Dye-It signed the number-one country singer, Marlee Jayne Johnson, as the voice and face of their ad campaign and in no time Born That Way spread across the southwest like a hot virus in the dead of winter. And down here in the land where the harsh sunlight bleached out a woman's color almost the minute it was applied, Born That Way flew off the shelves. Darlene had long aspired to be named Texas' Top Beauty Rep of the Year, and Born That Way had finally pushed her over the top. Loretta's held their annual statewide banquet in her honor, where she was presented with the highly coveted Golden You Glow Girl trophy along with a check for five thousand dollars. Money and praise pocketed, she knew she was at the top of her game professionally. Curiously though, she left the hall feeling hollow.

The emptiness had been there since meeting Christian, but work had allowed her to keep a lid on it. Driving back from Pearsall to San Antonio the day they met, she'd reveled in the promise of that charged encounter, attributing it at the time to hormones and the fact that she hadn't been with a man in months. Now, a month later, when she still couldn't get him out of her mind, she knew it had to be more. The rush of work behind her, she had far too much time on her hands to obsess, and obsess she did. Over and over she replayed their conversation, convincing herself she wasn't wrong about the frank desire—and kindness—she'd seen in his eyes. But a month had passed with nary a sign from him. In an effort to get him off her mind, she called up an old fling, but the mindless sex did nothing to relieve her want.

Never one to let grass grow under her feet, she decided the time had come for her to pay another call at Ina's. She would go on Wednesday at two on the off-chance he had a standing appointment. If not, at least she could prod Ina and learn if Christian had spoken of her. If her luck held, he'd be there, and she could take his measure for herself. No matter, anything was better than waiting for a silent phone to ring.

❖

It was eighty-nine degrees in the shade when she pulled up to Ina's, and she could only hope her deodorant would hold. She wore her best dress—a slinky hot pink jersey that followed her every curve, its vibrant color accentuating the red of her hair. A blast of cold air welcomed her as she pushed open Ina's back door, her heart high in her throat. To her great disappointment, though, the manicure station was empty.

Out front Ina, elbows deep in a washbasin, scrubbed away at a woman's thinning scalp. Looking up to see Darlene, Ina whooped, "Well, well, well, look what the cat dragged in. I was just sayin' to Deena here that we had ourselves such a run on Born That Way that I done run out. An' who should sashay on in but Red herself? My, my but don't you look tasty today? Got yourself a hot date?"

Darlene's laugh sliced through what felt like an undercurrent of jealousy. "Hot date? Hah! Don't I wish? No dearie, I'm out makin' calls is all, checkin' in on who needs more product. The way Born That Way's been flyin' outta the warehouse, I wanted to see how you're fixed."

Deena Brolly chimed in, "This the Dye-It lady? Lordy, as I live and breathe, if this ain't my lucky day. I jest finished tellin' Ina my color's faded off into the next county an' I come in today hopin' for summa that Born That Way my danged sister-in-law's been braggin' on, an' Ina tells me she's plumb run out."

Darlene chortled, "It *is* your lucky day then. I've got plenty out in the car. Ina, tell me what number Deena needs an' I'll fetch it for you. Then, when you have a minute, we'll go over your order."

"Bring me a #3 and we'll have ourselves a happy customer, ain't that right, Deena? Lean your head on back now. I got to rinse you off."

With a bottle of Born That Way #3 delivered to Ina's station, Darlene returned to the manicure room. Her heart resumed its quickened pace as she went to the mirror, reapplied her lipstick and ran a comb over her teased hair. There remained a few more minutes before the clock struck two, but hope was beginning to fade.

Then the back door swung open and in walked Christian.

They looked at each other with the force of mutual surprise. Darlene's cheeks, flushed a deep red, mirroring his own. Flummoxed at first, she quickly found the necessary presence of mind to begin a conversation.

"Well, if it ain't Pastor Man! An' they say lightnin' doesn't strike twice in the same place." If Darlene had touched a finger to Christian, he would have fallen to the ground, he was that surprised. The truth was she had rarely been far from his mind this past month. He had struggled mightily every day against the urge to contact her, knowing full well where that one call would lead. But instead of throwing her card, and thus the temptation, away, he stashed it in a small box hidden in the back of his jumbled bedroom closet. Inside the box were his two most prized possessions, both photographs: one, the picture of his mama that he'd stolen from Mason's dresser, and the other a photo taken the afternoon he was named captain of the East Baptist Warriors. He hadn't looked in the box since the day he married, afraid of the feelings the pictures would evoke. But for his adulterous thoughts, he would have tossed Darlene's card instead of concealing it in his secret hiding place. Despite his best efforts to put her out of mind, Darlene had continued to haunt him. He began to take the card out of the box almost daily, his resolve eroding bit by bit. Now here she was in the flesh. He didn't know how he'd find the strength to stop himself.

It seemed an eternity before he found the wherewithal to speak. They were both so awkward and self-aware that neither noticed the other's anxiety. "Miss Steeger," he murmured tremulously, "May I say how very pleased I am to see you?"

She began to relax. "Why thank you, sir. An' I might add that you're a sight for sore eyes yourself. I hear you were preachin' up my way last Sunday. Seems folks cain't sing your praises enough. I been hearin' a lotta mighty good things 'bout you. Maybe one day, I'll even make it to one of your events."

There it was. She'd rehearsed her lines on the drive to Pearsall, but it was spontaneity that broke the ice. He threw back his head and laughed with gusto, "One a my events! My, my, you *do* have a way of puttin' things. In my business, we tend to refer to our *events* as *services*." Still chuckling, he motioned graciously with his hand to the two chairs where they'd first talked and they sat down together for the second time.

Though he was hardly familiar with Catholic doctrine and practices, there was something in Christian's bearing that invited confession, particularly from members of the female sex. Ever since shedding his delinquent past, the lonely child in this oddly charismatic man caused many a woman to fantasize about wrapping her maternal arms about him. Not only that, but his pastoral gravitas encouraged both men and women to share their innermost secrets and desires with him. With Christian and Darlene—the perennial man-child and the femme fatale faux-feminist—the combination of their joint wants and needs was wildly combustible.

Conversation between them came easily—perhaps too much so. Christian had never been around a woman like her— one who so brazenly invited thoughts of wild fantasy even as she opened wide the doors to her own troubled past. Darlene hadn't come today to reveal anything more than physical desire, and a strong one at that. But when Christian laughed, his kind eyes crinkling up with joy and trust, she opened up, talking as if she'd known him forever, exposing parts of her psyche that she had kept hidden for much too long.

She told him how her daddy ran off when she was three, leaving her mama to support them on what she made cleaning offices at night. Her eyes welled up when she described how hard her mama had worked, scrimping and saving, and all of it for Darlene. How finally she scraped together enough money so that, by the time Darlene was thirteen and coming into her figure, her mama had accrued enough to sign her up for the local teen beauty pageant.

The thought of this sexually ripe woman perched on the cusp of puberty was so arousing to Christian it was all he could do not to erupt right there on the spot.

By the time Darlene was fourteen, her mama felt the need to be around evenings, so she traded in her nighttime janitorial job at Loretta's, the beauty supply house in which Darlene had recently risen to the top of the sales force, for the day shift. The job came with an important perk: free cosmetics and hair products, both of which were enormously helpful for a burgeoning beauty queen. Physically precocious, Darlene took to pageantry, and it took to her. She won the Texas Beauty Teen title at fifteen. Along with the crown and a small sum of money came an obligation to travel throughout the county, speaking at 4-H Clubs and the like. Exciting as this was for a girl who had never left home, the world of pageants had its dark side.

"I can't believe I'm telling you this. I never breathed a word of my shame to another soul before." Christian held her gaze and she steeled herself to continue.

"After a coupla more wins, I started to get a lot of attention, 'specially from the men. Mama came 'long with me when she could but most times, she hadda stay behind to work so I was on my own. I'd been lucky growin' up, it always bein' Mama an' me, an' her carin' so much 'bout me but that also made me awful naïve. Sometimes, when I was away competin', I was so lonely I liked to die. I don't expect you ever been to one a these pageants?" He shook his head. "Well, if you had, you'd understand the kinda men who hang round 'em, an' I'm here to say, none of 'em have anything good on their minds.

"The first one what paid me any real notice was old enough to be my daddy. He started out all nice and seemingly innerested in my welfare, talkin' to me like a father might talk to daughter, an' like I said, I was pretty wet behind the ears. So I let myself believe he was jest a kindly man, maybe a little lonely was all. Deep down I probly knew something wasn't right but growin' up fatherless like I did, it felt good to think he was lookin' out for me.

"It didn't hardly take any time at all though afore he started in on me. A hand where it shouldn't be, his eyes checkin' me out all the time, always tellin' me how pretty I was. Then one day he told me he had a special treat. He had planned a photo shoot in his motel room, jest for me, the kind like the models do. Only thing is, he was the photographer. I was a little nervous 'bout bein' alone with him but I went 'long with it. He started right in posin' me in all kinda positions, all the while tellin' me this was *art* photography. That a girl who wanted to go places had to have these shots. An' that was when things started to turn." She looked away, her hands gripping hard the sides of her chair.

"He had ta be fifty if he was a day, an' I wasn't but fifteen. Fifteen!"

Christian touched his black handkerchief to her tear-stained cheeks.

"He ripped my clothes off and then he *forced* himself on me. I wasn't more'n a hundred pounds soakin' wet. I couldn't fight him. I jest couldn't. I didn't have the strength." She was crying full out by now and Christian, the pastor, didn't know what to do. Christian the man, however, did. He took hold of her hand. "I went to the head of the pageant an' you wanna know what he did? He laughed. Tole me straight out that lookin' how I did, it wasn't any wonder a man would take to me. Said that what happened musta been my fault. That I asked for it. Said if I didn't leave it be, he'd enjoy a taste a my sugar himself.

"So I packed up and hurried back to Mama fast as I could. An' I never did tell her. It woulda broken her heart. How could I after all she'd sacrificed?

"When I got home I told her I lost an' I was done with pageants. I saw the disappointment in her eyes but she never got mad. She was like that. Never wantin' me to feel bad. I tell you though, awful as it was, I learned somethin' back then. I learned that I'm the one has to look after myself cause there ain't really no one else can. I grew up an awful lot then an' damn fast, that's for sure."

Her confession complete, she couldn't look him in the eye. Having never told this to anyone, she had no idea know how he would take it. For his part, Christian was glad she didn't look his way. When he imagined her as a young teen, he couldn't help but feel more than a little like the men about whom she spoke. He certainly understood why no man could be around her, be she fifteen or fifty, and not want her so desperately he would be willing to risk everything to have her.

He was a man of God now, an ordained pastor, albeit by mail order, and he couldn't afford to surrender to temptation because, for the first time in his life, he had something to lose. On the other hand, he rationalized, how could it be wrong just to listen to this lovely woman unburden her unbearably heavy load? It was what God expected of him, that much he knew.

Finally, she turned and looked him squarely in the eye. "I hope you don't see me different now that you know. I don't know why I told you, us practically bein' strangers. It's jest that you seem different than most men. So decent, so—Christian."

Before he crossed the proverbial Rubicon, Christian reached into his pocket and fingered the compact Bible he always kept with him, praying somehow that its touch alone would transfer to him a much-needed fortitude. "My dear, I am not here to judge. That task belongs solely to the Lord. I too have a past, one which I gratefully left behind when I found Jesus. Someday, like me, maybe you'll welcome Him into your life so that He can ease your pain, as He did mine. If you do, not only will He wipe the slate clean, but then you too can forgive yourself."

She reddened with anger. "Forgive myself? Pastor, I never thought *I* was the one needs forgivin'. I only told you all this because it seemed you'd understand. Maybe I'm wrong about you."

The heat of moments ago evaporated. Hellfire and damnation! He shouldn't have spoken so high and mighty. He cleared his throat to buy time as tears rushed to his eyes, "My dear, what I'm tryin' to say is that I do not judge you. Not in the least. That's not my place. I sit before you today, a man of God, with you tellin' me a story that near to breaks my heart. You have to know how hard I'm strugglin' to maintain my pastorly dignity. Your being next to me, so close I can feel your heat, smell your sweetness—why, it's all I can do to stop from takin' you in my arms."

Softly, she began to weep.

"There, there, my angel. Don't you see what you do to me? An' how very weak I am?" To his relief, she reached for his hand and smiled at him with her warm green eyes.

At that moment, Ina entered the room and, guiltily, they pulled apart. "At it again, are ya Miss Darlene?" she cackled, filling the basin in front of him. "Lookit the two of you! If

I didn't know better, I'd think somethin' was goin' on here. Good thing I come back to chaperone."

Like the rest of Pearsall, she knew all too well about the marital hell in which her beloved pastor lived, and like most, she wished he had a way out. She also knew that if he'd ever so much as looked her way, she'd have left Earl so fast his head woulda spun clear off. Taking her age into account and knowing full well that she was hardly the kind of woman any man would ever look at in that way, she only hoped that one day Christian could find the happiness he deserved. But honest to Jesus, did it have to be with Darlene?

Christian popped his hands into the warm, sudsy water for a soak while Ina placed her order with Darlene. That done, the three chatted amiably while Ina tended to Christian's nails. Darlene, unsure whether to stay or leave, was surprised when she realized that all she really wanted was to stay at this man's side. Her spirits soared at Ina's generous suggestion.

"Christian, why don't you drive Darlene out to the church this afternoon an' show her 'round?" To Darlene, she boasted, "Pastor's performed miracles with what used to be an ole pony keg. Now folks travel as far as fifty miles every week jest to hear him preach. We got two restaurants what are now open Sunday lunch for churchgoers, and hot-damn, if they ain't full to burstin'. This one here, why he's practically a one-man industry for Pearsall. He'll be the rebirth of us all," not realizing her unintended play on words.

"I was just tellin' the pastor here that I been hearing 'bout him a lot lately," Darlene said. She sent an intimate look Christian's way, one Ina didn't miss. "I'd love to see the church, that is, if you're not afraid lightning'll strike the minute I enter?

Many a moon's come an' gone since I last entered a place of worship."

Slowly, he released his breath, relieved they were back on track. "Ina, now that's an idea. Tell me. You got any other customers comin' in today?"

"You're my last."

"Then how's about the three of us go on over there together? Dorothy could use the help decoratin' for Soul Train, though she'd never admit it, an' I'd love to show Darlene my pride an' joy."

Darlene's heart took a nosedive. Even with all he'd just said and the way he looked at her when he said it, it looked as if he meant to keep her at arm's length. When Ina answered, "Why not? A girl's entitled ta a day off every now an' then," the lights inside Ina's Beauty Nook seemed to dim.

Damn Ina to hell.

12

Grace Be Mine

July 2, 1984

THEY DROVE ALONG IN silence, the pheromonal neurons singing and zinging their way across the front seat all the while Ina filled the back of the car with her inane chatter. Steering his ship into harbor, Christian spied Dorothy Brae at the far end of the property, exactly where he knew she'd be. Dorothy, a lonely, middle-aged woman, her children long gone and her husband paying her no never mind, had too much time on her hands. When it got down to it, it was either serving as a surrogate church-wife or spending her days at home alone with the bottle. She chose the former.

Possessed with an artist's soul, Dorothy's relatively recent love of Christ had delivered her and her questionable talents to Grace Be Thine. When Christian pulled up, she was so involved creating a poster that she didn't hear the car. From the beginning, she made it clear that she preferred to work solo when it came to artistic ventures, but with the Fourth only two days away she was overwhelmed with all that was left to do if the Soul Train decorations were to meet her standards. So, instead of her trademark snippiness, she showed relief when Ina sallied up with an offer of help. Years of catering to women in the shop gave Ina the inside track on how to deal with the often crotchety woman.

"Dorothy! Look at your beautiful handiwork! I rode out with Pastor C so's he kin show my beauty rep the church, an' I came along ta see if you need an extry setta hands. That is, long as you know that the only kinda artistic talent I got is the hairdo kind. But if it's help with spray paintin' you need, I'm all yours."

Another set of hands was precisely what Dorothy needed. She looked to the heavens and muttered, "Thank you Jesus. Ina, you come on over here an' I'll show you what I need."

As the women began their collaboration and Ina settled into her perpetual blather, neither noticed Darlene and Christian slip away into the church. With Ina out of the way, Darlene's excitement returned. She looked around her. If she were to be objective, there was little in any aspect of the small building to recommend it. To her eye, it looked very much like the retro-fitted pony keg that it was. But to Christian, Grace Be Thine was nothing less than the eighth wonder of the world, and it was with a compelling sense of pride that he showed her around. He left nothing out, not even the smallest detail. Before long, she found herself thinking she might indeed be in the presence of something great.

It had been a long time since Darlene had entered a church—she didn't go in for religion. Still, she found herself wondering about Grace Be Thine's lack of religious symbols. Three flags stood prominently in the front of the chapel: The American, a Christian banner, and the flag of Israel.

Darlene was puzzled as to why a Jewish flag would feature so prominently in a place of Christian worship, but the thought disappeared as the temperature in the room started to rise. The more Christian talked, the less she heard. Words muddled together and she found that all she wanted to do was to silence his mouth with her lips. Everything he touched provoked her jealousy—she wanted her flesh to be the object of his caress. As she witnessed his passion for his church, she felt as close to religion as ever she had, praying silently, *Dear God, please let him take me here and now.*

Glancing around the insignificant building, she felt a certainty that the structure had yet to be built that could contain this man. An aura of greatness suffused him, and whether or not it came from God she was hardly qualified to say. At the moment, she didn't much care where it came from. She simply wanted to be part of it.

A calm exterior belied the inward torrent that at the same time pummeled Christian. As he guided Darlene through the small church, all redemptive thoughts dissipated in the face of her nearness. He babbled on mindlessly, all the while his loins cried out for release. On the pretense of sharing his collection of biblical figurines, he led her down a dark flight of stairs into a small, dank cellar. Taking her hand, he pulled her into a small storage room, letting the door close firmly behind them.

For a moment, they stood apart, each wanting the delicious moment of first desire to go on forever, their rapidly weakening flesh drinking in the tension. If Darlene were to look down, she would know with certainty that here stood not just a man of God, but more simply, a flesh and bone man who wanted what only this Earth could provide.

He lifted his hand to touch her cheek ever so slightly, and with that touch, the match was lit. All thoughts about right and wrong vanished in the face of his unstoppable, demanding need. He pulled her to him, softly intoning Solomon's erotic words from so long ago: "Open to me, my sister, my love, my dove, my undefiled."

With the first kiss, a kiss born of overwhelming hunger and need, their bodies melded together. She was dwarfed by his size, yet somehow it seemed they were made to fit. His hands wandered slowly, languorously, delighting in every curve and crevice, fondling copious breasts while his fingers sought out the source of his desire. To his nearly eruptible excitement, he felt two lacy garters high upon each thigh. He stood up and fumbled to unfasten them, letting the old-world silken stockings slip to the floor. When the ghost of the Righteous sent a last S.O.S. to his animal brain, he made a weak effort to pull away, but to no avail.

Thy kingdom come, thy will be done, he intoned and then his conscience went mute. Willingly, thrillingly, he watched her go down on bended knee and he surrendered to the magic of her mouth, after which he gave as good as he got. The entire act took less than five minutes, but they were five minutes that were to change the course of their lives.

When they heard footsteps overhead, they pulled apart without a word, wiping, zipping, snapping, adjusting. Upon exiting the closet, Darlene placed one of her garters, fragrant with her scent, into his palm. He closed his hand around it, a sacrosanct gem, and when his eyes adjusted to the light, he saw it was embroidered with the initials DMS.

It was then he knew that one day soon, other initials would grace her lovely thighs. Whatever it took, he would find a way to answer to God for what they had started today and somehow, someday, they would join together, and in *this* life. After a few interminable minutes, they heard Dorothy's car start up and up the stairs they climbed, the church ladies, having vanished, none the wiser.

❖

Little was said on their way back to Ina's. Neither had the language to communicate what had just taken place. They made a simple plan: they'd meet again in ten days and spend the night together. Christian had a preaching engagement at the First Calvary Assemblies of God in Pleasanton one week from Sunday, whereupon Darlene Steeger would experience a service for the first time since girlhood. With Pleasanton only an hour away from San Antonio, they decided to play it safe and spend the night an hour farther west to make it less likely they would be spotted.

In the interim, Darlene would use the time to figure out how to make herself indispensable, no matter what obstacles Christian's wife, or Jesus, might throw in their way.

❖

Back in San Antonio, Darlene relived the afternoon's every detail in a state of dreamy half-consciousness. She neither saw nor spoke to anyone, unwilling to let something so sacred turn into just another cheap sexcapade. No stranger to random sex, she knew that what had happened was of another order entirely.

Christian, unwilling to face home and Elena, headed back to the church. He parked the Lincoln out back, went inside, and locked the church doors. Then, kneeling down, he wept unrestrainedly, wept with the release from a lifetime of loneliness. Finally, his head throbbing and his mind a muddle, he arose and went to his office. Seated in a hard-backed chair, his Bible spread before him, he set to work.

A knife-like pain sliced at him when he read:

> And I say unto you, Whosoever shall put away his wife, except it be for fornication, and shall marry another, committeth adultery. —Matthew 19:9

Even if today's transgression paled in comparison to what had come before, it was nonetheless a betrayal of the highest order. Yet if the Lord had forgiven him the sin of murder, didn't it stand to reason that mere adultery couldn't possibly cancel out the good he'd done since then? Still, the question nagged at him: just how many strikes is a man permitted before the promise of Salvation is withdrawn? Was there a limit, he wondered? He plodded on in his quest for scriptural redemption, continuing his search late into the night, until finally he found something. It wasn't perfect, but it was a start:

> Be not deceived: neither fornicators , nor idolaters, nor adulterers, nor effeminate, nor abusers of themselves with mankind . . . shall inherit the kingdom of God. —1 Corinthians 6:9-10

Abusers of themselves with mankind: If he was reading this correctly—and he was sure he was—it said right here that, with Elena's coat-hanger abortion she had become an *abuser of the entire human race*. That meant that, thanks to that murderous act, Christian, a newly reborn shepherd of souls, could not possibly be meant to spend life on Earth in partnership with such a beast.

His heart thundered with both fear and hope. There had to be more. The Bible, unlike his fellow man, had never let him down before and, he was sure, it wouldn't now. Then there, in Deuteronomy, he found it. God spoke to him from the age of the Jew, showering him with the vindication he so desperately sought:

When a man hath taken a wife, and married her, and it come to pass that she find no favour in his eyes, because he hath found some uncleanness in her: then let him write her a bill of divorcement, and give it in her hand, and send her out of his house. —Deuteronomy 24:1

Damn. They didn't call it the Good Book for nothing.

13

In Darlene We Trust

Mid-July 1984

THE RAINS CAME, CLEANSING the ever-dusty roads and turning the sun-baked parking lot outside the Vogue Bar & Grill into a mud-slickened hazard. Darlene and Christian sat next to an open window and every time the wind picked up, droplets of cold rain spat through the tattered screen, dampening their skin, lending a physical chill to the thrill-chill that pulsed across the table. It was the middle of a Sunday afternoon and they were the only customers in the bar. The locals were likely at home enjoying or, at the very least tolerating, family time after their post-church suppers. A muscled bartender stood guard over his liquid treasures and upon setting a bottle of scotch and two glasses at the ready, he never looked their way again, his eyes fixed on the images and grunting thuds emanating from the wrestling match on a screen above the bar.

Since their vertical romp at Grace Be Thine, Darlene's spirits had risen and fallen with a will of their own. Her heart, serving as her daily alarm clock, awakened her every day at four a.m., sounding, pounding. Ten days seemed too long to wait. Ten days gave her too much time in which to scale the heights only to find herself back in freefall, staring across the chasm of fear that is spelled A-B-A-N-D-O-N-M-E-N-T. And when the fear came, it was with a terror so piercing it grabbed her by the throat and skirted along every nerve in her being, finally burrowing deep inside her bones. Hers was a heart-clock, sounding and sending her off to do battle with her bowels. Up and down, bed to bathroom, she raced. From Hope to Faith to Panic to Dread, then back to Hope, Desire never once leaving her. Desire, the link between all things.

It was surprising that a man of religion should have such sway over her. Aside from physical chemistry, what did they have? He was no different than the tens of other bible-thumping pretenders she'd spent her life avoiding. Darlene had never understood the mindset that permitted otherwise rational human beings to blindly set aside reality when it came to the subject of religion. The way she saw it, if there really was a greater being, where had He been the day she was raped? If she had an ounce of sense, when Christian told her that the only laws worth following were biblical, she should have bolted. But alas, here she was, afflicted with emotional and physical diarrhea—and an unstoppable sexual yearning.

She hoped he was less serious about his extreme beliefs than he appeared. She hoped religion was more or less a gig to him— one that could be quite lucrative, as she well knew. If not, how could she possibly accept Christian's willingness to follow laws written before science and knowledge had had the chance to replace ignorance? It wasn't that faith didn't have its place, but to live in a world as backward as the one in which Christian purported to believe was, she thought, at best, ignorant, and at worst, dangerous. Darlene might have grown up with little in the way of a formal education but she was smart enough to know truth from fiction. Here in the Bible Belt, when a person turned his life so completely over to God it was usually because he was running from something. When she learned the reason for Christian's turn to Jesus, then she'd know the man.

Until then, why not have some fun?

❖

From the opposite side of the table, Christian drank in the sight and smell of her, his finger twirling lazily around the rim of his glass. Like her, he'd been in a fever pitch ever since their afternoon delight at Grace where, indeed, her grace had been his. A few surly remarks were the only contact he shared with Elena these days, their masquerade irrevocably shattered. Now that he'd experienced the feelings a man could have for a woman, the question was no longer if, but when, he'd put the beast of his marriage out of its misery.

He poured himself another drink and quickly threw it back. "I don't know where to start."

She picked up his hand. "Start at the beginning. Say what's in your heart an' the rest will follow."

Maybe it was the softness of her voice that moved him to share. Probably, it was the memory of her flesh. But once begun, the act of sharing was exhilarating. He spoke of his childhood; his mother's death and the abuse he'd suffered at the hand of his father. He described his shotgun marriage and how it had become a prison of unbearable torture, especially after he learned of the baby-killing evil in Elena. He told her how he stayed up all night searching for biblical justification to understand the magnitude of the sin that he'd committed with Darlene in the church basement. How when at last he found the liberating passages, it was if a millstone had been lifted from his neck. But he didn't tell all, his instincts warning him that certain parts of his past belonged only between him and his maker.

And in the telling, their relationship jumped to a higher plane. The physical attraction remained as powerful, but with their mutual revelation and acceptance, what had been purely sexual enlarged into something more.

"Christian, just because you're a pastor doesn't mean you're different from us other mortals. All of us, we got our problems. It's just that while you might try to solve things in a godly way, others of us use the brains God gave us. Ya know, when I was growin' up an' things got to overwhelmin' me, my mama would say, 'Darlene, take your problems, dice 'em up into bits an' pieces you can handle then go out an' take 'em on, one at a time. It's the only thing you can do when life's got you by the short hairs.'

"An' you know what? She was right. When you do that, then the big things don't seem so big an' one by one, you find your way 'round each hurdle. As for you an' me an' whatever we got goin' here, what do ya say to us puttin' our heads together an' figurin' it all out, piece by piece? First, we take it apart and get ridda what doesn't work. After that comes the fun—puttin' it back together the way *your* God meant it to be." Inwardly, she cheered her unplanned but skillful use of the Lord.

Running a bare foot along the inside of his thigh, she lingered just long enough to raise the flag of his desire. "I think we can do this, don't you?"

He trembled in answer, as waves of want crashed over him. Encouraged by the raw hunger in his eyes, she pushed forward,

"Look, we haven't known each other long but if you could put yourself in my hands, I believe I might be the one to change your life. Not that I claim the powers of your God—nothin' like that—but I will tell you this: life's yet to get the best of me, try as it might."

He looked down at the small hands clutching his and answered, "My angel, you probly see I don't do this easily." He paused, the sensation of emotional honesty overwhelming him. "I never been blessed with the love of another. But if you look into your soul right now, you will know that not only do you hold my hands, you also hold my heart."

As for Darlene, whether what she felt was love, lust, or dreams of a future paved with gold, only God himself could know.

14

Cat-ricide: A Tale of Blood Redemption

November 1984

THE DIVORCE WAS SIMPLE. Grace Be Thine, a non-profit, didn't belong to them, they didn't own the house, and Christian's stash of blood money remained hidden. The judge declared simply, "No alimony," and their ten-year nightmare was over as abruptly as it had begun. In a gesture of uncharacteristic generosity, Christian offered Elena the TV. Together in the house for the last time, he sat by as she packed up her few possessions.

Concerning the divorce, Elena had no regrets. On the contrary, still terrified of his mood swings, she couldn't leave fast enough. Having barely survived, but never forgotten, the vicious beating he inflicted a year after they married, she suffered no illusions that he was a changed man. She knew it was only a matter of time before the violence resurfaced, and when it did she planned to be as far away as possible. Besides, she was leaving with the only thing she had ever wanted from him—the promise of citizenship. As for the television and the cats, he could keep them. She couldn't care less.

On her way out, she couldn't help lobbing a departing grenade his way. "Ir al infierno, bastardo! Truth ees I was already pregnant when I let you fuck me first time. My uncle, heem an' me, we treeked you, Señor Impotente!" Before he could answer she was out the door, slamming it shut on their marital disaster.

Fuck me. Did he hear what he thought he heard? That she was already with child when they fucked, meaning the wedding had been just another Farley scam, with Christian as the mark? Then his brain registered the word "impotente," melding the duplicity with the Masonic slurs on his manhood, and he saw red. Rage pounded a drumbeat in his head: *GET HER, GET HER, GET HER* and while every fiber of his being strained to give chase, to catch her and drag her back by her greasy spic hair, to leave her with the furious parting blows that her disrespect demanded, he stayed as if nailed in place. That his inner demons continued their whispers made it all the harder.

Don't let her go, not like that. You can't let that filthy whore speak to you in that way. Go on. GET HER. Show her what a real man is. His fury was matched, though, by the overwhelming desire not to destroy all he'd achieved, especially his chance of a future with Darlene. So instead of going after Elena, he went for the cats.

The first, a striped tabby, was curled up asleep in the corner when he grabbed it by the tail and hurled it with all his force against the peeling living room wall. The animal was killed on impact, its limp body crumpling onto the sofa, blood oozing from its mouth. His rage not spent, he went looking for the black cat, the one that most reminded him of Elena. It was fast asleep on their bed. Christian noted the irony as he approached.

Bad luck little cat. Black as night little cat. Adios little cat.

He seized it by the tail, dirty black tail just like Elena was a piece of dirty black tail. He swung it round and round and round and round, like he'd like to be swinging Elena. With each rotation, he felt his wrath begin to slip-slide away. Finally, dropping the lifeless animal on the ground, he wiped cat-blood from his eye and collapsed onto the bed, a childlike rhyme playing over and over in his head:

Pastor killed the cats.
What d'ya think of tha – aat?
Blood in the eye
Made them die
Pastor killed the cats.

He lay down as darkness made its slow creep into the room, an ominous silence surrounding him. He felt dirty, not the greasy grit-under-the-nails kind of dirty, but a seamy-like-a-porn-shop, dirty-in-the-eyes-of-God dirty. And all that dirt, it made his heart break. He needed to get clean more than he'd needed anything in a long time. But first, he rifled around in the kitchen for a garbage bag. Gingerly and with a sense of horror, he collected the small, dead, warm cat-bodies, threw them into the bag, and tied it off. As any murderer worth his salt would do, he threw the bag into the trunk of his car and drove off to stash the bloodied, lifeless animals in the dumpster behind the Food-Mart before speeding off. No Ho-Ho's for him tonight.

Back home, he shed his clothes and tossed them into the washtub, then stepped into the shower. He scrubbed himself raw, stopping only when he drew blood—his own for once—and watched the scarlet color join with the clean, clear water to disappear down the drain in one more blood sacrifice. Crying out in terror, he implored, "Jesus, my Lord and Savior, I cry out for your forgiveness yet again." Then he remembered the words he'd shared with congregant Joe Tansey not long ago. "Joe," he'd said, "there's no sin in this world so big that God won't forgive you." He had also reminded Joe: *Then Peter came to Jesus and asked, "Lord, how many times shall I forgive my brother when he sins against me? Up to seven times?" Jesus answered, "I tell you, not seven times, but seventy-seven times."*

Feeling cleansed, Christian stepped out of the shower to once again seek the numbing comfort of the bottle.

15

Movin' On Up

November 1984

FOR THE REST OF THE summer and into the fall, Darlene and Christian met in motels across South Texas. It was the first joy he had ever known, enhanced all the more by the titillation that accompanies illicit sex. Violating his way through the Ten Commandments, no bolt of lightning had yet struck him down, leading him to believe that his standing with Jesus had not been compromised. Elena was little more than a bad memory and the time had come to move the ball forward.

They returned to the Vogue, the site of Christian's first confessional, and sitting there with her he found himself too dizzy with arousal to even finish his first drink. Next door at the Moonlight No-Tell Motel, a hunchbacked desk clerk with a nametag reading "Slider" grunted in a gravelly voice, "How long you want the room fer? S'twenty-five dollars the first hour, thirty-five fer all night. Payment up front. Makes no matter ta me."

Christian cleared his throat in an effort to muster what dignity he could under the circumstances, and answered, "Excuse me, but my wife and I shall be paying by the night."

A lascivious snicker leaked from the gnome's mouth, making Christian blush as he slapped thirty-five dollars onto the counter. Darlene squeezed his hand to convey she felt no shame and then, regally, swept up the key and led him by the hand from the motel office, sorry for his embarrassment but feeling none of her own.

Room number seven, noted Christian. Seven. The holiest number of all. It was a sign. Had to be.

The shabbiness of the room did nothing to dampen their passion, and practically before the door slammed shut, they were tearing at each other's clothing. The simple sight of the ever-present black lace garters never failed to drive him wild. Panting, they fell upon the bed. His body buzzed electric and then everything melted away into her softness.

Thy navel is like a round goblet, which wanteth not liquor: thy belly is like an heap of wheat set about with lilies. Thy two breasts are like two young roes that are twins. The Song of Solomon was the only scripture he cared about right now.

When he entered her this time, it was like that terrible-wonderful South Texas night when he felt the spirit of Jesus Christ. A feeling of oneness came over him like it had back then, convincing him more than ever that what he was doing was right. Hour after hour, they lay siege to one another in as many ways as the body and imagination permitted. Their lovemaking vacillated between frenzied fury and languid, erotic exploration. All the while the night moved toward its inevitable dawn at both a snail's pace and warp speed. By the time the sun found its way through a gap in the heavy curtains, all indecision was gone. Damn the torpedo, but he wasn't going to throw this away. His life had been a train wreck up to now, with fate the cruel conductor. From this point on *he*, and *he* alone, would drive the future. With sheer effort he unlocked himself from the tangle of their half-asleep embrace and climbed out of the warm covers to retrieve his travel bag and the two small boxes within.

The first held a ring, the other a garter monogrammed with the initials DSH. Kneeling down on the rough brown carpet, he spoke in what Darlene called his "sermon voice," intoning words from the book of the prophet Hosea. "And I will betroth thee unto me for ever; yea, I will betroth thee unto me in righteousness, and in judgment, and in lovingkindness, and in mercies. I will even betroth thee unto me in faithfulness: and thou shalt know the Lord."

When he finished, tears were streaming down his face as Darlene tried to ascertain what in the world he'd just said. Thinking it possible he'd just asked for her hand, she answered with a question, "Forgive me if I'm way off base here, but is it crazy to think you just asked me to be your wife?"

Still kneeling, Christian roared with laughter. Leave it to Darlene to bring humor into the moment. "Yes, my little greenhorn. Will you *marry* me? I may have the gift of inspired preaching, I may have spiritual knowledge and think I understand the secrets of the world, I may have the faith needed to move mountains, but if I don't have you, I have nothing. Now—my knees are startin' to give, so a speedy answer would be much 'preciated 'bout now—that is if you think you're ready to love, honor, and obey."

Paying no heed to the obedience part of the equation, she yelped, "I thought you'd never ask! Yes, I'll marry you! Of course I will—that is if you're willin' to have a wife as religiously illiterate as me. Oh Christian. I'm so happy, I'd marry you today if I could."

"Soon enough my love, soon enough. Having failed so miserably once in marriage, it has to be right this time 'round." He took hold of her delicate hand and slipped a small chip of a diamond onto her fourth finger. "This here's what I call a holding ring. One day, soon's I can, I promise you'll have the biggest diamond you ever did see.

"An' this," he said handing her the other box, "this I had monogrammed special for you," and he placed the more intimate symbol of their love in her hand. She peeked inside, letting rip a lusty laugh when she saw the initials DSH woven onto a black garter.

Laughter turned to desire as he pushed her down again, rolling her back into day and another night. Trips to and from the Vogue kept them in food and drink, in between contortions of love and talk of the future. The shadows and shapes of his past had never suggested that John Christian Hillcox, born to lose, would one day find himself on a winning streak. But here he was, and with Jesus to thank for it. He knew with great clarity that the Almighty had brought Darlene to him so that, together, they could go out and conquer the world.

"You sure your God's alright with your bein' divorced and all?" she asked.

"I got it covered, my sweet," he answered, fingers tapping the Gideon's Bible next to the bed. "But," he continued, "there is something important I have to ask before you give me a final answer. You see, when I married Elena, even though it wasn't by my choosin', I made a covenant with God which, as you know, I broke. This time, I need for it to be different. The commitment we make to each other truly must mean till death do us part."

"Aw, what d'you think? That the two of us're gonna wake up one day, look 'cross the kitchen table and say, I'm outta here?" she chuckled, carelessly caressing his chest. "I hardly think that'll happen."

"Darlene, be serious." The abrupt change in his tone silenced her as her heart surprised her in her throat.

"What I am sayin' is that this is no ordinary proposal. The only way I can marry again is if it's a marriage where we're joined together in a covenant with God. Our vows have to be more than what's written on a piece of paper. I learned the hard way that paper is easily ripped up. I want us to be wedded, not jest to each other, but to another, so to speak. Do you follow me?"

She hooted, jabbing him in the gut, "Oh you! You're havin' your fun, aren't ya? Tellin' me we're gonna start our married life in a threesome. What are you up to anyways? Turnin' all free-love on me, are ya? If that ain't a hoot, I don't know what is. Meet the Hillcoxes—Pearsall's first polygamist family. Jesus f–in' Christ!"

Disapproval was branded on his face, putting her on notice. "Darlene, while you might choose to take Christ's name in vain, it *is* the Lord we are speaking of an' this here is no joking matter." He leaned in close, his eyes searing her psyche, sending an involuntary shiver through her. "As I said, I'm not looking for a flimsy contract we can walk away from on a whim. If we go through with this, mark my words, it will be as three. That means, you, me, and the Holy Spirit. Only then will we own the blessing that marriage can bring. If you can't say 'I do' for Eternity, then we have nothing."

Christian dropped back to his knees and softened his voice. "Now that you know the depth of my commitment, I ask again: Will you, Darlene Steeger, agree to be my covenantal partner in this life and in the hereafter?"

Darlene inhaled deeply and, taking a plunge she knew she didn't fully grasp, answered, "Will I? You're damn straight I will."

At the same time, all she could think was *Jesus Fucking Christ*.

❖

That Sunday, Christian confessed his marital infidelity from the pulpit at Grace Be Thine, his disgrace on show for all to witness. "Brothers and sisters, I stand here today, my head bowed in sin for I have come to confess—to lay myself bare before Jesus. *Father, I cry out for your forgiveness.*

"While I was still married to Elena Escamilla, I turned from God and the covenant of my marriage and committed adultery. I have no excuse. I am an adulterer an' accordin' to the Bible, I ought be stoned for this offense. Instead, I ask God's forgiveness, and hope that you good people will one day find it in your hearts to accept me for the sinner I am. Believe me, my transgression is equaled only by the shame that I bear.

"It is therefore with the deepest regret and sadness that I am compelled to tender my resignation as Pastor of this most glorious congregation, effective immediately. With what I did, I can no longer, in good conscience, serve as your spiritual leader."

There was scarcely a person present who didn't have his or her own transgression to hide, so none was willing to send him packing over a failing they so easily understood. In their exhortations to cajole, sympathize, and coax him to stay, no one knew that Christian's mind had long been made up. Much as he looked with gratitude upon the pony-keg church as his salvation, he was ready to move on to bigger things, with Darlene at his side.

He had one last announcement, an offering of sorts. "In hopes of bringin' some communal healin', I humbly ask that you, my friends, join me and my bride-to-be, Miss Darlene Steeger, next Saturday as witnesses to our covenantal marriage." The church fairly vibrated with this last piece of the puzzle.

"I've thought long an' hard about how to right myself in the eyes of the Lord and as a result, Miss Steeger and I have made a commitment not just to marry, but to do so in a way that binds us together in a marriage that no man can put asunder. As it is written in Matthew 19:6: 'So what therefore God has joined together, let not man separate.' I vow to you and the Lord on High that this one's for keeps. An' your presence as witnesses will help hold our feet to the fire. When we pledge our eternal commitment to one another, it will be before you and Jesus Christ, our Lord and Savior. Dare I hope that after you witness our marriage, it'll become somethin' of a tradition and that one day soon, some of you will choose to follow in our footsteps an' renew your own vows in a covenantal union right here, in this sacred space."

In the space of a few short moments the folks at Grace Be Thine learned that they'd lost this man who had insinuated himself into their lives and their hearts, and that they'd lost him forever. Only now that he was leaving did they understand that he had always been too big for them to hold onto and that they had been blessed to have him for as long as they did. It was hard to imagine their world without him, he who had brought hope, light, and sometimes even salvation, into their lives.

One week later, after a simple but moving ceremony, Christian and Darlene became one with God. They bade farewell to the good people of Pearsall who saw them off with tears of awe and sadness. Waving sadly as they drove off, the moment they turned the bend, Christian accelerating as fast as the roads would let him. Speeding forward to the deeper waters of San Antonio, neither one so much as gave a backward glance at the town that had made Christian Christian.

16

Headship

November 1984

SAN ANTONIO. LAND OF MILK and honey. Metropolitan population: 1.2 million. Christian's past was a mere fifty miles to the south, but he might as well have crossed the continent for the liberation those miles gave him.

In no time the newlyweds established themselves in San Antonio's Word of Faith community. From the get-go, Christian emphasized male superiority as a defining characteristic in the name of their proposed church, The Male Headship Church of God.

Having given Loretta's her notice, Darlene and Christian ventured out to find a location to set up shop. Thinking about the long term despite his burgeoning interest in the End Times, they wanted a property where Headship could not only grow but dominate. When they happened upon a sprawling one-story recently vacated department store, replete with a huge parking lot, they knew they'd found home. Christian was well aware that his reputation as a preacher had preceded him, but was still surprised at how easily things came his way. Darlene's legendary high school stature here in her hometown didn't hurt either.

"Well, well, if it ain't the love a my life, Darlene Steeger!" whooped Dale Jessup, the manager of San Antonio Heritage Savings and Loan. "Ooo-eee. If you ain't still good enough to eat! You got the prize with this one, didn't you?" he whispered to Christian in a low voice. "Mmm, mmmm. She never was hard on the eyes. Glad to see that hasn't changed none."

"Dale Jessup. What're you tryin' to do? Get me in hot water with my man here?" Darlene laughed, linking her arm in Christian's. "Damn, but it sure is good to see you," she smiled at Dale.

Turning to Christian she said, "Dale here, one a my former beaux, is now the hotshot at this here bank. An' Dale, in case you haven't heard, this here's my *husband*, Pastor John C. Hillcox. If you weren't payin' attention, I did say *Pastor*. I'm thinking you might wanna show a tetch more respect," she tittered. "Anyways, how the hell you been? I reckon a boatload a water's passed 'neath the proverbial bridge since we had our fun together. Tell me, you ever settle down?"

He held his hand out to Christian. "Sorry, Pastor. I was only foolin' with ya. I'm greatly honored to make your acquaintance. Don't let my adolescent talk get under your skin. Hate to say it but Darlene was one a the good ones. So good in fact she let a passel a us boys down. Anyways, the two of us, we never got into any real trouble, though I can't say I didn't think about it.

"To answer *your* question, Darlene, yes indeedy, I'm married. Wouldn't have it any other way, ain't that right Pastor?" He gave Christian a friendly nudge. "Fact is we got ourselves three little Jessups runnin' 'round, with another on the way. But that's enough 'bout me. It's the pastor I wanna hear about. Seems everyplace I turn, someone's spoutin' off how you're offerin' up a whole new way a preachin'. The town's practically in a lather what with the news you're gonna be one a ours. Darlene, I cain't say how grateful we are for whatever part you played in snookerin' this great man into settlin' here in San Antone. I know we'll all be the richer for it. Now what can I do you for?"

From then on, it was like water rolling off a duck's back. Dale arranged for an immediate low-interest loan, bundling together a house and church mortgage, and within a couple of weeks they had settled into their new life. After tending to the home front, Christian and Darlene promptly set to the business of preparing Headship for opening, all the while devoting any leftover energy to making babies. With an empire over the horizon, there was no time to spare if they were to establish the Hillcox lineage.

The church grew, and fast. Once word spread that Male Headship was up and running, the flock flocked, the tithers tithed and countless seeds were planted. Even so, money wasn't coming in fast enough. Expenses were higher than revenues, and Christian continued to pay Luke, so it was difficult to see how things would change. That is, until one evening when Darlene came up with what could only have been an inspiration from above.

They were chatting amiably on the front porch swing, Christian enjoying an ample portion of Sara Lee pound cake drenched in Darlene's homemade strawberry syrup. An ominous cloud looked to be headed their way when Darlene unwrapped an idea that had been bumping around in her head the past few days.

"Christian, I think I have a way for us to make some money an' I'm not talking small change."

"Do tell, Mrs. Hillcox. You know I like to talk money almost as much as I do the Bible. An' of course, sex," he grinned.

"Well, you know how every time someone comes to you with a problem an' you always find that perfect bit a scripture that pertains to what they're about? Now suppose you an' me sit down together and come up with every kinda life situation we can think of—the type a things what trouble people every day. Bein' a woman, I can already give you a boatload a situations, and that's without even tryin'. An' you, you got all the things you've seen an' heard ever since you started pastorin'. Anyways, we write 'em down fast as we think 'em up an' you go to the Good Book an' find a biblical answer for each one. Sorta like the time you found the perfect piece of scripture that took care of your gettin' a divorce in a way that was acceptable to the Lord."

She went on to say that her cousin Bobby was an artist and printer and could take these biblical answers and print them as pamphlets. Her excitement growing, she squeezed Christian's thigh, reminding him that he had indeed won the prize the day he married her.

"Okay. Now. This is where it gets good. I take the pamphlets 'round to all my old beauty accounts an' ask if they'll display 'em in a special rack we'll have made. Think about it. Each pamphlet sittin' there in its own individual compartment, screamin' out to save or fix someone's life. It'll be irresistible. After all, what is a beauty parlor but a place where women gab for hours, pourin' out their hearts to their hairdressers, all a 'em with some kinda trouble, and every one in need of godly direction? They'll fall over themselves to get your words of wisdom an' for fifty cents or even a dollar. Besides, this way they don't actually have to tell you face to face about their shame. Kinda like Confessions Anonymous.

"Imagine it. All those captive women. Maybe one's thinkin' about how her husband likes to look at girlie magazines, when all of a sudden, poof, she sees a pamphlet directed to that very topic. Bam! Fifty cents an' it's hers. On down the row, another one is tellin' her beautician how her son was caught stealin' an' her beautician walks over to the rack, picks up a pamphlet about the godly way to handle such a problem. Another fifty. It'll be never-ending, because you can write 'em as fast as we come up with the situations. An' beauty parlors are only the start. There's grocery stores, barber shops, military bases—and San Antonio's just the beginning."

It was a brilliant idea and her excitement was contagious. Christian chimed in.

"Darlene, this is genius! We'll accomplish two things at once: we'll spread the gospel while at the same time we're gettin' fat offa the same lamb. I swear, the moment I laid eyes on you, lightning struck. We're not two ships that passed in the night, more like two super-tankers that collided, spilling our oils all over this great land," his nascent double chin quivering with excitement.

Startled by a sudden, brilliant flash of lightning, they jumped from their chairs.

"Ooo-eee!" Christian squealed. "That one's a tad too close for my comfort. Breasts get inside," he hooted. "There's a hard rain gonna fall."

Interlude

Beam Me Up, Scottie

HIS YEARS AT HEADSHIP HAD been a lark—a spinning, dizzying lark. It was as if a Hollywood production crew had descended upon San Antonio and set the stage for the likes of Christian and *his* Male Headship. Thanks to the great minds before him, the time was ripe to plant a church—to plant a church and watch it grow. To sow a seed that came back so fast and so big that there was no end in sight to the great, gushing fountain of money that poured forth into Headship's—and Christian's—coffers. Since the Word was Faith and the Faith was fertile, then the money poured in and the proof—er, the Faith—was in the pudding.

From pamphlets to books to radio to TV, an empire was born and with it, the emperor, King Christian. Courted and coddled, the swag flew in, increasing the cycle of fame and seduction. Power. But not to the people.

A week-long journey two hundred miles to the northwest morphed into a six-month sabbatical. Except for monthly conjugal visits coinciding with her menstrual cycle, Darlene stayed at home to mind the Headship. Who knew that self-anointing awaited one overly plump Christian at, of all places, The Ranch for Jesus?

Spinning and dizzying his way through the days, days when America's Christian royalty lay hands on Christian, filling his mind with prophetic thoughts, discipling away at him, He, the soon-to-be Prophet of Man.

"Submit to his Lordship for *you* are the chosen," saith the Lord's messenger, Pastor Ron Steeple, another mail-order Jesus freak-on-the-rise. Make that, already risen.

Six months to revel in Revelation, six months that left him nearly panting on the ground, filled, finally. Filled with the knowledge of that mystical book—that bookend to Genesis—that his mission was made so plain he felt newly energized, freed, and blessed. Blessed and empowered to take to the halls of government, to teach and preach about the role of the Jews and of their place in Israel, to hasten the day, hasten the day, of the Lord's return.

Six months to revel in Revelation and then to go forth and spread the Good News.

> And Jesus came and spake unto them, saying, All power is given unto me in heaven and in earth. Go ye therefore, and teach all nations, baptizing them in the name of the Father, and of the Son, and of the Holy Ghost: Teaching them to observe all things whatsoever I have commanded you: and, lo, I am with you always, *even* unto the end of the world. —Matthew 28:18-20

Lo, He is with Me always, even unto the end of the world.

And so it began. The beginning of the end. At least in the mind of the overly plump Christian. Tasked to set up a Kingdom for God, his mission on Earth expanded beyond Earth's boundaries, beyond time immemorial. Material wealth was good and fine and pleasure-producing but power, *power* was the necessary ingredient for Prophecy to go as planned. Christian would return to *his* world and do what must be done to ready the greater world for its End, praise be He, our Lord and Savior. And when that day comes, John Christian Hillcox, formerly known as a white trash sinner, now forgiven and anointed, would be second only to His Son.

Glory to the Lamb of God.

PART 2

Eight Years Later

17

Countdown to Jesus SWBN, Spread the Word Broadcasting Network

1992

"LIGHTS!"

Stage lights come up, audience lights dim.

"Music!"

An organist keys in CTJ's theme song. Up-tempo and churchy. Bass guitar and drums add a backbeat as the director signals:

"Action!"

Enter: Christian, Stage Right, his eyes raised to the heavens. More performance than hymn, his voice builds in song, his voice itself an act of worship and slowly he sings:

Jesus paid it all,
All to Him I owe;
Sin had left a crimson stain,
He washed it white as snow . . .

The camera pulls back, panning slowly across an audience of enraptured women.

Christian ascends to a throne-like moderator's chair.

Today's guest: Danelle Billup.

Today's show: "Do it Right Tonight!"—a tremendously risqué topic for Christian television. The episode had been keenly anticipated by housewives across the nation, thanks to two weeks of nearly R-rated media teasers that have blanketed the Christian airwaves, each one a titillating come-on for the highly salacious show.

"Welcome! Welcome! Welcome one and all to . . ."

Drumroll . . .

"COUNTDOWN . . . TO . . . JESUS!"

A jolly, jovial Christian calls out with false modesty, "Thank you. Thank you. Thank you very much." Canned applause further whips up the already excited live audience as the crowd greets Christian with whoops and hollers.

"We have with us here today a very special guest, Mrs. Omer Billup. Among friends," he stage whispers, "we call her Danelle. I think most of you out there in TV land know Danelle but for those of you who don't, let me tell you a little bit about her. Danelle is the founder of *Teach It, Don't Breach It*, the nation's largest home-schoolin' resource. Now I *know* you've heard of *that*."

An infectious sense of jubilation brings the audience to their feet.

"Without Mrs. Billup's tireless, often unheralded work, Christian home schoolin' wouldn't be half what it is today. Danelle, why she's a national treasure and we are thrilled and honored to have her with us here today."

More thunderous applause, both canned and live, fills the airwaves.

"Fair warnin': what Mrs. Billup's gonna share with us today will be some a the most explicitly intimate information you ever heard. She'll be givin' specifics, an' I do mean *specifics*, of how you ladies—the ones here with us today in our studio audience, as well as those a you at home—can satisfy your husbands sexually, even *after* a long day servin' as mother, teacher, cook, laundress, and housekeeper. I tell you, this is one time we can be grateful for cable TV's lax moral standards, Praise Jesus."

Enter: Danelle.

A curvaceous woman walks seductively onstage to be warmly greeted by her host while the audience stands and cheers.

Christian watches as she walks across the stage. *Fuck me. This is my kinda woman, ripe an' ready ta burst* he thinks. *Dressed like a woman oughta dress. None of that hard-nosed-career-look-at-my-pantsuit-I-got-balls look.* He clears his throat. "Danelle here's a godly woman, an' I do put the emphasis on *woman*. She has been tasked with the role of sharing with you everything she knows 'bout how best to fulfill His word by submittin' to your husband's manly needs."

Inwardly Christian fights the sexual distraction: *Look at her. That sweet pink blouse, drawn up so tight against her, a man can't help but light upon them bazookas. An' that tight skirt positively singin' hosannas to hips that could breed a sow.* Here he was. Preacher Man, Christian megastar and television sensation, broadcasting live on national TV and he couldn't keep from fantasizing about his guest wrapping her legs tight 'round his engine. He gives himself a mental slap and loudly clears his throat, albeit a bit huskily, careful to maintain his outward bearing.

"Danelle, uh, I'm not exactly accustomed to discussin' such, uh, shall we say—sensitive a topic with a woman to whom I'm not legally wed, so if you'll forgive my modesty, I'm gonna turn the whole ball a wax over to you. But first. You viewers at home, set your young uns up in another room. Make sure they got plenty a toys, pop in a Gerbert video—do whatever it takes to get 'em out a the way—then buckle your seatbelts. Make sure y'all got paper and pen at the ready cause I *know* you're gonna want to take notes on what you're gonna hear in this next hour.

"Congratulate yourselves, ladies, because startin' tonight, you're gonna be givin' your husbands what they been achin' for an' it don't get much godlier than that!, Dag-nammit Danelle, if we ain't gonna have us some mighty satisfied cowboys, after this!"

He turned to the camera crew and grinned large. "Do me a favor, boys. Shine the camera on the back a me. I'm afraid I'm 'bout to turn redder than a hot chili pepper."

❖

That was Monday. On Tuesday, he was off to Washington to meet with select congressional leaders, give a talk at the American Christian Heritage Foundation, and conduct a one-day training seminar for local pastors in northern Virginia. Then he was back home Thursday for a full-day strategy session with the San Antonio chapter of Texans for Life, who were busy recruiting individuals to run for city council and local school boards in the upcoming primaries. Ordinarily, he was nothing but energized by the frenzied schedule, but he hadn't been sleeping well of late.

The nightmares had returned, and this time around they were on steroids. He'd sweat and thrash his way through the nights, through the gruesome reels of his past, and Darlene could not help but notice. In his dreams the dead and the dying, the putrid smell of rotten flesh were more real than the jasmine-scented woman lying next to him. He became increasingly concerned that he might start talking in his sleep. Every night before bed, Darlene coaxed and cajoled, trying her best to get him to open up, but to no avail. It was only in the middle of the night, after his personal demons had come out to play, that he was closest to her. At these times, she would gather his moist corpulence to her body, rock him gently, encouraging him, "What is it, JC? C'mon now, share it with Mama."

At these moments, feeling emotionally and physically cocooned, he would come close to unburdening himself. But a lifetime of sublimation kept his defenses on full alert. The consequences of confession loomed so large that the most terrifying of night-dreads had so far not been enough to supersede his basic defensive instincts. In many ways, Christian needed Darlene more than ever even though, sexually, the thrill was gone—only to be replaced by the thrill of women like Danelle Billup.

So far, despite the years of unremitting temptation that had accompanied his rise to power, Christian had remained faithful. Because self-denial didn't come naturally to him, he had had to settle for substitute forms of excitement. The closest thing he got to a rush these days came from hanging with the big boys in Washington. Since his televangelism career had taken off, conservative politicians from all over the country wooed him fiercely, treating him as if he was the Second Coming himself. These leaders were all in hot pursuit of the golden ticket that the evangelical voting bloc promised. Christian was awash in money. Pamphlets had evolved into books, leading to a multi-million dollar television empire, *and* he was the recipient of substantial sums from the donation baskets passed around on Sundays. Whether a check in the basket came from an oil baron or was a widow's Social Security check signed over to Headship he was equally pleased to add the amount to the ledger and bank at least part of it safely into his personal account.

Yessir, he had it coming and going, and for the simple reason that he had been Chosen. As long as he kept his demons at bay, the abandoned child in him flourished. Money and power were the gravy that fed his ego and, being a man of insatiable appetite, he took in as much as he could. Thankfully, he rarely crossed paths with his father anymore, and the few times he saw him down Pearsall way, he took great pleasure in twisting the knife, never missing an opportunity to shine the light on who the *real* man of the family had turned out to be.

Aside from his tortured nights, the one other area that continued to dog him was that he and Darlene had been unable to conceive. In the early years when Darlene fulfilled his every urge, sex came easily and often. But time passed and, narcissist that he was, his desire for her waned. He remained hot on her ovulatory trail, though, following her cycle like a hound on a scent. If that meant dashing from a meeting when her egg-time came, then that's what he would do. After all these years he had convinced himself that if there was a problem, it had to be hers.

But Elena's parting words, long buried, still stung, even if subliminally. Especially when he heard through the grapevine that she had remarried and gone on to give birth to five children, popping them out one after another. Maybe one day, he thought, when he was on his own and far from San Antonio, he'd find a doctor and get himself checked out. He sure as hell wasn't about to let a local doctor put his manliness to the test on the off chance the problem was his. No fucking way.

"Manliness is all." His father's words played over and over in his mind as he'd recall the only lesson his father had thought worth teaching. Christian presided over a megachurch *he* had named Male Headship, he was the constant recipient of calls and invitations from senators and congressmen from all over, and he was the biggest name in Christian television—yet none of this had ever been enough to earn the respect he still desperately craved from one man: his earthly, if contemptible, father.

❖

From the outside, Darlene seemed to have a golden life. As Christian's wife, she was treated with near celebrity status wherever she went. She had never looked better or been more vibrant. A lifelong devotee to beauty, she was spending increasingly more and more time at the gym, in between indulging herself with the not infrequent nip-tuck. Christian thought her expenditures excessive, but he knew it was money well spent. Not only did her good looks and sensuality confer masculinity onto him, but on the Sundays that she stood beside him at the pulpit, donations picked up. Darlene still had a powerful effect on men of all ages and from all walks of life. The desire she evoked in others would excite him in the moment but it rarely transferred to the bedroom, their moments of intimacy having become scheduled, mechanical, and joyless.

❖

No matter what Christian had accomplished in his life, the idea of image continued to trump all. If Darlene were unable to display his manhood by giving him a child, then he would find other ways to burnish his self-esteem. That was why he decided it was time they find an estate worthy of his stature. Darlene, tasked with the enviable duty of finding a place that the world would covet, called on Bunny Eller to help with the search. Bunny, a tithing member of Headship, also happened to be San Antonio's most successful realtor. After weeks of looking, Bunny surprised Darlene early one morning, the excitement in her high-pitched voice evident.

"Darlene, it's me. Throw on your clothes this instant an' I do mean *now*. Sugar Creek jest came on the market only this minute. This is the one—but we gotta get out there right away cause it's gonna go faster 'n a stack a hotcakes. I know of two couples already on their way. Can you be ready in ten?"

"Sugar Creek!" Darlene screeched. "Hells bells, Bunny, come get me *now*. Whatever it takes, I want this! To think, lil ol' me at Sugar Creek. If only Mama was alive."

A few minutes later, flanked on two sides by graceful rows of live oaks, they wound their way along a half-mile drive, until the lane opened to a vast white-pillared replica of the Mississippi River Road plantation, Oak Alley. The mansion's exterior was a near-perfect copy of its antebellum predecessor. Its Greek Revival architecture, the evenly spaced grand columns that ran the height and breadth of the building, its second floor wrought-iron exterior gallery—all of it screamed wealth. Sugar Creek, built in the late eighties was, at that time, a gross tribute to the excesses of the era, its crassness an insult to the elegance of the original Oak Alley. The sweeping veranda was populated by far too much, too-white statuary. The Olympic-size pool was large enough for three Olympic teams, and the heart-shaped hot tub and overly elaborate formal garden were all testaments to the kind of gaudy materialism Darlene found irresistible. But best of all was the land. Sugar Creek sat on nine hundred acres of prime grazing land, complete with a large and pristine barn. It was here, Darlene realized, that Christian could trade in his disappointment with her barrenness for his odd but growing passion for animal husbandry.

In the time it took Darlene and Bunny to complete a tour of the property, the house and grounds had filled up. Many had come to gawk, for it wasn't every day a place like this came on the market, but there were two couples Bunny recognized as serious competitors. With the cunning of a hunter, Bunny made certain they would be first in line, approaching the seller and staking their claim, while Darlene stole away to phone Christian.

After several minutes of pleading with Christian's secretary, Tammy, she finally put her through to a clearly peeved Christian. "Darlene, what the fuck you want? I'm a busy man. How many times I gotta tell you not to bother me at work? I've a lot more important things to do than listen to your crowin' 'bout your new shade a lipstick, or whatever the fuck you have to say."

His assault on her dignity took a backseat to her desire for the mansion. "Christian! Please! Don't hang up! You remember Sugar Creek? Well, it just came on the market, an' Christian, it's what we been waitin' for." Over the years, he'd heard a lot about the estate, seen pictures in the society pages of the hi-falootin' galas held there—photographs that never failed to raise his hackles. Even with the stature he'd achieved, he knew that a certain strata of society would never accept him – that he would never be good enough to warrant an invitation to Sugar Creek. He would have *never* dreamt of living there. But now . . . it was available and he had money enough to buy it outright several times over. Still, he wondered. Would he be mocked as the country bumpkin who overreached? Then Darlene began to describe the barn and its acreage, and his doubts vanished.

Lately, no matter what he did, he felt flat. Like an addict, he had to find a way to satisfy his habit for more, bigger, better. The truth was, he'd been thinking that, with no heir of his own, what kind of legacy would he leave when his time was up? When he got to thinking that way, he realized that it wasn't enough that he be remembered as a prominent pastor. That, in and of itself, was almost meaningless. No, he wanted the world to see him for the prophet he knew himself to be. And Sugar Creek would be his means to this end. With the combination of land and his financial resources, he could hire the expertise he needed to help him successfully breed a spotless red heifer, the cow that would change the world.

> This is a requirement of the law that the Lord has commanded: Tell the Israelites to bring you a red heifer without defect or blemish and that has never been under a yoke. —Numbers 19:2

No matter how long it took or how much it cost, Christian was determined to one day hand-carry that heifer's ashes all the way to Jerusalem, where he would purify the way for Christ's return. Then, John Christian Hillcox, the impoverished son of a ghost and a monster, would go down in history, known to mankind as the prophet who set Armageddon in motion. When that day came, he'd be second only to the Son of God.

Brusquely, he interrupted his wife. "Dar—stop blathering. Go as high as you gotta to get this. No matter what they want, you do what it takes. An' call me the instant you get it. I'll make sure Tammy puts you right through."

It was that simple. Darlene was the high bidder and by lunchtime Sugar Creek was all but theirs. Three months later they moved in, lock, stock, and barrel, christening the estate Second Coming. That was two years ago.

❖

Second Coming served as a temporary Band-Aid for Darlene and Christian's marriage. Between her church duties and working with the decorator, there was enough to keep her busy. The house had a schizophrenic air about it. Every conceivable space was occupied by religious paraphernalia, Judaica included, squeezed in alongside plaques and photographs of Christian's religious, political, and social worlds. Rooms clad in pastels, ruffles, curlicues, and Texas kitsch echoed the gaudiness outside.

Things between Christian and Darlene had not improved. Staying busy prevented Darlene from dwelling on her continued infertility, but still it was never far from mind. Always a favorite with the congregants' children, Darlene hid her pain with the contrived sense of warmth she showered on them. Every month, the appearance of her womanly bleeding deepened the scar of emptiness she carried within. It had been ten years of barrenness, and the disappointment had never gotten any easier.

She was losing Christian and utterly helpless to stop it. Aside from mechanical monthly sex, it was clear that he no longer desired her. The flirtations he engaged in with the young women who came to him for advice were growing more and more blatant. The only thing that could possibly bind him to her was a baby, and it didn't look like that would ever happen.

Like Darlene, Christian faced a moment each month that tested his resolve and shed an unwelcome light on his life and ministry. On the first day of every month he wrote a check to Luke Farley—Luke, his "public relations consultant." The amount increased monthly, along with the animosity that accompanied each payment. If the twenty percent he paid Luke would at least salve Christian's tortured soul or put an end to his growing nightmares, it would be worth it. But the payments achieved neither of those outcomes.

The only thing Luke's blackmail had done was to keep the law from the door. Human trafficking was increasingly in the news and Christian pored over every article he saw, learning all there was to know about the gruesome deaths blamed on the traffickers. He followed stories of their arrests and once even attended a trial. The transporters who had the bad luck to be caught ended up with life sentences or worse. So Christian kept his mouth shut and continued to pay Luke. Month after month he gritted his teeth, never once missing what he considered to be his personal tithe to the Devil.

❖

The arguments between Christian and Darlene started slowly, but over time they became more frequent and impassioned. One Sunday morning before church, having learned that another barren month had passed, he snarled, "If I'd a checked out your plumbing 'fore I married you, I wouldn't a been in such a rush. What's so fuckin' hard about getting knocked up? Seems to me, any teenaged slut can do it. What the hell's wrong with you?"

"Fuck you. How *dare* you put the blame on *me* when you never even had yourself checked out? For your information big man, I went to the doctor and I checked out fine. All I can say Pastor, is go plumb yourself. Or here's an idea—why not ask the Almighty to fix it for you like you tell everyone else? Ask and ye shall receive? Hah! Don't see you on the receivin' end here. You an' all your talk about plantin' seeds? Seems to me you got yourself a problem sowing one that's fertile, don't you Mr. High and Mighty?"

If it hadn't been forty minutes before the start of church, nothing could have stopped Christian from striking her. To think, that by seeing a local doctor, *without* his permission, she had revealed the problem to be *his*! What was he supposed to do with this? Biting his lip, he tasted his own blood, and everything that was subliminal and unresolved rose up in him, but he fought to keep the rage tamped down. It took a Godlike, superhuman control to keep from going after her. Swallowing hard, he turned to leave.

"Make sure you look hot this mornin'. It helps pay the bills." Had he waited for an answer, the demons would surely have gotten the best of him.

18

Left Turn Ahead

Inauguration Day
January 20, 1993

THOUGHTS FROM A CHRISTIAN:

Unhappy day. The country has come to grief. We are under the sway of the evil-secular do-it-till-it-feels-good liberals.

Don't ask, for I shall tell . . . homosexual-perverse-sodomite-backdoor-faggot-tolerant, no make that Tolerant with a capital T—

BLASPHEMERS.

Baby killers-murdering-bloodletting-court-loving stain on mankind.

A*bor*tion.

A-A-A-A-A-A-A-A-A-A-A-A-Abortion.

Abortion for all. Sex 'n drugs 'n drink 'n lust 'n fornication 'n priests with altar boys 'n show all/tell 'n Hollywood nigger loving, Jew loving, Spic loving, Chink loving Tolerance.

Marrying sin to sin 'n mankind's downward fall towards H-E-double hockey sticks and that's where WE get 'em.

The end is nigh.

World Bank Commies + dirty, life-hating, small brained Muslims—the faith that is no faith that lives to die = WAR, glorious WAR and SOON.

Gotta get dem Jews back to the holy land 'n fast.

Shalom = Peace over their dead bodies.

White stallion vs. Satan 'n fire 'n trials 'n tribulation 'n blood, oh glorious oceans of blood 'n eternal H-E-double hockey sticks 'n RAPTURE.

Bye-bye love, bye-bye happiness, hello H-E double hockey sticks, but not for US. There is only ONE, and His name shall be ONE, and the meek shall inherit the Earth . . . or is it the Kingdom? . . . no matter the sin . . . small, medium, large or jumbo size . . . a seat at His side is reserved for you IF YOU BELIEVE.

If you BELIEVE.

All the rest of you, you're goin' down down down down down.

DOWN.

Take along the sunscreen, but it won't help none. 'S time to reap what you sowed.

HAVE A NICE DAY.

19

Come Again

April 1995

OLD HABITS DIE HARD. Hard habits die old. If Mason disappeared today, there'd be no mourning down San Antonio-way. Alas, the fates had something different in mind for father and son when, one brilliant April morning, Christian opened his front door to find, not only the San Antonio Express-News, but his dear old dad, hand poised above the doorbell. For the first time since Christian left Pearsall, Mason had come a-calling.

Still living hand to mouth, job to lost job, Mason scraped by except for when the hard drinking days came a-knocking. That's when he'd look to Luke to bail him out. Luke, the son he should have had. The one who was always there for him, unlike the faggot of a bible-thumping son he'd sired. Through the years, Luke had kept him up to date on the world of Pastor Man— from the drug-runnin' murderin' fuck to *Male* Headship's faggot-assed Jesus flim-flammery. He knew all about how the muckety-mucks kissed Christian's ass as he pranced about full of airs and it was sickening to imagine. If the high and mighty had a clue as to the pastor's past, chances were they might not be so eager to link their names and reputations with his.

This time though, Mason had really hit bottom and he knew it was now or never if he were to claim what he saw as his paternal rights. In other words, the time had come to climb aboard the gravy train and ride it for all it was worth. If he played his cards right, he'd be sitting on Easy Street faster 'n you could say, "It Takes a Licking and Keeps on Ticking," which was how he felt most days. See a Christian, be a Christian, help a Christian.

❖v

No matter his success, Christian, the man, remained an emotional infant. Neither the love of a good woman nor the spirit of the Good Lord himself had been able to replace the fatherly love he so deeply craved. When he opened the door that fine spring day, he allowed hope to creep in ever so slightly.

"Whoa Becky," Mason whooped. "Wouldja look-ee here! Where the fuck am I? The White House?" It was the second time in Christian's life that Mason expressed anything close to awe concerning his son, and as a result he greeted his father in a far more gracious manner than he deserved. Christian held out his hand in peace, shuddering at the grime-encrusted paw Mason offered in return.

"Ain't this the surprise? To what do I owe the pleasure?" Christian asked.

Pushing past his son, Mason entered the house. Christian glanced back at Mason's chariot, a badly beaten-up Ford Bronco. Thanks to a recent rendezvous with a telephone pole late one drunken night, the car was as dented as its driver, the crumpled passenger door topped off by a sheet of plastic where the window should have been.

"Sheeee-it!" Mason hooted, letting loose a long, low whistle. Unable to control his constitutional venom, he muttered under his breath. "Must be some kinda scam you got goin' here, boy. I take my hat off. You're livin' like a king."

Mason was limping from an old bar fight when Darlene, who had met him once and only briefly, descended from the second floor looking like an angel, and her innate kindness replaced the shock she felt at seeing him. "Mason? What a surprise. Never thought we'd see your face at our door. But look at you. You're limpin'. You hurt?"

It clicked right then in Mason's mind. *Why, the dear lil fool. She don't realize the sweet angle she just lobbed my way.* He hadn't thought of it before, but why the hell *not* play up his accident for all it was worth? Smiling down at her, his eyes focused on her amplitude and he saw gold in them thar hills. She wasn't hard on the eyes so, quite amiably, he hooked his arm into hers, flashing a charmed smile, not unlike his son's, upon her as she steered him further inside.

"Decent of you to notice my dear," he crooned to Darlene. "Y'see," and he pointed to the the Bronco, "a coupl'a two weeks ago, I was on my way home from Lytle, where I was workin' as night watchman fer the big food enterprise they got over there, when this ass-fuck, pardon my French ma'am, son-of-a-bitch drunk slams into me. I'll tell ya this much. I'm lucky to be alive. As is, I been dealin' with my share of bodily pain."

"You poor thing," she fairly cooed.

It was inevitable in that moment that the rutted pathways of deeply ingrained loathing that Christian had spent a lifetime nurturing would kick in, and they did, making him stiffen at

Mason's self-proclaimed injuries. This train track could have only one destination.

Mason looked back his way. "Make yourself useful boy an' fetch my duffle," he snarled, his voice filled with condescension. "Be sure you watch yourself with my car. You always was a lummox an' I don't want nothin' more happenin' to Bessie out there." Christian steamed as he fantasized about his fingers closing around his father's neck. Old habits do indeed die hard. What a fool he was to have expected more, even if momentarily. He should have known that Mason was incapable of change—yet the hurt struck with a resonance so fresh, it seemed to Christian they'd never been apart. Out in the car when he saw the size of Mason's duffel, he realized his father was planning to stay a while.

A glowing Darlene, happy to have company—any company—was busy showing him around the house. After a grand tour indoors, she led him outside, whereupon he let out a second, low whistle.

"Holy shee-it! This here's the real thing." He took in the grounds, which looked to extend forever. "That a hot tub over yon? Jest what the doctor ordered for my achin' bones," And he rubbed his lower back. Smiling again Darlene's way, he said, "Ya know what sweetheart? I think I'm gonna like it here at the Hillcox Ritz."

Christian joined them in time for Darlene's answer. "You most certainly are, my dear man."

Dear man, my ass, Christian snarled to himself.

"We're gonna take good care of you for however long you stay. It's been far too long since you an' Christian had time together. Only thing I wanna say is I expect you two to try an' get along for once. It's past time. An' I mean it. Now I'll go on in an' set you up in our nicest suite of rooms an' after that, I'm goin' to make you a doctor's appointment an' get that leg looked at. Seems to me you need a woman around who'll treat you like a king."

King? King of hate and destruction was the only kind of king Mason ever would be, thought Christian.

Lately *anyone* who came to the house was a welcome distraction for Darlene. The marital renewal she had hoped would result from living at Second Coming had never materialized. If nothing else, Mason's arrival gave her an excuse not to accompany Christian next week on a trip across the Midwest. His pilgrimages always turned out the same; the saving and converting, the promises and intimidation, all of which had become increasingly more difficult for her to stomach. No matter how long she'd been in the game—and it was a long time now—no matter how convincing her act, she had never bought into it. Never had. Never would.

As for Mason, she had to wonder whether he was really as bad as Christian had made him out to be. She'd only ever heard Christian's side of things, and his alone. If she could keep Mason from drinking while he was here, who knows, maybe father and son could find a way to get past old wounds. If so, then Second Coming would live up to its name. In spite of herself, the Darlene of old resurfaced, hoping to turn the bitter brew that had become her life into something far sweeter.

It took her a few moments to settle upon Mason's room, ultimately deciding that the one farthest from hers and Christian's would be best. Darlene picked up a flower arrangement from the hall and placed it on the bureau in Mason's room, suffusing the air with the overly sweet scent of gardenias. She fluffed feathery pillows and filled a sterling silver carafe with water.

Returning downstairs, the tension between Christian and his father had already turned explosive. Left on their own for just a few minutes, Christian's customary ease at small talk fell flat, leaving him without the resources with which to disguise the old feelings.

As water finds its opening, so too does hatred.

Ignoring the tension, Darlene offered a bright smile and clucked, "Mason dear, c'mon on upstairs where I insist you take a nice lie-down. When you wake up, it's outside for you. A long soak in the Jacuzzi'll do you wonders. Christian, take your father's things upstairs to the back room."

One look at the size of Mason's duffel and Darlene too was taken aback. "Looks like you're plannin' on stayin' a spell."

"You bet your bootie. That is, unless you tire a me an' throw me out on my keister. Ain't nothing like spendin'—what's that they call it these days?—quality time—with my family, is there? Speakin' a which, 'fore I go up, bring on the grandbabies, wouldja? Gotta be a passel of 'em by now."

Darlene and Christian traded glances and she jumped in, sparing Christian this particular bullet.

"Sorry, Pops," she said. "We been so busy, what with growin' the church an' Christian's television show an' all, we haven't had the time to start a family yet. It'll happen." More than grateful, Christian relaxed ever so slightly. Maybe this time, things didn't have to be so bad. When it came to dealing with Mason, he'd never had an ally before.

But Mason wasn't finished. "Say boy, what 'bout that kid you an' that Spic had? You know, the one what made you a dropout. Love to meet the brat. He's got my blood runnin' through his veins too, ya know."

Thwap.

"Trust I ain't tellin' tales outta school, am I?" he grinned.
Bam.

Never underestimate the power of your adversary.

"Fuck you," Christian snarled. He slung the heavy bag over
his shoulder and instantly shot back. "From the clinkin' in this
here bag, I wager it's safe to surmise you're still the same shit-
faced drunk you always was?" He headed up the stairs without
giving Mason the opportunity to reply. On the way down the
hallway, he glanced at the photographic hall of fame lining the
wall and stopped to pick up two. One was of him laughing
amiably with the former president, and in the other he was
standing alongside the presiding Chief Justice of the Supreme
Court. He placed the photos on the bedside table in Mason's
room, muttering, "Put this in your corncob pipe and smoke it,
you ass-fuckin' son-of-a-rat-fuck-hillbilly," and upon flinging
the bag onto the ground, he exited the house via the back stairs,
but not before first scrubbing his hands clean.

❖

His brain near to exploding, Christian stormed out to the field
where his cattle grazed—the only place on Earth that seemed
to calm him these days. The moment his eyes lit upon his
prize cow, a magnificent reddish-colored beauty named Queen
Esther, he felt his anger slip-slide away.

To ensure that he be the one to develop the flawless Red
Heifer, Christian had engaged the services of the internationally
renowned Australian bovine breeding expert, Exeter Tibbett.
A devout Evangelical, Exeter lived on the premises, dividing his
time between lab and field. Although he had yet to deliver, so
to speak, they were both confident that he soon would. Unlike

with other things, when it came to prophet-making events of such magnitude, Christian was a patient man.

Tibbett had put Queen Esther out to stud with a roan-colored bull forty days prior and they would learn any day if the seed had taken. When Christian had first seen this magnificent animal, God whispered in his ear that this lovely lady-in-heat was the one to bear him the biblically mandated Red Heifer necessary to set the Rapture in motion. Whether or not they succeeded this time mattered little. Christian knew that one day, be it this year or ten years from now, it would happen—and when it did, the world would finally recognize him as the Lord's *true* emissary. Come Judgment Day, Christian would take his seat at the right hand of God, humbly and with grace. And when he looked down to see his father hurtling downward to Hell, Christian would wave a joyful farewell to the man who'd robbed him of all that was good, so long ago.

Recently, Christian had been giving a great deal of thought to what he'd become. To be wined and dined by the powerful—ferried about on their private planes, to speak before thousands of adoring people—it was all pretty heady stuff. Not long ago, it would have been unimaginable to think that anything *he* said could affect a Congressional vote, but such was the case these days. Now that was a mind-fuck if ever there was one.

It wasn't all glory and power, though. For him, the real test came in the quiet moments when he was alone, face-to-face with his tormented soul. Nightmares have a tendency to bleed into a person's waking moments, and bleed they did. At least once a day, he'd find himself battling the most violent urges, and these urges were becoming more and more difficult to control. Some days he felt that, instead of the bones and flesh of mortal man, his skin concealed an explosive interior of brush and tinder, all of which awaited the spark that would set him afire. With the passing years, the accumulation of repressed self-doubt and anger made a conflagration increasingly inevitable. In these rare moments of reflection, Christian wondered if God had truly forgiven him for what he'd done along the border so long ago. Had he forgiven himself? And suppose one day, the world learned the truth? Would he be man enough to face the public, with faith his only refuge?

Fear of exposure made him all the more committed to doing whatever it required to guarantee that that day would never come.

20

Stiffed

April 1995

"HEY YOU! OUT THERE IN THE kitchen. Carmelita, or whatever the fuck yer name is, bring in s'more a them sausages. An' make it snappy."

Darlene glared at him. "What'd I do?" Mason mugged. She was surprised at how well he had cleaned up since his arrival. He was quite presentable really, considering how derelict he looked when he first arrived.

"How many times do I have to tell you, when you're at our table. you ring the bell if you want service. I won't have this yellin' and screamin'. This here's a civilized place, by which I mean we don't behave that way. Also, for the last time, her name is Consuelo, not Carmelita."

"Consuelo, Carmelita—s'all the same to me. She ain't a bad lookin' hump," he cackled. "Sure as shit wouldn't say no to a game a fumble an' tumble with la cucaracha—not that she holds a candle to you, *Mrs.* Hillcox."

Darlene blushed as much from his crassness as from the unexpected compliment. In the few days he'd been there she had come to see vast contradictions within Mason, and didn't quite know what to make of him. He could be one way with her—charming even—and another to those he looked down on, like Consuelo. When it came to Christian, he was nothing but mean.

"Do please forgive me Madame. I shall try to behave bettah in the futcha." She couldn't help but laugh, even knowing her laughter would encourage him.

She heard Christian descending the stairs and, forcing the gaiety from her voice, called out. "Honey-pie, c'mon in an' join us for breakfast."

Looking in at the happy domestic scene playing out before him, his disgust was visceral and unconcealed. He was on his way out for the "Midwest Salvation Tour," and he'd paid special attention to his attire this morning, with the express goal of intimidating his father. That he had a thick head of hair contrasting with Mason's thinning pate, and that his expensive designer clothes put the elder's synthetics to shame didn't hurt his game either. Additionally, Mason's abusive lifestyle had left his body something of a wreck, particularly when compared to Christian's tanned and overfed girth.

"My, my, what *do* we have here?" Christian sneered. "If this ain't the cozy twosome. *Mrs.* Hillcox, while I'm gone, I expect you to spend your days over to the Headship. I will not abide your lollygaggin' about. So long as you choose not to be at your rightful place, which, by the way, is at my side, I expect you to keep a tight rein on the ship. As for you, my ass-fuck of a father, you never was a father to me an' guess what? You ain't one now.

So I'm not askin'—I'm *tellin'* you to get outta my house before I get back an' that means get out *forever*. You ever come here again, I'll call the law on you, you hear?"

Not one to shy away from a challenge, it was with great effort that Mason bit his tongue. Inwardly steaming, he retained enough presence of mind to answer, "Y'want me gone, pansy-boy? Well, ya ain't gotta ask twice. Truth is, I've had more'n nuffa yore phony-ass religiosity an' I'd already decided—*on my own*—it's time ta move on. So don't you go worryin' yer purty lil head no more on my 'count, Chris*tine*. Me an' Bessie'll be outta here soon's I pack up."

Christian ignored the familiar taunts. "You do that. F'you know what's good for you, you'll make this the last time I ever lay eyes on you. Sorry I cain't wait to see you out, but my chauffeur awaits. Darlene, Tammy'll be expectin' you every day an' you better know, I'll be checkin' in." With no further goodbye for his wife, Christian turned to go.

Why that fat fuck, Mason fumed to himself. *Thinks he's better 'n me, does he? I'll show his ass.* He had originally come to San Antonio to horn in on the lucre, but now it seemed that his hoity-toity faggot of a son had upped the ante. *If it's blood he wants, then it's blood he'll git.*

While Mason simmered, Darlene ran out to the car, her feelings of guilt for not accompanying her husband driving her forward. Christian had settled himself in the backseat of the Lincoln and waited while his driver arranged his luggage in the trunk. Poking her head inside the window, she pleaded, "Christian, please don't go away mad. I'm so tired, I feel like I need a break jest this once."

In a voice devoid of expression, he answered, "You know very well, my dear, that in my world it is customary for a wife to be at her husband's side, particularly someone of my position. My question to you is, what part of honor and obey have you forgotten? Truth be told, your act with that old bastard inside turns my stomach. 'F you think your charmin' an' flatterin' him is suddenly gonna turn us into one big happy family, well then, you're a bigger fool'n I thought.

"Anyhow, like I said, I'll be checkin' on you."

His pointed and callow dismissal aimed to hurt, and hurt it did. With a scarcely perceptible gasp, Darlene took a step back. Christian closed the window, nodded to the driver, and without so much as a glance, drove off.

Like a character in an old cartoon, Darlene felt steam issue forth from both ears. How dare he condescend to her that way after all she'd done for him? Why, he'd be nothing but a two-bit country preacher if it hadn't been for her. She should have told him what she really thought—that she was relieved not to be traipsing around after him—that she looked forward to a few days away from the same old tired, sanctimonious platitudes, that this was to be the first time she could be herself in years. Glancing toward the house, she saw Mason scurry away from the open front door back to the dining room. Since he'd witnessed their scene, she had nothing to hide, giving herself full permission to vent to Mason before he left for good.

"Damn that holier-than-thou son of a bitch," she seethed. "Talkin' to me like I'm his slave. Did you hear how he ordered me 'round?"

Seeing an opening, or perhaps more accurately, a new scheme, slowly, ever so slowly, Mason crept in.

"There, there. I'm sure he didn't mean nothin' by it. He's jest peeved you ain't goin' with him. Top it off, it ain't pleasured him none, I'm sure, t'see you an' me gittin' on. You mighta noticed, but he an' I still don't take ta each other. Seems we never will." He heaved a sigh.

"Don't know what all he's tole you, but God's truth Darlene, I did my damnedest to be a father to that boy. All the times I tried . . . asked ta take him fishin' or huntin' jest t'have him turn me down. I'd ask, 'How 'bout we toss a football, why don't we?' an' every time he'd turn me down. No matter what I did, it wasn't never right with him." He pushed on. "It weren't easy on me, what with his ma so sick in the head she went an' done herself in. Why, I had to be both mother an' father to the boy. Sure, I made mistakes. Who don't, 'specially when the luck never seems to break yer way? An' now, my not bein' so young anymore an' achin' like I do, I came in peace, hopin' he'd let bygones be bygones."

Like his son, Mason could be the consummate actor when he needed to. With Christian out of the house, he slipped into the role of martyred father. He was so good, in fact, that Darlene started to wonder if maybe there *were* two sides to the story. To see Mason like this, his head in his hands, brought out instincts she'd been forced to sublimate for years. All she could think was, *the poor man*. After all, he hadn't had it easy either. To think Christian considered himself a godly man, yet he was so unforgiving, so completely incapable of seeing past the hatred and disappointment he so carefully nurtured, even if that hatred was poisoning him. Despite Christian's earlier ultimatum, Darlene made her first independent, if willful, decision in years. She asked Mason to stay on a few days. Company was company, and anyhow, if somehow she could bring father and son together, then maybe things between her and Christian would improve. It was worth a try.

For the rest of the day, Darlene carted Mason along with her in the belief that she was meant to be the fixer in this family drama. With Christian's "orders" still on her mind, her first stop was the church.

While giving Mason a tour of the facilities she stopped at a large all-purpose room that was being repainted to check on the progress of the job. Mason stood near the doorway as Darlene crossed the room to speak with the foreman, who was high atop a ladder. She stepped up onto a scaffold, unaware that the sunlight streaming through the tall windows behind her caught the white, knee-length dress she was wearing at just the right angle to outline a perfect silhouette of her thighs and bottom. She moved about and talked, seemingly flirtatious, Mason thought, as he watched her every move. The foreman said something that elicited a throaty laugh from Darlene at the same moment she turned her hips in what Mason perceived as a stripper's grind. He saw her wink at the foreman as she stepped back down to the floor, then she walked toward him, took him by the arm, and ushered him out for the rest of the tour.

From that moment on, Mason saw his daughter-in-law from a different perspective.

Some might say he'd had himself a religious experience. As for Mason, he'd seen the light.

21

The Jew in Me

April 1995

WITH GOD HAVING STEERED Christian into a world of wealth and power, it was clear He had bigger plans in mind for his earthly son. Why else would He have tapped the fallen man and brought him so far if not for greater purpose? With Queen Esther's future offspring soon to herald the Way, Christian had legitimate reason to see himself as more than just another servant of God. Like countless zealots before, he was confident that he had been "chosen" to usher in the Kingdom, that all that he'd attained so far was the means to the only end that mattered: the fulfillment of Biblical prophecy as foretold in The Book of Revelation. And because Christian knew the Bible to be the gospel truth, he also knew that, however vile his past, it didn't amount to a hill of beans in the eyes of the Lord. With God playing the role of Supreme Director, it was clear that, from the beginning, He had charted the course of Christian's life for Such a Time as This.

Christian had taken to preaching in the traditional Jewish garb of prayer shawl and skullcap. With each passing day, world events convinced him that the oncoming and inevitable Rapture was nigh. The "Jew" in him had recently emerged as if from a chrysalis, presenting him with his most difficult challenge to date. In sermon after sermon, he skillfully led Headship's congregation through the genesis of their collective Hebraic roots, explaining that the time had come for all good Christians to see themselves as "completed Jews," the *truly* chosen people. Such teaching was an uphill climb for Christian, having to walk a delicate balance between encouraging a sense of commonality with the Hebrews while not completely hiding the anti-Semitic disgust he shared with the members of his congregation. To tell *his* Christians that there was Jew in them didn't sit well with the long-held notions of hook-nosed moneychangers that skittered across their ignorant minds. But he kept at it, hoping to find his way around the resistance engendered by long-ingrained imagery.

Then, all at once, he saw his path.

"Folks, I think I finally get why you been resisting me so hard on this," he said one Sunday morning. "You been thinkin' I been comparin' us to the shyster Jew lawyers, or the bankers or maybe even the master-Jews of the universe who run our government. Maybe you're even thinkin' a the ones what control the media." A laugh issued out from a place deep inside of him. "And, I say, let that go! We're not *that* kind of Jew! Not at all!

"Listen up and listen good. Here's the real deal. If we wanna see Judgment Day—and I know we do—if we wanna see it in our lifetime, then we're gonna hafta put aside our *true* feelings about the Yids. The only way I know to help you with that is to tell you that without their Old Testament, Christianity wouldn't exist at all. Like Paul said in Galatians 3:28, 'If you belong to Christ, then are you Abraham's seed.' That means that whether or not we like it, whether or not we can get comfortable with it, the time's come we own up to the fact that we're every one of us descended from the Jew. Like Jesus was. How do I know that, you ask?" He paused—a long, pregnant pause. "C'mon now—say it with me—"

Prompted by Christian's oft-asked nursery-school-style question, the congregation responded as one, musically chanting, "'Cause the Bible tells us so."

Christian pushed on. "Herein lies the important part, the part we gotta keep to ourselves so's not to have folks label us 'Jew-haters,' a label we can't afford to have attached to our movement. Remember, we can *think* whatever we want—but we can only let the outside world in on the parts we *choose* to let them know.

"Here it is in a nutshell—*we* evolved with Christ while *they*, the unbelievers, the ancient *Jews*, turned their collective backs on him. So instead of the constant hammerin' away that they're the Chosen, doesn't it follow that their rejection of our Lord and Savior deemed *us* to be the *true* Chosen?"

He paused to ponder the word *us*, enjoying the unintended but rather brilliant play on words. "An' that *US* also means that the good ol' U-S-of-A was Chosen at *its* birth as the *Christian* nation that it is—a nation what answers *only* to *His* law.

"Come the Rapture, who do you think'll be flyin' on up to meet our Lord? I'll tell you this. It won't be the kinda Jews you're thinkin 'bout. No Sir. No Ma'am. It'll be *us*, the COMPLETED JEWS! WE, who knew THE WAY when we came upon it. WE, who knew THE TRUTH when we heard it. WE, who knew THE LIGHT when we saw it." He paused to maximize the impact. "WE, who are GOD'S TRUE CHOSEN.

"Or, to put it in more contemporary terms, if I were a Jew today, let's jest say I'd be plannin' my retirement in a place far hotter than Miami Beach."

Over time, Headship members accepted the difficult and foreign concept of their Jewish roots. Sunday services evolved to absorb specific Jewish rituals and holidays, the congregation ultimately claiming them to be their Christian ancestral right. Sales of Judaica in the church gift shop grew rapidly, often outpacing traditional Christian items. Within a short time, mezuzahs graced more doors than not in certain neighborhoods, making it next to impossible to identify a Jewish home from a Christian one. Try that on for Tolerance.

❖

Out in Omaha, midway into his whirlwind tour of the American Midwest, a pastor named Christian, looking more like Moses than any Christian should, shared, not bared, his soul with an eager crowd of holy rollers.

"I stand with you today, here in this glorified place, for one reason and one reason alone. An' that reason is to wish all of us here today a gigantic *re-birthday*."

"I have come to these hallowed halls with the sole purpose of *guar-un-tee*-ing each an' every one of you your *own* personal seat in Heaven. To any one a you who pays attention to today's news, it oughta be clear we are livin' in the most exciting times in history. *We* are the generation that shall witness the last days of life on Earth, as we know it. *We*, who have front row seats to the greatest show on Earth, the *End of Days*, need to rejoice because, believe you me, it don't get more excitin' than this. Those a you here today whose walk with Jesus is strong, maybe you can help this morning by layin' a hand upon your neighbor. Could be the person next to you, or maybe in the row in front or behind you, someone who might *not* have completed his or her relationship with the Almighty. That's right, put your hands on 'em an' send some of *your* energy their way.

"Let it flow good people, let it flow. Let it wash over the lost among us so that they, like you, can know Him before it's too late. An' that time—that time—it's drawin' near. Because the time is *now* to bring home as many lost souls as we can.

"To those a you not quite sure how to do this—an' you know who you are—just as sure's you know you came here today for a reason, I beg you, *seize this moment.* Close your eyes, let the glorious music in this sacred space wash you away and *let Him in!*"

On cue, the organist began to play, slowly at first, building, slowly building until the music reached a stirring and heart-rending crescendo. "Feel Him," Christian proclaimed, "I say *feel!* For *He is here. Here.* HERE with us. *Now.* For *such a time as this!* Let go and feel His Glory enter you. Feel it enter you so fully that your very soul aches with wonder at the sacrifice he made for *you.*"

Mopping his brow, he looked pointedly around the auditorium, convincing each member of the audience that he spoke expressly to them. The timbre of his voice rose and fell with perfectly timed theatricality as he continued.

"There is no act, no sin, *nothing* in your past that *He* will not forgive."

After another calculated pause he asked, "Who is ready to take Jesus today? Come on down. Come on now. *He's* waitin' for you. Get up now. Get your fannies up outta those comfortable seats an' come on down here to meet *His son for He is here with us now!* Waitin' to bring you on *home*, sins, blemishes an' all.

"We are all, an' I mean *all*, born into sin. Each and every one of us a sinner. Why, we *bled* sin the moment we slid out of our sweet mamas' birth canal into a world *teemin'* with lust.

"Who among us today can lift up his head, look God squarely in the eye an' say he has never succumbed to temptation, be it lust, addiction, infidelity, bloodletting, or thievery? If any a you says he can, to you, I say—*you're a liar*! A bald-faced *liar*! Sinners, I say, each an' every one a you.

"So, come on down! Here we go. I see one, two, three, six, Lord—look at you good folk pouring down here. Praise Jesus! C'mon. I wanna save more!"

The more people came forward, the more Christian upped his rhetoric. "Why, I'd be willin' to bet we got ourselves a woman here today who thinks herself unworthy because she's committed murder. You heard me. I said *murder*. A woman—maybe even a girl, who, through grief or fear or evil advice, let the devil convince her she was better off aborting—*no*, let us call it as we see it, *murderin'*, the life inside her. Why, you ask? Why? I'll tell you why. Because maybe it wasn't a convenient time for her to have a baby or maybe she'd lost her job or she wasn't legally wed. Maybe she was poor an' she didn't know where to turn, when along comes the Devil persuadin' her that rippin' the precious life outta her womb was the only way out.

"But that was *then* and this is *now* and today, this woman-child grieves for what she has done. If only she could find forgiveness, she thinks. Forgiveness. Salvation. Well, to this tortured soul, an' to all of you I say, *Yes you can! Forgiveness is yours for the takin'.* You need only come forward and *repent* and *forgiveness is yours.*

"To everyone out there who suffers in other ways—be it financial, or illness—maybe it's loneliness or addiction, or maybe it's the sufferin' of self-loathing that comes from homosexual urges. To you—as to all, I say, *Come home to God. Come home to Jesus. His love is yours if you'll let yourself take it.*"

Dabbing his black hankie at the rivulets of perspiration streaming down his face, he paused, slowing his cadence, purposely calming himself, as he spoke to the audience in a conspiratorial tone. "Now I wanna say somethin' a mite bit off topic, but if you listen closely, it'll all come together. Bear with me.

"Lately, I been doin' some thinkin' 'bout the way we use language. Seems to me we've let the media—and by that, you know who I mean—get away with bastardizin'—yes, *bastardizin'*—our native tongue. Let it be known henceforth that I *do not now*, nor shall I *ever*, condone the purposeful intent to muddy up our Christian values through the misuse of words so prevalent in today's media." Blank faces looked up at him suggesting he hadn't broken through.

"Lemme explain. How many times you hear someone on television talk about a person bein' gay?" Loud hissing and the stomping of feet were his answer. "What are we really talkin' 'bout when we say *gay*? We talkin' 'bout *happy*? Is that what Joe Liverlips Newscaster means when he says a gay man is the same as you an' me?"

The audience howled, "Nooooooo."

"You better believe it. Joe Liverlips ain't talkin' happy. No, he's talkin' *queers. Faggot-faced sodomites.* An' *that's* what he *should* call 'em, if he wants to call himself a newsman. But he doesn't on account a the great big liberal agenda out there. You know what I'm talkin' 'bout—the one what's eager to grab hold a your children's minds by trickin' 'em with words. It's happenin' on TV an' it's happenin' in the schoolhouse. I'll tell you what else. It's happenin' on the street corners and playgrounds in our towns and cities. It's one a the slippery ways Satan works. Sure, you parents can turn off your TVs, you can homeschool your kiddies, but now? You gotta keep 'em off the streets too? Outta the parks and playgrounds?

"You're *damn straight* you do, else they're gonna go out there'n learn that what's perverted, what's against God's word, is not only *fine*, it's good. It's happy. It's *gay*.

"So how 'bout we make a pledge, here and now, that we ain't nobody's fool an' we ain't gonna fall for their wordplay no more. I promise you this—you'll never hear *me* use the word *gay* to describe the *sin* of man on man. It's *in the name of Tolerance* that these Lefties, many of whom are Jews and Commies, by the way, think *they* have the right to teach our young that their perverse ways are normal when the real honest-to-goodness truth is, they're the ones blinded to the Truth, and that, my friends, is *Truth with* a capital T.

"As for us, we tell it like it. We call the perverts *Sodomites*, like they're called in the Bible. I do not now, nor shall I ever, have any use for *Tolerance* unless it is the *Tolerance* of the *Bible*, the *Tolerance* for the *inerrancy of His Word*. On the contrary, the Tolerance the pagan Left rhapsodizes over is none but a *tool of the Devil* and when you know that, you'll know that everything you need to live a righteous life is writ here in this book." He held his Bible high. "When you acknowledge that herein lies the literal and ONLY Word of God, you will live not only a godly life here on Earth but, more important, your future will be an eternity paved with gold, beginning on that glorious day we are raptured up to the heavens."

He put aside his Bible, exchanging it for an elegantly curved piece of animal horn.

"Here in my hands, I hold the horn of a ram. This is called a shofar. If you already know that word, you most likely also know it is a Jew symbol. What, you ask, is Pastor Hillcox doin' with a *Jew* horn?

"We are, each of us, full-blooded descendant of the Hebrews, and as such, I declare our collective right, no, make that our collective responsibility, to take on the earliest traditions that come out of the history of our faith."

Christian took a deep breath, put his lips to the sterling mouthpiece, and let the shimmering wail of the shofar fill the air. Then he proclaimed, "The great Rabbi Maimonides explained the shofar's call when he said, 'Wake up from your (moral) sleep.' Because you *are* asleep. *Get up, awaken from your slumber.* Get up from your lazy ways. Search out our past and accept the Truth. On bended knee, remember always the Lord—He who created you—your Rock and your Redeemer.

"*Because* we are evolved from the Hebrews, I declare; the time has come to claim *their* symbols as *our own*. An' for the record, this is the *only* kind of evolution you will ever hear me speak of." Laughter bubbled up from below.

"Know this, oh good people of Omaha and know it well: We, the *true believers*, are the *completed Jews*, the *Chosen*. From this time forth, we shall blow the shofar as we proclaim this the Year of Release, the Year of Our Jubilee, the Year of Our Rapture. Glory to the Lamb of God. When you hear the shofar's call, a call that harkens back to the beginning of biblical times, understand that what you are hearing is the proclamation of the re-gathering of the faithful in announcement of Christ's return."

His voice quieted to a stage whisper, taking on an ominous tone. "There are those outside these walls who spend their wealth and their time plotting our downfall as they seduce and lead us down Satan's path. They use the temptations of riches and bodily pleasures to draw us in. Oh, we have all met the Devil. Why, he walks among us every day. We have tasted, yes, and even enjoyed his ways. Some a you might think yourselves not ready to renounce the earthly pleasures you currently enjoy. You might feel you have not yet satisfied your desires. Maybe you think you *cannot* or *do* not want to turn away from temptation. But remember, every day you partner with the devil is a day that pulls you deeper and deeper towards the eternal quicksands of Hell.

"Trust not in the Lord, leave not behind your sinful ways, continue to yield to temptation, and I *promise* that one day very soon, a boilin' river of blood shall open wide and plunge you deep into the fires of Eternal Hell. And so shall it come to pass. *Judgment Day manifests its arrival in all things around us.* We see its approach every day in the news. The closer we get, the faster it comes. Biblical prophecy is bein' fulfilled at this very moment while the sinners sleep. But *we*—we shall NOT sleep!

"No matter your sins, be they great or be they small, know this—*it is not through your deeds on earth, but through His grace alone that you will be saved.*" He paused to let his words sink in, leaving a moment for the audience to visualize an Eternity free of pain and suffering. Or conversely, to imagine Eternity at Satan's side.

There is a special rhythm to a successful sermon, and Christian had become a master. If he went in too early for the kill, he failed to give fear enough time to do its job. If he waited too long, doubt might set in. But when he timed it *just right*— and he had learned by now to *always* get it right—he was in like Flynn.

He cued the singers on the choir platform and they began to chant the eerie, repetitive entreaty they'd practiced earlier in the day. The voice of an angel rose above, a voice so exquisite it was impossible to ignore. A delicious shiver ran up his spine as he remembered what had transpired a few short hours ago in his private dressing room adjacent to the altar. Her name was Tiffany and she had just turned fourteen. She was virginal, blossoming, a girl on the cusp of womanhood, a youth volunteer and a member of the choir. As Christian exhorted the crowd to renounce their sins, his thoughts turned to the lithe, youthful body and the afternoon's delight.

"Tell me, *Are you ready?*" he cried out, just as earlier he had moaned the same question to the budding Tiffany. A thunderous cry shook the room. "I ask, *Are you ready?*" as he remembered prodding Tiffany, stroking her hair.

"I am," the willing child had answered, as gratefully, eagerly, she yielded to him her sweet virginity, certain that with this act she was submitting to God Himself.

The hysteria he drew from the audience grew into an almost sexual roar while the memory of the afternoon's climactic cries raised high his spirit. Lifting the striated horn to his mouth once more, he let the ancient sound of the Hebrews fill the space for a second time. From on high he rejoiced, both in the scene below and in the memory of the girl, not yet a woman, surrendering to him. Tears flowed down his face at the sensual joy he felt at the bodies gyrating before him and the sounds of Amens and Hallelujahs filling the air.

This was his show and he was in control—producer, director, writer, star. Entitled to everything, he took it all.

Here he stood, in the middle of an Omaha church before a vast sea of desperate and earnest faces, each one there with the hope of finding something better, there because they needed to believe in what he had to offer. He had performed this scene hundreds if not thousands of times before, always upping the histrionics. But nothing had ever come close to the emotional high he felt today. Glancing back at a reverent and glowing Tiffany in her glimmering choir robe, he bowed his head as the music quieted. Silence held the audience in its thrall.

Then the room exploded in a cacophony of thundering percussion, clanging cymbals, and the rich melodic strains of the undulating organ, all of it perfectly orchestrated to manipulate the human spirit just as today he had manipulated Tiffany's tender youth.

Ah, sweet Jesus, you get the best of my love.

22

It's About the Seed, Stupid

July 1995

"FUCKIN' GARDEN GNOME," Christian snarled as he signed a check in the amount of twelve thousand dollars, payable to Lucifer Farley, the word *Consulting* inked on the memo line. The bank wouldn't notice the given name even if it was made out to the Devil. He had paid Luke a stunning one hundred forty-four thousand dollars so far this year and it was only July. Cringing, he thought about how much more Luke would make off him next year if Headship's growth continued as projected. He scrawled the words, "Growing bigger to serve YOU, you pasty fuck" on a scrap of paper and stuffed it inside the envelope with the check. Christian was making Luke a wealthy man and there was nothing he could do about it.

As the revenues of Male Headship and its subsidiaries grew, there were times Christian thought about chucking it all and heading for the hills—and his burgeoning Swiss bank account. Then, if Luke talked, no one could touch him or his money. But the reality was that he would never walk away from the circle of power he had worked so hard to be the center of. Shit, he'd practically become the Don Corleone of The Church of America, or, better make that, The *Non-Denominational* Church of America, not the fucking white-bread *Church of the Pasty-Fucks*. He saw no conflict in that all the while he professed to serve Jesus, he was truly at the service of Mammon, the God of Riches. As the Good Book says, "Seek and you shall find."

Closing the unwieldy corporate checkbook, he returned it to a vault hidden behind his latest acquisition, an oil painting of Christ in the style of Raphael. Christ smiled down on him even as a crown of thorns pierced his scalp. Some days Christian saw himself in the painting, minus the smile that is, for his own crown of thorns got mightily sharp at times. He had purchased the painting by phone through an auction house in New York for 1.4 million dollars, knowing full well he could turn around tomorrow and sell it for four times that, if need be. Christian was a firm believer in physical assets. Should Hell break loose before the Rapture, he wanted to make sure he had insurance.

Locking the dirty business of extortion away for another day, he followed his nose toward the kitchen. His appetites, both sexual and gastronomic, were still king. He eagerly anticipated Consuelo's culinary delights, only to be outraged to find Darlene seated at the kitchen table in intimate conversation with Consuelo. Time and again, he had explained to his wife why it was a mistake to get too friendly with the help. If they didn't maintain clear boundaries between themselves and the staff, he was certain they would awaken one day to find a full-blown mutiny on their hands.

❖

Christian's trip to the Midwest had been a great success, in terms of money made and souls saved, but he was surprised to realize that, except for the time spent in Omaha, he had missed Darlene. Not long after his tryst with Tiffany, the singing teen, he had found himself beset by gut-twisting comparisons between Luke's pedophilia and what he'd just done and, like an alcoholic, he foreswore forever the sweet whiskey of young flesh, promising himself that from then on he'd drink only from the marriage well. It was funny how certain sins bothered him more than others. This time it wasn't the infidelity that troubled him, but the likeness to Luke.

Tiffany was turning into something of a concern. Convinced that their coupling was ordained by God, she wanted a repeat performance. Not only that, but having experienced womanhood, she was ready for another go-around. Her most recent phone message ended with the promise to take a bus to San Antonio as soon as she could. The thought thrilled him momentarily, but the similarity to Luke killed that feeling in an instant. What kind of a man did she think he was? After she'd left two overtly sexual messages on his private phone line, he knew it was time to put a stop to it. Jailbait or not, her voice alone had a strange ability to elicit visceral memories of her flesh, so much so that hearing her sweet young voice aroused him to the point that he was forced to complete the act by hand. Thankfully, the Lord was looking out for him and the frequency of Tiffany's calls diminished, allowing Christian to put the misstep in the past. He gave no thought to the possibility that the young girl might be struggling with his callous dismissal. All that mattered was reassuring himself he was no pedophile. He was no Luke.

❖

He leaned down and surprised Darlene with a deep kiss like those long ago. "Consuelo, how many times have I specifically asked you not to draw my wife into the seamy details of your life? I'm late and I'd like my breakfast served now." He took Darlene by the hand. "We'll be in the dining room."

His superior tone filled Darlene with a feeling of profound shame. Christian's vitriolic flare-ups toward Consuelo and the rest of the staff revealed a despicable bigotry entirely inappropriate in a man of God. She and Consuelo had become friends, and their relationship was something she didn't take lightly. From the beginning, Christian had stifled any attempts Darlene made at friendships he could not control or oversee, and to befriend a woman of Consuelo's background heaped additional fuel onto his insecurities. She came from the upper class, the product of a generations-old manufacturing family that had lost its fortune in the early 1980s. Consuelo had had no choice but to join the legions of laborers fleeing Mexico. Harkening back to Elena and his trafficking days, Christian had no control over his deep-seated hatred of immigrants, and thus, Consuelo. She would have left them long ago, Darlene or not, if she hadn't needed the job so desperately.

Reluctantly, Darlene followed Christian into the dining room. Awkwardly they settled at opposite ends of the long table, an ostentatious flower arrangement arching up between them. She looked down when Consuelo brought in their breakfast on a silver tray, silently laying everything out. "Will there be anything else, Pastor?"

"That'll be all for now," he answered superciliously. Consuelo reddened with anger as she backed away from the table, turning only to close the door. Darlene heaved an angry sigh. "Christian, why must you be so hateful? What is it with you? She needs the job and she performs it well. But you give her no choice but to despise you. They all despise you."

"Well fuck you and fuck your mother too." His momentary affection for her vanished. "That woman, and alla them for that matter, they got it so good here it would make any wetback's head dizzy with envy. You need to trust me on this. I'm the one knows how to handle help."

"You must be right as always, Pastor. I apologize if, from time to time, I forget you were to the manor born." With the first bite of huevos rancheros, she turned an unappetizing shade of green and, pleading sickness, ran from the room. A few minutes later, wan and weakened, she returned.

"Christian," she stammered. "I—we—we been so outta sorts with each other for so long I don't hardly know how to tell you this, because—well—I don't even know if it's what you want anymore. Y'see Christian, I'm—I'm pregnant." Through half lowered eyelids, she searched his face. "Did you hear what I said? We're gonna have a baby."

Those two words—*I'm pregnant*—silenced him like no others could. After all this time and shame—the lifelong reminders, first by Mason and Luke and later, by the doctor— that he wasn't a man, at least not in the real sense, and he had confounded them all. Well fuck that doctor and his tests and fuck him all the way to Hell and back. This unfamiliar sense of manhood swelled in him and in that moment he experienced the closest thing to an emotional connection he'd ever known. He went to her and they embraced with a passion they hadn't known in years. Towering above her, Christian felt all-powerful. Wordlessly, he took her hand and gently led her outside to the pasture, desperately wanting his beautiful, fecund bride to commune with the now-expectant Queen Esther, the female on whom, until now, he'd placed his hopes for a miracle birth. Hallelujah, an heir to the Hillcox throne was to be born after all. God was good.

❖

After all these years of playing the pastor's wife, Darlene remained as unconvinced as ever that God was good. Or that he even existed at all. Life was far too complex for her to accept the simplistic explanations that satisfied Christian and his flock, and she had little patience for the convoluted Zionist themes with which Christian had become consumed. Having been in the "business" with him from nearly the start, she knew all too well that however sincere his original conversion, his present motivation had more in common with a con artist than a saint. For Darlene, this knowledge was accompanied by the painful awareness that she had been his accomplice along the way. Every time Christian convinced a trusting congregant to exchange hard-earned wages for empty promises, she had been right there with him. And there was no question but that she was his equal when it came to spending the vast amount of money he brought in, despite the immoral, if not illegal, ways in which it was obtained. Indeed, a few souls along the way may have found relief in Christian's words, but Darlene couldn't help but think that most people who came to him for help needed a lot more than the cheap salve of Jesus-talk to fix the real-world problems confronting them.

When he advised someone suffering from cancer not to seek medical help because faith alone would heal, Darlene knew his words were tantamount to a loaded gun. Or to tell a man with a wife and four children that the job he lost didn't matter because God would provide—that is, once the man sowed a proper seed into the church's coffers, was the basest kind of theft. Time and again she'd heard him give godly advice for something that demanded human action only to be astonished by how willingly the desperate and frightened accepted his advice, eagerly handing over their hard-earned money as well.

Pastor Christian Hillcox was the anti-Robin Hood—he took from the poor and gave to himself.

He and the Word of Faith Movement skillfully abused the human desire to believe in something greater than oneself. Believers came, they listened, and, almost always, gave generously when asked, never realizing how much of their money was destined to feed Christian's—and Darlene's—profligate lifestyle. Devious and predatory, he manipulated congregants with the ease of a confidence man: plant your seed, make your tithe, send your child to Bible school, and one day that child will grow up to take his place as a victim in the cycle of deception. Over the years Darlene had remained a silent and, consequently, willing agent in the creation of the monster that Christian had become.

Early on, when they worked together as a team and she was the planner-in-chief, when the first dollars trickled in, she suffered no qualms. But the years ticked by, and with no children to distract her, Darlene became increasingly aware of the change in Christian. He seemed unaware of his own hypocrisy, and as before, she remained silent. Now that his increasingly apocalyptic zeal had spun out of hand, her only hope was that taking responsibility for a human life might anchor him to a more earthly future.

The times she overheard him telling one politician or another, "The Rapture is nigh, and when it comes, the world will look to you in Congress as the Lord's Council, but only if you *serve* as the Bible demands," she could no longer fool herself into thinking that his words had no consequences. His clout with conservative lawmakers was no longer about the ego boost he derived from rubbing elbows with power. No, Christian was determined to do whatever it took to protect the biblical boundaries of Zion, illegal settlements and all, and *only* because of the Hebrew nation's role in the Rapture. She'd hear his crazy talk about nuclear first strikes against Iran and Syria while at the same time, lawmakers lined up at his door hoping to gain the favor of his significant voting bloc. The stakes had grown increasingly dire with each passing year.

Satisfied that he was doing as much as was humanly possible to sow and nurture the seeds of strife in the Middle East, Christian intended to satisfy his every appetite in the time he had left. If not for his political connections he would have been just another religious con man in a long line of con men—a modern-day Elmer Gantry. The difference was that this new-world charlatan lived in a nuclear age and that he actually wanted to *hasten* the world's end.

Had Darlene deliberately set out to destroy him, there could have been no better way than to have danced with his real-life devil. To have danced so well, in fact, that Mason left a piece of himself behind in her. She could have aborted the devil-child in her belly—she'd have had no regrets about that—but the thought of Christian learning about what it was to care for a child, to be grounded to this Earth, made her think she just might be able to pull it off. Seven months from now, the living indictment of her shame would come into the world. She might not have been a virtuous woman before they'd married, but at least back then, she'd had a moral code. Now that she fully acknowledged what she'd become, she had no alternative but to live with it. She would forever own the truth, and for the sake of her position and her unborn child she'd carry her secret to the grave. That is, as long as Mason never returned.

❖

It all began the day Christian left for the Midwest. Mason all too gleefully accepted Darlene's offer to stay on while Christian was gone and now, at dusk, father and daughter-in-law sat outside on the porch, watching the sunset. The sky shimmered with color, not that Mason noticed—he was focused solely on his scheme. All day he had played the perfect gentleman. It was warm for an April evening, and the night's warmth increased the heat that had been building between them ever since Christian had left. Smiling over at her, Mason's voice turned raw and guttural, setting loose a thrill of the forbidden within her.

"Darlene, I probly shouldn't be sayin' this to you since yer married to my son, but dammit to hell, I cain't figger out, fer the life a me, how he coulda left you behind even fer a day. If you was mine, I'd never let you outta my sight If you ain't the sexiest woman I ever laid eyes on, I don't know who is."

She knew fire when she saw it yet she did nothing to extinguish it.

"Don't get me wrong," Mason continued. "I'm glad he did. Leave, that is. It's been, as his highness would say, heaven on Earth fer me. Bein' here alone with you, gettin' to know each other with none a his poison interferin.' I tell you, these are memories I'm gonna keep forever. Gonna lock 'em away in a special room in my heart marked 'Darlene' so's I can take 'em out long after I've moved on, which I 'spect I oughta be doin' sooner rather than later."

Something ominous hovered in the air, exciting and repelling Darlene at the same time.

"Been a long time since the likes of someone classy as you paid me no never mind." He held up one of the bottles of liquor he'd brought with him. "Any chance I might could entice you to join me in a drink?" She deferred with a weak shake of the head.

"I promise there ain't no sinnin' in it. Never was, never will be, far as I'm concerned."

With faint conviction, she pushed the bottle away. "When I married I promised Christian I'd never so much as touch a drop of alcohol, an' I've been true to my word."

"Well then I wager you ain't had much fun," he chortled. He took a swig from the bottle, their proximity on the swing both taunting and exciting her.

"Damn but that feels good," he murmured. "Nice 'n warm. All a the vice an' none a the virtue."

He eyed her, his desire-filled eyes never once straying from her. They sat in silence for a time as Mason continued to put bottle to mouth. "Why my fool of a son is such a tight-ass, I'll never unnerstand. Sure you won't take a nip?" He held the bottle out to her. She looked at him, really looked at him, and in that moment, she saw not the evil man Christian deplored but instead a sad and lonely man. He wasn't bad looking for a man his age and she began to feel stirrings from another life weave their power over her.

A quiver in her voice betrayed her. "I—I don't know. I guess—I guess I'm jest afraid. Afraid what might happen if I let go, even a little. One thing I know is that all these years,

I never heard your side of the story. Always believed whatever Christian said 'bout you. Since you've been here, well—all I can say is you're not what he described." By now she was leaning against his arm, touching him, all the while a voice inside her head screamed RED ALERT! Ignoring the voice, she nuzzled fully and intentionally into the crook of his arm and speaking throatily, said, "I believe I been enjoyin' myself as much as you."

Mason was in a holding pattern, cruising gently, poised and ready to come in for the landing. He stroked her cheek softly with one hand, caressed her shoulder with the other, lightly brushing against her breast.

"Lately I've been feelin' more like a forgotten piece of furniture than a wife. Guess I've only got myself to blame," she said. She reached for the bottle and took a long deep drink. "Oh, to hell with it. Let's have ourselves some fun." The old Darlene Steeger was back and, already feeling the warmth from yet another pull, she went with it. "Hell, let the devil take tomorrow." Little did she know how prescient that thought would turn out to be.

It might have been minutes or it could have been hours when, swooning with drink, they tumbled inside and stumbled upstairs. But what began tenderly morphed with frightening speed into a scene of horror. When Mason hurled his pants across the room, she thought nothing of it. It was when he ripped her dress from her that she felt his passion turn into rage and her desire into fear as he pushed her onto the bed. Screaming, she begged him to stop, and he responded with a firm slap in the face.

"Shut your fuckin' whore trap," he shouted, as he entered her roughly and pumped away with vigor. She looked into his eyes and saw therein a bottomless pit of hate, realizing all too late that the evil in this man was real. "Now you're gettin' some real male headship, and it sure as fuck ain't what that faggot son a mine been givin', is it?" he roared. She began to wail. "Shut the fuck up, bitch." Grimacing as he came, his body contorted with animal satisfaction and he bellowed, "Take that, you fuckin' pansy-boy. Yer wife'll never forget what a real man is after this." Then he collapsed at her side and fell soundly to sleep. For sleep comes easily to those without conscience.

Darlene lay there a while, whimpering, not knowing what to do. She slid out of bed, tears streaming, and and pulled on a long robe. Equally frightened of Mason as she was of the future, she reached for the phone and held it high. Shaking him, she shrieked, "Get out of my house! *Now*. Or I'll call the police, I swear I will." Dazed, he slit one eye open and slurred, "You ain't callin' no one 'n you know it. 'Sides, if you do, I'll tell 'em you was beggin' for it, an' that won't be no lie neither, so do us both a favor an' shut yer piehole so's I kin sleep. Then maybe we'll do it agin if yer lucky." He grunted and passed out.

When Mason awoke, it was just past five in the morning and for a fleeting moment he wasn't sure where he was. When he realized he was in the "Master's" bedroom and saw the bedcovers strewn wildly about, he surmised he'd scored. Touchdown Jesus! Alpha rules again and all was right with the world. Once more, he'd gotten the best of his son. Wandering downstairs he was amused, if somewhat taken aback, to find Darlene sitting in wait on a stool by the front door, a long shotgun in her hands.

"Morning, daughter," he said, stretching languidly. "Damn if you ain't one hellcat in the sack. Lookee-here—I got me some claw marks all over my glory," as he examined his naked body. "Slam, bam thank ya ma'am. I gander I could be ready fer another round." He took a step in her direction. How 'bout it sweetheart?"

She raised the gun and, squinting her eyes, pointed it at his forehead. "Take another step and I'll blow your head off an' don't think I won't, you sack of shit. Nothing in this world would give me greater pleasure than to see your brains splattered 'cross my white carpet. I want you outta here an' I mean *now*. Not only that but I don't ever want to lay eyes on you or hear your voice long as I live."

He took stock of the wild look in her eyes and backed away slowly. He had had his way with his son's bitch, and satisfying as that was he still hadn't scored any cash. Almost as an afterthought, he snarled, "I'll leave. A man can see when he's not wanted—though I must say, it breaks my heart to hear you say I cain't see my son agin. So much so that I cain't imagine *not* comin' back, if you git my drift."

Cheerily, he disappeared up the steps to pack up his belongings, singing all the while.

Oh when the saints go marchin' in,
Oh when the saints go marchin' in.
Lord I wanna be in their number,
When the saints go marchin' in.

A few minutes later, duffle in hand, he descended the grand staircase for the last time. Darlene kept the shotgun ready with one hand. In the other she held out a plastic bag, tied shut. "What happened last night ends here," she said. She tossed the bag outside onto the front steps. "There's twenty-six thousand dollars in that bag. It's all I got to my name. Take it an' get the hell outta my sight. I ever hear your voice or learn you contacted

Christian, I'll hunt you down. An' you'd be wise to believe me."
She gestured adamantly, both hands on the gun, gesturing to
Mason the way out.

Like Luke, Mason wanted more. After all, Christian was his
biological son, meaning Christian owed him. Unfortunately,
he wasn't dealing with the businessman here, but with the
businessman's wife. As he stepped toward the bag of cash he
snarled with false gratitude, "Thank you ma'am. You are most
generous in addition to being one helluva fuck." He looked
deliberately at the diamond on her hand, and amped up the ask
while he still could. "Actually, I'm, uh, thinkin' a somethin' say,
a tetch more personal, if ya git my drift."

"This?" she spat, following his eyes to her ring. Wresting the
ring from her swollen finger, its four carats of marital brilliance a
mockery, she hurled it at him, shrieking, "Now get the fuck out!"

He scrambled to pick it up. Slowly he examined it, turning it
round in the bright light. "Yeah, this'll do me. I'll keep it as a sort
a betrothal trinket," he leered. "Never know what the future'll
bring." With a tip of his hat, he grinned a toothy grin. "It's been a
pleasure doin' bizness with you ma'am, a real pleasure." Creaking
open the rust-coated car door, he called back, "All in all, not a
bad coupla days work. Maybe we'll meet agin. Never kin tell."

Darlene raised the gun and released a shot into the air.
"I ever see you again, you breathe a word a what went on here,
an' I swear to God I'll find you an' blow your brains all the way
back to Kansas. That would be *my* pleasure." The look on her
face told him she meant business, and with a nasty smirk, he
pocketed the ring and drove off.

PART 3

Growing Pains

23

Raising Hell

December 24, 2000

WITH CHRISTMAS EVE BEHIND, Christian resigned himself to the grueling twenty-four hours ahead. Two years earlier, Headship's board voted to follow the lead of megachurches across the country and shutter its doors on Christmas. It seemed odd for a church to be closed for the birth of our Lord, even verging on the irreligious, but a day off was a day off, even if did leave him with no means of escape from his clinging, watchful wife. The reality for most people is that Christmas Day spent at home with your loved ones is the definition of Hell. Too much time together in close quarters more often than not magnified tensions usually obscured by the business of everyday life, and the results were evident. On December twenty-sixth the outer sanctum of Christian's office looked more like the local mall the day after Christmas than it did a pastor's waiting room. Last year alone, he'd spent most of a week dealing with the aftermath of widespread drunkenness, abuse, one case of incestuous rape, and a suicide. They came for advice, but just as often to beg forgiveness for sins committed on the Nativity of their Lord. Christian pastored and lectured, railed and put the fear of God into them, leaving no one unscathed. The "Good News" was that no matter how bad the deed, forgiveness was there for the taking—especially if certain conditions were met by the seeker. If he carried a business card, it would read:

> Christian John Hillcox
> Southwest Texas Distributor
> "Get Out of Jail Free"
> Come One, Come All

Christmas or not, Christian was depleted. His nightmares had returned and this time he looked, not to Jesus, but to a little blue pill called Xanax. Nights when the coyote came a-howlin', Christian checked out, courtesy of Upjohn Pharmaceutical.

❖

Male Headship was flourishing, its membership well above 12,000 and still growing. Plans to open a satellite church in an impoverished rural exurb forty miles outside San Antonio were on the drawing board. With the idea of branches, each one a virtual Headship ATM, Christian and the board hammered out their five-year plan. All they had to do was to find the areas where the Devil already had a foothold—for example, places with the highest murder and prostitution rates. Or maybe next door to an abortion clinic. Plant a church there and Headship guaranteed itself a built-in market. And after all, how many businesses can promise that?

Syndication and reruns of *Countdown to Jesus* brought in millions annually and his latest book, *Nuclear Dawn*, due out next June, promised to be his biggest yet. His earlier books had done well, but this was the first one to be marketed internationally. Thanks to the early projections, he had already received a quarter-million-dollar advance.

Food, drink, women, power, and now at long last, a son. Christian had it all. With his night terrors under drugged control, there were only the occasional times when, alone with himself, he felt the seductive lure of depression. When that happened, the usual background noise in his head would morph into a clanging, clattering racket—a sort of death rattle that sent him back in time to that terrible night on the border. When that happened, try as he might, he was unable to quash the image of the dying woman's pleading eyes, eyes he had so callously extinguished. Or of the other bodies, stiff from death's grip, deaths he had directly caused. It didn't matter how much time had passed, the sounds and images, when they came, were as vivid as ever. There were times that these visions could be so real to him that the thought of following in his mother's footsteps held more than a little allure.

Christian's life had turned into a circle of irony that began and ended in the trash bin of self-loathing. And then he'd think, *Fuck this.* If his past was morally indefensible, it was exactly that—the past. Christ had died for his sins, and Christian's debt, in return, was that he forgive himself.

❖

Darlene was particularly unsettled by today's "Tumbling with Jesus" gym class. John Jr., or JJ, as they called him, was a decent little gymnast and he had taken to tumbling with vigor. To watch him leap and roll about, so carefree and jubilant had, up till now, been pure joy. At this morning's class, though, the teacher had had to stop him from pummeling a handicapped child, and Darlene saw, for the first time, the ghost of Mason in JJ. Viscerally repulsed by her son's callous cruelty, a shiver of foreboding ran down her spine. Misty Madsen, another sad-looking mother, chanced to catch her eye at just that moment, and Darlene realized she wasn't the only woman there wearing a mask. But Misty wasn't married to the most prominent pastor in Texas.

"Darlene, everything okay? You look like you seen a ghost."

Darlene forced a smile. "I'm fine dear. Musta been something I ate." She looked back at the children, relieved to see her son once more and not the ghost of his birth monster.

❖

One evening early in JJ's fifth year, Darlene was on her way out the door when she met Christian in the driveway. "Look-ee here. What do we got? Looks like my wife but she's dressed like a schoolmarm, so it can't be her, can it?" he sniggered, as roughly, he held firmly onto her arm to keep her from leaving. "Where you think you're goin'? The Librarian's Ball?"

"For your information *Pastor*, I'm goin' to the school to register JJ for kindergarten next fall and I purposely dressed this way so as to fit in. First impressions matter when you're dealin' with teachers." She added, "I s'pose you have no interest in goin' with me—you know, as his *father*?"

"Well, fuck me. There ain't gonna be no registration because no son of mine's goin' anywhere near no public school. You think I'm gonna allow my boy to be exposed to what goes on in those liberal hotboxes? If you think that, then you don't know me at all. My boy'll be homeschooled an' if it ain't by you, then I'll find someone else fit to teach him. No ma'am. I ain't about to have no fairies puttin' their dirty paws all over my boy."

Darlene, long having anticipated this fight, was ready with a retort. But it was at that moment that Christian noticed, for the first time in the five years since Mason had absconded with her diamond, that the ring now encircling her fourth finger was not the one he had given her. "What's that on your finger? It sure as hell ain't my diamond," he snapped.

Darlene trembled as the blood rushed to her cheeks.

"Where is my diamond, damn it?" Bile rose hard and fast, as his temper went reeling back to the days of Elena.

"Christian, calm yourself. I misplaced the ring not long ago and I didn't tell you, figurin' it'll turn up. This here's only a cubic zirconium so it's not like you need worry I bought myself another diamond."

"Wait one holy-fuckin' minute here. You're tellin' me you lost a four-and-a-half carat diamond and decided not to tell me?"

"I didn't tell you, precisely to avoid the scene we're havin' right now. Look at you. You're a ravin' lunatic. Calm yourself. The ring's not gone, it's only been misplaced—so I'd appreciate it if you wouldn't talk to me like I hocked it or something worse. You think *I'm* not upset? It *is* my ring after all." Holding up her hand, she tried to lighten the moment. "Not bad for a fake, is it? Kinda like the holding ring you gave me when we got engaged."

He didn't smile. "Let me get this straight. You lose a four-and-a-half carat diamond an' you *figure* you'll find it? C'mon, you gotta do better than that, sweetheart. How in the fuck could you lose it anyhow? I thought you never took it off?" With each word his voice took on a sharper edge.

"You know I don't, that is not unless I'm workin' in the garden. I'm sure that was when it went missin'. I put it on the counter one day 'fore I went out to do some plantin' an' when I came back in, it wasn't there." Darlene saw he wasn't buying it so she went on, "There was no one home that day 'cept for Consuelo, but she was upstairs and didn't hear anyone come in. I musta picked it up when I came in and somehow unknowingly put it down somewhere."

"Well, fuck me blind," Christian scoffed. "Seems my own wife's got herself a sweet little cover-up. Indeedy-do. An' I'd be willin' to reckon it's a cover up for our own resident-in-thief, Señorita Consuelo." The discussion had veered in a direction Darlene had not foreseen. The last thing she wanted was to implicate Consuelo in her web of lies. But that was precisely what was happening and she couldn't see any way around it. If she didn't come up with something fast, Consuelo would be the one to pay for Darlene's sin.

"Christian, let's not talk anymore about the ring. You're right. I shoulda told you an' when it turns up, which it will, we'll laugh about it, but for now, let's finish up the conversation we started 'bout JJ."

They went inside and Darlene removed her jacket to signal she wouldn't be going anywhere. "I apologize for thinkin' JJ could to go to public school. I don't know what I musta been thinking, what with your position. You're right. It's hardly fittin' to put our son in a public school, when I'm the one who should be directin' his education."

Inwardly, Darlene seethed. Her attempted bait and switch had committed her to homeschooling her son, something

211

she had sworn she would never let happen. Cartwheels and somersaults with Jesus were one thing, but pseudoscience and revisionist history were another entirely. Just because she'd made her bed in Christian's stone-aged world didn't mean she intended to make JJ lie in it. But suddenly she was trapped.

"That's settled then ," Christian said, matter-of-factly. "As for the ring—"

Damn it to hell, not only had she just agreed to homeschool JJ but Christian was back on the ring.

"Way I see it is you got a choice. We either report Consuelo to the police right now or you march inside an' fire the thievin' bitch."

"Christian! You have no proof she took it."

"Christian!" he mocked. "An' you have none that she didn't. I never trusted that uppity Mexican, her thinkin' she's better 'n me. An' like you always say, she only stays with us because a the money. Think 'bout it Einstein. One day, while you're out in the garden, la *puta* happens upon your rock. Without so much as a thought for *you*, she pockets it, *knowin'* you'd never accuse her. That's frenship for you."

"Christian," she sobbed.

"Don't *Christian* me. You listen up an' you listen good. It's only because I'm a godly man that I'll agree not to press charges even if it means I lose a four-an'-a-half carat stone. I'll do it because, after all, I'm a *forgivin'* man. But that means you'd better go on in an' give her her marchin' orders, an' that means now. Without references. Make sure she's gone by dawn's light." Darlene hesitated. "What's it to be? Do I turn her in or are you gonna handle this?" Angry as he was, he enjoyed watching Darlene twist and turn herself inside out. He walked over to the phone and began to dial.

Darlene rushed over to stop him, "Fine. I'll fire her. But it's wrong, terribly, terribly wrong."

"Now, that's a good girl. An' don't you go believin' it's wrong. It's best for everyone. This way, she walks out on her own two feet 'stead of leavin' here in cuffs. Jest be sure she's gone by morning." He started to leave the room but turned back with an afterthought. "Oh, an' on the other thing we discussed, I'm relieved you came to your senses 'bout schoolin' our boy."

A parting slap on the buttocks—a slap that stung—reminded her who was boss. Then he was gone.

Darlene's fear of discovery far outweighed the guilt she felt in betraying her friend, but she had no choice. Letting Consuelo go was minor compared to what would happen if the truth about the ring were discovered. Still, it was one thing to go along with Christian's dishonesty and deception, and another entirely to put an innocent woman, and a friend at that, out on the street like so much trash. Helpless to do otherwise, she steeled herself and went inside. Her voice cool and direct, she told Consuelo that her services were no longer needed. The conversation was brief and she offered no reason. Backed into a corner, Darlene took a page from Christian's book and did whatever was necessary to protect herself. Lies and deceit had become as much a part of her life as they were of his, and they were bound to catch up with her one day. Fortunately, today was not the day.

24

"Do You Not Think an Angel Rides in the Whirlwind?"

Inauguration Day
January 20, 2001

"CHRISTIAN GOT BY WITH A little help from his friends. Yessir. He was in . . . In like Jesus. Scratch that. In *for* Jesus."

"Out of sinnin' 'n snortin' coke. Frat house, now White House. Not Black House. Hell no, he didn't go. But heavens yes, he will be blessed."

"We know the race is not to the swift nor the battle to the strong. Do you not think an angel rides in the whirlwind and directs this storm?"

"Georgie-Porgie puddin' 'n pie. God bless you. God bless Amurica. Make that, God bless ME for puttin' YOU here."

From the second row, Darlene looked at Christian up on the viewing stands as he wiped away a telegenically perfectly timed tear. "Land that I love. Fuckin' right. This is *me* up here, *me*, John Christian Hillcox, seated smack dab behind the first honest-to-goodness godly President of these U-nited States of Christ."

He smiled tenderly at Darlene, clad in ermine and pearls. "Yessir, the lady is a tramp."

"Oh dear Lord, with you up there an' me an' the president down here, we're gonna do great things together. Awe-fuckin' inspirin' things."

"God bless my overcoat. It's fuckin' freezin' out here."

"Faggots, you better run for the hills. Better run fast cuz we're comin' for you."

"Abortionators, prepare to meet your maker. Repent ye, your slaughterous ways."

"WE'RE ON OUR WAY. We don't know when He's comin'. We're on our way. Takin' our time but we'll be there. Goodbye Satan, King of Gehenna, sayin' me an' Jesus, down by the schoolyard."

Hand on Bible.

"Do you not think an angel rides in the whirlwind and directs this storm?"

25

Trials and Tribulations

January 28, 2001

"THAT'S IT, SON. TAKE A deep breath an' blow. One,
two-ooo, three!" It was John Jr.'s fifth birthday and Darlene
had orchestrated the most flamboyant, if Christian-themed,
party the community had ever seen. The invitation list topped
three hundred, most of whom were churchgoers and board
members, all invited to pledge fealty to the heir of the Headship
kingdom. All that was missing from the picture were the doting
grandparents, aunts and uncles, and cousins. The engraved
invitation sported a photo of the little prince taken the previous
summer in Oberammergau, Germany during a family trip to
the "World's End Conference." In the picture, John Jr., clad
in edelweiss-embroidered lederhosen, looked the perfect Aryan
specimen as he gazed out reverently across the German Alps.

Like Jackie and J.F.K., the Hillcoxes had their own John
John. As John John had been graced with the best of both parents,
JJ benefited from Darlene's green eyes and full lips, gentled by
Christian's delicate features and coloring. True, he'd inherited his

father's penchant toward heaviness but hopefully time, and a few good whippings, would take care of that. Christian, for his part, drew the Kennedy parallel even further with an outsized sense that both boys had been born of American royalty. His son—the spermatic miracle—was as royal as they came, praise the Lord, having overcome the doctors' pronouncements showing them and their science for the balderdash that they were. Here was living proof that with God all things are possible. Far be it from Christian to ever proclaim the struggles of his seed to make a point from the pulpit.

The party was a success from the start. For the children, there were pony and elephant rides along with an enchanting carousel sporting seraphs instead of horses. Seven hundred Christly-purple balloons dotted the landscape, each one attesting to the feted one's royalty, the balloons bowing and scraping above the crucifix-shaped pool. The chill in the air, which disappointed the would-be swimmers, enhanced the breathtaking spectacle of hundreds of fragrant white lilies that floated in the water.

The pièce de resistance was an elaborate birthday cake, a twenty-one layer likeness of Gabriel blowing his horn, each layer filled with strawberry crème anglaise and the entire cake topped off by light-as-air, purple-tinted marshmallow icing. The height of the custom-built platform on which the cake was displayed required that JJ climb a ladder beside it to blow out the candles. Laughter filled the air when the boy missed the candles completely. Darlene clambered up to help, and in her ascent, she unknowingly, or perhaps not, offered a view of her scantily pantied bottom, lacy garter and all, to the crowd below. Christian fumed. How shameless of her to put her wares so plainly in sight, wares which were by all rights reserved for his eyes and his alone.

Being Christian

With a harsh tug on her skirt, he yanked her down and snarled, "Have you no decency?" In an effort to distract the lascivious onlookers from her pubic show, he bellowed out with false jollity, "John Jr.! Look here what Pappa's gone and bought you." Christian, a man with a less than stellar history of private affection, was a master at showing his love when the world was watching.

The wide-eyed boy ran to his father, Christian, with grand ceremony, whisked a sheet from atop a large object in the center of the great hall, unveiling a miniature motorized Corvette coupe. He lifted the over-excited boy high in the air and deposited him into the driver's seat. The crowd pushed back as Father showed Son the Way, and after revving up the small car's engine, Christian sent him off. JJ motored along the floor at a snail's pace until he was stopped by an unfortunate collision with a costly Louis XIV ormolu commode. He burst into tears, more out of fear of his father's reaction than from the accident.

Ever the savior, Christian scooped up his son while, undetected by the guests, he pinched the child's bottom so fiercely it brought tears to the boy's eyes. JJ would do well to learn here and now that Christian would not stand for having his things damaged. Not now, not ever. The severity of pain rendered JJ momentarily mute before he burst into tears, bringing forth Darlene, nanny in tow. She knew her son had to be crying from something more than the inconsequential collision and, glaring at her husband, she snatched JJ to take him upstairs. Christian scowled at her, unable to forgive the shame of Darlene's indecent display on the ladder. Darlene knew all too well what she had to look forward to once the last guest had gone.

❖

Even with John Jr. gone, the party continued in full swing. Christian was deep in conversation with two board members when he sensed a man staring at him, hovering out by the fence. Christian excused himself to confront the stranger whose eyes remained trained pointedly upon him.

"Pardon me, but do I know you?" he asked politely.

Luke looked him in the face, square on. "Dickhead. Ha! D'you *know* me!"

Christian staggered backward and kept from falling by grabbing hold of a fence post. "Luke," he gasped, regretting the unmistakable display of fear. Desperate to regain his composure, Christian took a deep breath and brought himself back to a standing position, physically dwarfing the scrawny man. "Pardon my shock, but what the fuck 'r you doin' here? Have you forgotten the part of our arrangement that states my never having to set eyes on you again? Seems to me this here's a clear violation an' if you know what's good for you, you'll take your degenerate body off my property right now. Make me say it twice an' you'll be leaving with an escort of armed guards. Your choice."

"Still king of the mountain, ain't we? How's about you take the stick outta your ass an' listen why I come, Pastor Shit-For-Brains. I'm not here to make trouble, only to protect my investment. Thought it'd be best for both a us if you knew that the law's been sniffin' round, askin' questions 'bout illegal trafficking. I didn't hafta come, ya know, so perhaps a little courtesy for your partner-in-crime would be in line."

Christian leaned back again onto the fence. "Are you shittin' me?" He looked around to make sure there was no one in earshot. "You sayin' they can come after us fer somethin' happened nearly twenty years ago? Well, fuck me." He felt as if he had just taken a punch in the gut. "I, uh, I'm sorry I was so harsh. You hafta know what it's like for me to see you all of a sudden here, in my world. I always figgered, that as long as the checks kept comin', our paths'd never cross again. But, well, you're right, you didn't hafta come warn me, an' I am grateful." Christian pulled out a thick wad of bills, a gesture reminiscent of their shared past, but with the roles reversed, and he stuffed several bills into one of Luke's sweaty palms.

In recent years, there were times when the Devil had used Christian's body as a satanic host, causing him to commit sins of the flesh. He never worried because he knew God was on his side. Sunday after Sunday he would rail, cajole, warn, even threaten those whose walk with the Lord was weak, all the while knowing that, no matter what *he* did, he was at peace, thanks to his personal relationship with Jesus. Come what may, Christian knew where he was headed on Judgment Day. That said, he was not equipped, on this sparkling January evening or at any other time, for that matter, to deal with fear of an earthly kind. In the deeper recesses of his mind, he'd always known this day might come. But as time passed, he'd stopped worrying. Whatever came from tonight's encounter, one thing was certain. He wanted Luke out of there before he had a chance to speak to anyone. Leading him firmly by the elbow, Christian guided him to the far perimeter of the grounds, away from prying ears.

Luke was enjoying the distress he'd stirred up. Sniggering, he said, "Pastor, I wouldn't get my knickers in a twist jest yet. My informant told me the INS has only reopened a coupla the old cases. Don't know how old is old, but one of 'em was in the vicinity of our—uh—sitch-ee-a-shun. I cain't say if ours'll get noticed or even if they could prosecute after all this time. 'Sides, we both know there ain't nothing money can't make disappear, so I wouldn't lose sleep if I was you s'long as you always got the ready cash."

Maybe this was just another play for Luke to get a bigger piece of the pie. Still, Christian couldn't shake the feeling of the six dead Mexicans hovering nearby in the darkness. At the same time, memories from his youth reignited his hatred of Luke. Quietly, he hissed, "Listen to me, you Godless fuck. I pay every month so's you keep me outta trouble which is what I expect you to do. You remember this—the only thing we got between us is blackmail, pure an' simple. In the future, you got somethin' ta say, you stick to the arrangement an' call my office. I've come too far to have the likes of you muddyin' the waters. My life is filled with godly people now, important people, and by definition that leaves you out. You wanna hang with a Hillcox, you do it with my ass-wipe of a father. Fuck if I care anymore. The two a you deserve each other. I appreciate the warnin', *if* it's for real. You take care a this an' don't show your face 'round here again. You do an' you can kiss this sugar daddy goodbye, no matter what kinda threats you make. We clear?"

Squelching the desire to slam his knee into the fat man's groin, Luke lifted his hand to the sky and crisply replied, "Sieg Heil, Herr Pastor," and disappeared into the night.

❖

After the last guest had gone, Christian, deeply shaken, headed out to the pasture to think things through. Luke's visit had bothered him greatly and he hoped his herd would calm him down, but the animals were nowhere to be seen. He saw a light shining in Tibbetts' front window but it was late, so he let him be. Every step back to the house increased his anxiety. Ignoring the legions of Mexican workers scurrying about, cleaning up from the party, he climbed the staircase to his son's room with a sense of impending doom.

Bedtimes were the only times Christian saw his son. Having grown up with no role model on which to base a relationship, theirs was strictly religion-based. When he had the time, he'd read to JJ from the Bible. Sharing the Bible was, for him, one of the only joys of fatherhood and, literalist that he was, he refused to read from any of the watered down texts written for children. John Jr., bright but anxious, was ambivalent about "Bible Hour," but, yearning for his father's time and approval, he participated with whatever enthusiasm he could muster. He dreaded the dark and terrifying passages Christian usually chose. Too young to understand that the man was constitutionally incapable of relating to a child in a healthy way, JJ never let on how frightened he was of his father.

In tonight's dark mood, Christian selected a passage from The Book of Revelation. With nearly sadistic pleasure he recited some particularly gruesome verses that described rotting corpses, terrifying beasts, and rivers of boiling blood. As he read, JJ went white, all the while attempting to keep a brave mask on his small face. Satisfied he'd imparted the fear of God in his child, Christian patted the boy on the head, turned off the light, and left him alone in the dark. Juices flowing, he headed for Darlene's room where she stood waiting, her eyes ablaze with fury.

"What the hell is wrong with you? I s'pose you want for your son to grow up afraid a his pappy like you were?"

"Afraid? He's not afraid a me. What he is is respectful."

He advanced slowly, put his face up to hers, and pushed her deeper into the room, shoving her onto the bed.

"Furthermore, don't you go psychoanalyzin' me, missy. I'll teach my son as I see fit, despite your best efforts to sissify him, somethin' that, by the way, ain't gonna happen, leastways not on my watch. All yer coddling won't make a man of him, an' that's what he's gotta be to survive. Ain't no place in this world for pansy-boys. Or in the next, for that matter."

With the words pansy-boy a chill washed over her as she remembered the very same expression coming from Mason's mouth that terrible night. Despite the fact that evil had brought their child into the world, something good had come out of it, and that something was JJ. Thanks to her, he had developed enough empathy to overcome his earlier violent tendencies, growing into a kind and sensitive child. The fact was, he was the only decent thing to come out of the past decade-and-a-half of her life.

She tried to stand up, eyeing the door and her escape, but it was blocked. Christian and Darlene hadn't slept in the same room since JJ's birth. Back then it made sense, what with the nighttime feedings and all, but JJ was five now and so far, Christian had not demanded that she return to his bed. Her door remained open to his conjugal visits but, thankfully, he left her bed most nights as soon as he was satisfied.

Tonight, waves of violence and hatred hung in the air between them as he threw himself atop her, tearing at her skirt. No longer charmed by what was underneath, he saw her for the whore that she was. Over and over he replayed the images of the night's exhibitionism and with it, the mockery she had made of him. If she could share herself so wantonly in her own home, he could only imagine what she might be doing outside of it.

He was wrong on the one most important detail—the real Judas kiss had taken place in his very own bed nearly six years ago, a kiss that had been far worse than anything he could conjure up even in the darkest recesses of his mind.

Darlene recoiled at his touch as he slammed into her, manhandling her, thrashing away. She cared not a whit for the physical pain she felt. On the contrary, she welcomed it, knowing she deserved all the loathing and agony he could dish out.

26

Thou Shalt Not, or, The "Christian" Ten Commandments

AND GOD SPOKE ALL these words, saying: *I am the LORD your God*.

Thou shalt have no other gods before Me.

No problem here, that is if you don't count money, which I worship the freakin' fuck out of.

Thou shalt not make for yourself a carved image—any likeness of anything that is in heaven above, or that is in the earth beneath, or that is in the water under the earth.

Check, though I confess to a certain idolatry of the man in the mirror.

Thou shalt not take the name of the Lord your God in vain.

No comment other than I goddamn try.

Remember the Sabbath day, to keep it holy.

Check, unless encounters of the pornographic kind count against me.

Honor your father and your mother.
No can do.

Thou shalt not murder.
Been there, done that. Was forgiven.

Thou shalt not commit adultery.
Ditto, numero Six.

Thou shalt not steal.
No problem here. I don't exactly steal: I "merely enjoy" the "seeds" so willingly planted in my "garden."

Thou shalt not bear false witness against your neighbor.
What neighbors? I live on hundreds of acres.

Thou shalt not covet your neighbor's house; you shall not covet your neighbor's wife, nor his male servant, nor his female servant, nor his ox, nor his donkey, nor anything that is your neighbor's.
Fuckin' A. They coveteth mine!

27

Give and Ye Shall Get

March 2001

"GET TO YOUR PHONE AND call up the number on your screen: 1-800-LIV-4-HIM. That's 1-800-LIV-4-HIM. Your personal Lord and Savior is waiting for your call with *your* personalized miracle. Tell the operator, 'IT'S MY TIME LORD. I am ready to walk with YOU and as proof, I am calling to sow my seed.'

"Make the call an' I guarantee that when you back your devotion with dollars, you'll be declarin' to the Lord that you're ready to let your light shine out from under its bushel. What I promise you, good people, is that your devotion will come back to you a thousand fold." Then Christian picked up the ancient ram's horn dangling at his side, held it to his mouth and let it rip, his trademark perspiration pouring forth.

"Hear ye of God's Elect, this is my clarion call! God sowed His seed when he gave to the world his only son. In Jesus' victory over death, He's already risen once as He is soon to do again. It was in the giving of God's seed that mankind saw the greatest gesture of love of all time. He sent His *son* to die for *you*, for *your* sins so that *you* can live a life of wealth. Because *we* are the Lord's mightiest harvest."

Canned studio voices shout, "HALLELUJAH!"

"Operators are standing by now to take the pledge that will put you on the road to health and wealth beyond your wildest dreams, and most important of all, ETERNAL SALVATION." He modulated his voice downward, "There isn't a moment to delay. Every second you wait brings you closer to a self-imposed Eternity in Hell. Though we cannot know the day nor the hour of His Coming, we know it will be soon. In fact, if I don't make it out of the studio today—if the Rapture takes me before this show is over—why, I won't be one bit surprised. No siree. What I will be is *jubilant*.

"I ask, why would any one of you be willing to chance another minute out of His favor, knowing full well it might be your last? You *must* awaken *now* if you hope to reserve your place in Eternity."

A chorus of white robed young girls gathered behind Preacher Man and began to sing:

> Every one of us a sinner,
> Every one has made the fall,
> We are each in need of saving
> 'Fore the Devil takes us all,
> Take my soul, the good Lord Jesus
> Take my worldy goods as well,
> I am yours until forever
> All the rest can burn in Hell.

"Once again, call the number at the bottom of your screen, 1-800-LIV-4-HIM. As an added bonus, if you call within the next thirty minutes, I will send you a sacred vial of MIRACLE WATER." He held up a small bottle, a red fish embossed upon its gilded label. "This water, known only to a privileged few, derives from a secret spring in the Holy Land. A spring from which Jesus is *known* to have taken his last drink. Just a few drops of this water and your anointing will be complete.

"So call now an' receive this holy offer. Remember, give and ye shall get. Give not and ye shall regret."

The choir burst into song as the camera panned the fresh, angelic faces, the toll-free number never leaving the screen. The music built to a devotional frenzy before finally fading toward silence as the camera pulled back to show the entire chorus and Christian at his lectern, the holy book in the crook of his arm, a beatific smile on his face.

"An' that's all the time we have for today, fellow warriors, so remember, call and pledge your gift now. God-willing, I will be back tomorrow. *But if I do not see you again on this Earth, I pray we will be together as we ascend to His glory.* Amen, and God bless."

Christian and the chorus remained in place as the cameras jockeyed artfully while the lighting dramatically faded to black and the voice of the director was finally heard.

"*Cut*! That's a *wrap*. Great job, everyone!"

❖

It had been a long and fruitful day. *Countdown to Jesus* had turned out to be the biggest cash cow of them all. Originally shown on one station, it now aired in all fifty states and forty-two nations.

At the start it had been broadcast with a live studio audience, but the logistics of that endeavor quickly became too costly and time-consuming. Today, although the show was still promoted as "live," it was far from it. Christian set aside a couple of days each month during which they'd record enough for an entire month's worth of shows. Carefully edited audio and video gave the impression the show was still live. It was television, after all, and what is television if not artifice?

Each hour-long program required only fifteen minutes of actual face-time from Christian. The rest was an amalgam of infomercials cleverly packaged as news, singing choirs, and audience shots culled from actual Sunday services. Segments hawked golden promises in the form of "Manna from Heaven," the ubiquitous "Holy Water," or best of all, your own personalized "Mounted Crusaders Sword." *Countdown to Jesus* was a meticulously orchestrated propaganda machine, packaged and fed to the masses, by Christian and other Christian dignitaries, as the one and only way to guarantee an eternally blissful afterlife.

You pays your money, you gets your salvation.

Mopping his perspiration-soaked forehead with a freshly laundered hanky, Christian hauled himself up and out of his studio chair, cursing his ever-present flatulence, only remotely embarrassed by the rank odor sure to permeate the room in his wake. With an appetite like his, all sorts of bodily excretions could be expected. If appetite was to be his ultimate earthly downfall, at least he'd die a happy man.

❖

Two nights prior, Christian dined in a private room at a choice Washington, DC steakhouse with Senator Woody Mapes and

Congressmen Edsel Block and Warren Dyson. With a subtle wink that suggested an undefined intimacy between Mapes and the waiter, the senator told the young man, "DJ, bring me the usual." He turned a dour face Christian's way and said, resignedly, "Two scoops of cottage cheese and a house salad, hold the croutons, extra tomatoes and dressing on the side." Christian grimaced, an expression that Mapes saw as sympathetic but was actually a comment on the wink that had passed between the two men. The congressmen yielded somewhat to their desires and ordered filets, but picked at them guiltily when they arrived, all the while drooling with envy as they watched the lusty pastor inhale his bloody, twenty-four ounce porterhouse. These were men of titular power, but somewhere along the way they had lost their zest for life. Deeply covetous of Christian's *joie de vivre*, they followed each bite he took, slabs of bread serving as delivery vehicles for the fat-soaked bloody juices. No Catholics here, but who could ignore the Eucharistic symbolism? Whether their abstinence was the product of peptic ulcers or obedience to a cardiologist's orders, it didn't much matter. The forced control these dignitaries exerted over their appetites was proof that their power was fleeting.

Overweight though Christian was, he was free to have it all, to lust and to gratify, to want and to take. Unlike these men, he cared little about the number of years he had left on Earth. They might call themselves Bible-believing Baptists but they'd yet to free themselves of their corporeal worries, and for that, Christian pitied them. The security of knowing that Eternity was ahead of him had liberated him long ago to seek and satisfy his unbridled desires. You might not call him "Senator," but you could call him sated.

Dabbing at a globule of blood-red gravy splattered across his brand new silk tie, Christian belched unashamedly, looking at the congressmen and declaring, "Let the horse-trading begin."

Congressman Dyson stepped onto the verbal tightrope cautiously. "Pastor, uh, we asked you here tonight to discuss a highly sensitive matter. Knowing we share significantly overlapping concerns and issues regarding the Middle East, it is our hope you might be willing to work with us—well, not exactly *with* us—but, shall we say, on your own, but with like goals in mind. Call it something of a silent partnership."

"Gentlemen, I *am* intrigued. Do go on," Christian urged.

"It is our hope that you might agree to—and here's the operative word—*independently* devise a long-term strategy to point Christian voters in the right direction. Before we go any further, we need your God-fearing promise that whatever is said tonight stays among the four of us. I'll tell you now, if any of us are ever questioned as to whether this conversation even took place, the three of us will categorically deny it, as well as any relationship between us, lest we have the secularist mobs at our throats. Not to mention we'd find ourselves in the midst of a political firestorm. I hope this doesn't offend you."

"Congressmen, Senator, first let me say how honored I am that you place this kind of trust in me. As God is my witness, you have my word that whatever is said here tonight will remain among us. If there is another person alive on God's green Earth more aware of the delicacy and importance of what we're about to discuss, I've yet to meet him. As you know, up until recently, I have stayed on the fringes of party politics. Sure, I go to the inaugurations and have my share of friends who are politicians, but for the most part, I accomplish my goals from the pulpit and through my TV show. However, I no longer think that's enough.

It has become eminently clear to me that as true Christians, we can no longer afford to stand on the political sidelines if there is to be any hope of saving today's diseased world. Holding our tongues in the public square is what has brought us to this level of disgrace—this time of shame in which we live—this world littered with depravity and immorality beyond imagination.

"I had already decided on my own that as a Christian, I will be silent no more. Gentlemen, I accepted your invitation tonight in hopes of offering myself to you in any capacity possible because I have come to realize that in your own way, you too, are doing God's work. I don't know how much you already know, but the Christian-based strategy you're alludin' to is well in place. It has taken decades for the godly to get to where we are today, but I am happy to announce that in an institutional sense, we are so far ahead of the enemy we can't even see them in our rearview mirror. The Christian political machine that has long been in the makin'—in fact, ever since the Goldwater fiasco—is armed and ready for battle. We're organized, we have reach, we know how to communicate, an' we have the funds to back it all up."

The three men exchanged deeply satisfied glances, their enthusiasm evident.

"Today's secular world hasn't a clue as to how deep our pockets really are. If they did, they'd be shittin' bricks—pardon my French—or at the very least, trottin' out their liberal shills screamin' First Amendment. But because we are finally in place to genuinely influence elections by demandin' our leaders take on a Christian worldview, they're beginnin' to realize they've much to fear, if only because of the strength of our numbers.

"Senator, Congressmen, I am here today to assure you that there is indeed a vast right-wing conspiracy, praise Jesus."

The men were mesmerized as much by Christian's political knowledge as by his zeal. Each was contemplating the enormity of what was always topmost in their minds—guaranteeing their reelection through Christian's ability to direct votes. What he had just said was nothing short of revolutionary, and the excitement and concomitant power of hitching their careers to his wagon was exhilarating.

Block interrupted. "Correct me if I'm wrong Pastor, but am I correct in inferring that you—and your voting bloc—plan to throw in with those of us who share your Christian worldview?"

Christian sat back a moment, using the opportunity to make eye contact with each one. "As you might expect, there is, of course, another half of the equation. If I got somethin' you want, you can prob'ly guess, there's somethin' I want in return. As I explained, there is no other group so well organized or funded as what has been so ignominiously termed the Religious Right—a title that I, for one, wear with great pride.

"*Yes,* we are religious, and *yes* we are *right!* All of which means we stand ready to back the *right* sorts of politicians, that is as long as those politicians are willin', and I mean *really* willin', to go to the mat against the liberal, Godless Left. Senator, Congressmen, since I think you comprehend the number of voters I represent, I trust you'd be willin' to throw your support behind *the* issues that are important to me as a Christian.

"Here's the red meat, if you'll pardon my pun," he said at the exact moment the busboy removed his plate. "As Christians, we've had our fill of standard election-year lip-service. An' while the Rapture clock tick, tick, ticks away—an' trust me when I say it currently reads five till midnight—you and your party better get serious as a heart attack about, once and for all, *eviscaratin'* Roe v. Wade. I also expect to see the door slam shut on every pervert and sodomite who preys on our youth. If homos *choose* not to change their evil ways, then I say let 'em rot in Hell. But till God takes care of that, it's up to us to make sure their sick hands and minds stay offa our children."

Christian noticed a subtle yet apparent discomfort in Mapes' demeanor, and he stored the thought away for later.

"The same goes for the commie teachers and school systems who stand with 'em, all the while, teachin' our young-uns to strap on a condom and do whatever with whoever they want, in direct defiance of God's will. Hard to believe, isn't it, that we live in a society that *promotes* perversion—actually teaches our youth to have their way with each other—be it boy on boy, pedophile on girl an' sometimes even on boy. It sickens me, it's un-Godly and it must stop."

Block and Dyson bobbed their heads up and down in horrified agreement while Senator Mapes busied himself with a spilled drink. As Christian paused to maximize the effect of his words, Mapes gestured to the waiter, who hurried over to their table with what Christian could only perceive as a distinctly effeminate gait. After wiping up around Mapes, Dyson ordered more drinks and Mapes winked at the waiter again, "Thank you, DJ," and the young man headed for the bar. Christian watched intently as the waiter hurried away, one eyebrow raised, and said, "Now that's exactly what I'm talkin' about, my friends, exactly what I'm talkin' about." After taking a moment to refocus, Christian picked up again.

"There's more, much more, gentlemen. I wanna see prayer back in the classroom and God's words on the walls of every courthouse in the land. It's high time we put government on notice that we intend to put an end to the worship of Tolerance as the state religion it's become. For it is Tolerance, no question, that has gotten us where we are. Gentlemen, if you read your Bibles, as I know you do, then you also *know* that man was made in God's image. God was—and is—*not* tolerant, and he certainly didn't intend for Tolerance to become the law of the land. I say bring back stonin' and you'll see Tolerance meet its end. I for one—and the Christians I represent—am sick to death of fightin' the same battles against the amoral Left and their Jew lawyers over and over again. The time has come to put an end to it all. With your help, we can finally take life and death decisions out of the activist courts," he nearly spat out the words, "and put 'em back where they belong—into the hands of the states. When that happens, you'll finally see things turn our way. Trust me. The good and godly people of this land will stand behind you on this." He paused. "You with me so far?"

They nodded enthusiastically. Each one, God-fearing in his own right, was somewhat in awe of this mighty force who spoke his mind with the courage they lacked. Senator Mapes used the moment to assert his agreement. "I want you to know Pastor, that before you arrived tonight, the three of us had a conversation nearly identical to what you just said, though I admit none of us said it nearly as well or as clearly as you have. Whatever we can do to put God back in the public square, well then that's precisely what we'll do. If that means risking an election, we're each of us ready to take one for the team."

Christian nodded his approval. But he had hardly begun. In fact, he hadn't tackled what had come to be the guiding light of his life. "Thank you Senator. But even as moral depravity reaches an all-time high, we face an even more dire threat, one that reverberates with consequences that reach all the way to the heavens." The timbre of his voice shifted from the anger of effrontery to one of foreboding.

"Gentlemen, looming before us is nothing less than the mother of all battles— the final war. Stay with me because what I have to say now won't be easy to hear. Y'see, for me, it's not enough to try an' change the world through preachin' alone. Not at all. I may save a few souls here an' there—hell, I may even save millions. But millions are nothin' compared to what we're up against.

"Like it or not, it's a global world we're livin' in, an' in that world, there are over one billion—you heard me right—one *billion* Muslims, each one of 'em bound and determined to wipe us off the face of the Earth. We're talkin' the dark side here an' I ain't makin' this up. Mark my words, there never was an' never will be any reasoning' with a Muslim because they have *nothin' whatsoever* in common with us. You see, the Muslim is a different kinda animal. He's nothing like you an' me, not a bit—has nothin' in common with us. All he wants, point of fact, is to dominate—an' if that doesn't work, *annihilate* us because it's what their Koran says. Allah teaches 'em that life on Earth has no value, but to die a martyr's death will send them to *their* pearly gates to claim their seventy-two virgins. Hell, that almost sounds good to me," he chuckled. "The difference is that I'm a Christian—meanin' I *do* know right from wrong. That, an' I'm not *insane* like them. But if we don't stand up an' call out their insanity for the danger it is, if we don't do somethin' an' fast, mark my words, they *will* destroy us."

A collective shiver went through Christian's dinner partners. These were men who thought they had a reasonable handle on the various brands of danger out there in the world, at least in a political sense. In their own ways, each was equally devoted to Christ but their devotion hadn't prepared them to consider the kinds of thoughts Christian was about to float before them tonight.

"I don't know 'bout you, but I see the Book of Revelation playin' out with increasing speed each an' every day. Instead of mamby-pambyin' around, tryin' to stave it off for my children's sake or for their children's sake—and this might surprise you—I plan to do all I can to *hasten* the Final War between the heathens an' us." He paused, fidgeting with the cutlery on the table. When he looked up, he saw the three men exchange indecipherable glances. He hoped he hadn't gone too far, but this was no time for elected officials who had no balls. He stood up and slammed his fist down hard on the table.

"Listen up and listen good because I'm gonna tell you the hard truth, no pussy-footin' around."

His eyes narrowed as he sat back down on the edge of his seat. "You must know that the Muslims' foremost goal is to drive the Jews into the sea. Should they accomplish what Hitler didn't, do you think Christians'll be far behind? If you think the Commies were a force to reckon with, when it comes to wack-jobs, you ain't seen nothin' yet.

"I hate to use Hitler's words but this go-round, we're the ones who need a 'final solution'—not for the Yids but for the Muslims. If the opportunity comes our way, I say nuke 'em into oblivion. We'll only get one chance. Wait too long—they'll get us first.

Dyson, a Vietnam vet as well as a dyed-in-the-wool racist from Arizona, felt his blood begin to stir. The lust for battle had never left him entirely, particularly when it came to settling the non-white, non-Christian score. The congressman's evident excitement spurred Christian to continue.

"Gentlemen, *we* are the true Christians, the followers of the one an' only true God, praise Jesus, and as such it is our God-given duty to go into battle for our Lord." By now, his delivery sounded more like he was preaching a sermon than having an after dinner discussion with three highly ranked leaders of the government.

"Our goal, yours and mine, while perhaps not entirely identical, has more in common than you might think. Yours is to get re-elected so's to keep on runnin' the country. Mark my words, if the Muslims get to us first, there won't be any election an' none a this'll make a difference. In a different yet similar kinda way, I also wanna get elected, only my electorate consists of a constituency of one." He pointed upward to the heavens. "I'm here to say that the Rapture is barrelin' down on us at full throttle. Does that excite me? You bet it does. Am I gonna do what I can to help bring it on? Sweet Jesus, I most certainly will. It is why I study my Bible and why I seek the wisdom of today's scholars and prophets, the ones who understand what the Bible is telling us about the End. The thing is, we're not quite ready for prime time. There's still work to be done in Zion before Biblical prophecy can be set in motion an' I'm wise enough to know that that takes political clout. Which is why I'm here tonight. Y'see, I need *your* help in order to hasten God's plan, jest like you need mine in order to stay in power.

"What I need from you is your word that you'll make sure Congress stands up for the State of Israel, no matter what She does. Far's I'm concerned, Israel is the *only* foreign policy there is. If you sign on, then I can promise you the eternal voting bloc of your dreams. If we come together thusly for 'such a time as this,' God will take care a the rest. The march toward Armageddon is well under way. Your coming to me is, in itself, a prophetic sign. As for the Jews, we'd be fools to leave it to them. They gave up their prerogative long ago when they rejected His Word, and turned their back on Him. That, honorable gentlemen, is why it is up to us, and *only* us, to execute the final steps that will ensure His return. An' this can only happen when the Hebrews control the geographical boundaries prescribed in the Bible.

"I'll move heaven an' Earth to do what it takes to people the disputed territories with Jews. I'll bring 'em from Russia, from Ethiopia, who the hell cares where they come from? Those Hebes'll be so grateful for a one-way ticket outta their current hellholes, they'll think the Palestinian settlements are the Garden of Eden. But if our nation turns away from God's Will, if we push Israel to give up even one centimeter of Her rightful land, be assured, He will retaliate.

"One last thing—an' this time it's me who's gotta ask that this stays among the four of us. Personally, I don't give a rat's ass about the Jews. The only thing I care about is what I refer to as 'God's Pact.' I'm talkin' about Jeremiah, chapter 30, verse 3. 'The days are coming, declares the Lord. When I will bring my people Israel and Judah back from captivity and restore them to the land I gave their forefathers to possess.'

"There can be *no land for peace*, because such a peace would be *false peace*—the peace of *Satan*. Are we on the same page?"

The three leaders had not only just been promised the largest voting bloc since unionization, but a bloc that was certain to remain permanent, at least during their lifetimes. And although none of them had a problem with Christian's End Times scenario, each one privately hoped it might wait until his time was past.

With a nod to the others, Dyson, designating himself "Speaker of the Steakhouse," said "Pastor, it's clear you did your homework. Clearly, you were well aware of our stance on Israel before we met tonight. This leads me to believe that you are also aware of how passionately we want to re-inject Christianity into the moral fiber of this nation." With a small chuckle he added, "I'd say, we're of one mind here. Yes, we most certainly are."

Christian beamed. "So we are. You need my help. I need yours. You scratch my back, I'll be right there, scratchin' yours. You give me your pledge that you'll do your job from within, and I guarantee you'll have the votes to keep on doin' so. Together, we will take back the halls of Congress and pack the Judiciary with believers because, one day very, very soon we're gonna take back this shinin' city on the hill, our great nation, and ultimately the world, for Jesus. In the meantime, let's put our heads together and do what we gotta do to ready the land of Zion for Judgment Day."

By now, Mapes was trembling with excitement and he called the waiter over. "DJ, bring us your best champagne and make sure to keep it flowing." To the others, he grinned, "We got ourselves a deal so how about we celebrate?"

Flutes were filled and Dyson led the toast. "Christian, at this momentous occasion, we lift our glasses to you and all you have accomplished. We give you our oath that we will do everything in our power to achieve our common goal. Your leadership and courage are awe-inspiring and we are honored to be but pawns in this game of Eternity. There is nothing more important, nothing more historic. Fellow warriors for Christ, here's to a relationship which will outlast Eternity and exceed the boundaries of our planet, to a time and place when all who believe shall live in peace, together and under God's rule. Here here!"

Glasses clinked and toast followed toast as the attentive waiter kept watch to ensure the ever-brimming liquid never ran dry. Three hours later, four grotesquely inebriated men stumbled up the stairs from the cellar steakery, red meat of all kinds very much on everyone's mind. It had been a good night's "work."

PART 4

Revelations

28

As You Sow

June 2, 2001

IF CHRISTIAN HAD A SECRET vice, it was that he was hopelessly addicted to rock music from the 60s and 70s. Despite the fact that the nation's moral decline had been set in motion by the "tune in, turn on, tune out" generation, whose music was the call-to-arms that began the slide into free love, drugs and Communism, he was irredeemably attracted to it. Certain lyrics, in fact, came to his mind as often as Scripture did, and the music's visceral throb—it grabbed him by the gut and once there, took root. Whenever he felt the call, he'd slip downstairs to Second Coming's home theater and lose himself in the obscenity of word and rhythm. Considering his options one lonely night—Jesus or music—Christian opted for music.

He was unraveling, and at a frightening speed. In bed at night, in those fleeting moments before Xanax took him away, his personal ghost would make her nightly appearance. As if the nights were not bad enough, the dead Mexican woman's face had started to show itself during the daytime—in church, at the mall or, just this afternoon, in the face of a young Latina clerk in a Seven Eleven store. That twisted death mask, so real and seemingly in the flesh, sent him fleeing in terror, forcing him to forgo his daily fix of Hostess Snowballs.

Indeed, there was an unraveling going on.

Thoroughly unsettled, he went on down to the basement. This particular Saturday night, Christian cued up Cat Stevens on the sound system. That would be *the* Cat Stevens, aka Yusuf Islam. Heretic or not, Stevens understood the human heart, and with that understanding, the ability to touch Christian in a way that both bewildered and comforted him. Stevens's lyrics reached deep inside the places where loneliness and longing dwelled. Christian, a man who had spent his adult life guiding the human spirit of others, didn't have a clue how to deal with his own.

Earlier that night he and Darlene had had routine, even mechanical, sex, which had left him emotionally empty. The house itself resembled a tomb, but it all changed the moment he cranked up the volume on the stereo and settled into the plush armchair, a bottle of scotch nestled in his drink holder. Just to hear Cat Stevens share his emptiness—about being alone on a Saturday night, flush with cash from payday, and no one to talk to—gave Christian a feeling similar to what others must feel in the presence of a good friend.

"Tell it, Yusuf," he muttered between long deliberate draws from the bottle, "Every day's a payday for me an' fuck yeah, I'm in an awful way, Yusuf, you Muslim sonofabitch bastard. A far-fuckin' awful way."

If Stevens, traitorous vessel of evil that he was, so intuitively understood him, why then did no one else? Christian had never acknowledged to himself that he'd once had that chance, with Darlene, a chance he'd so carelessly thrown away.

❖v

Earlier that night, as they ate their dinner in front of the TV, they were grateful as always for the noise. Reminiscent of his life with Elena, television was the only sound that filled the silence between them. As usual, Christian was ravenous, inhaling his dinner as quickly as it was put before him. No matter. With biblical prophecy on the march, if there was ever a time to gorge, it was now. Why worry that his weight danced its way toward the top of the scale? Soon, very soon now, he would have a brand new and far slimmer chassis up there in the place whose credo would read "Let the Libido Reign!"

The teaser for tonight's lead news story concerned a sting and consequent factory shutdown due to a local meat processor's hiring of illegals. Feigning indifference, but fearing the topic would bring on another appearance of his ghost, he flipped the channel over to TRUE News, "The Only Truth on Television Today." A glance at the carefully selected beauty-caster sent his mind wandering down its familiar raunch-path, when all of a sudden, he snapped to.

"Senior officials in Moscow say plans are well under way for the construction of a tunnel that will ultimately link eastern Russia to Iran." At first, he puzzled at the story. On the surface, it seemed to contradict political expediency. And then it hit him—this small story heralded yet another sign of the beginning-of-the-end. Like the biblical prerequisite for a red heifer, the Book of Revelation states in no uncertain terms that Magog, a country from the Far North—in this case, Russia— will befriend the Muslim—obviously Iran here—unleashing Gog and his army to invade Israel.

If he remembered correctly, it was right there in Ezekiel, the thirty-eighth chapter: "And it will come to pass at the same time, when Gog comes against the land of Israel, that My fury will show in My face . . . And I will bring him to judgment with pestilence and bloodshed; I will rain down on him, on his troops, and on the many peoples who are with him, flooding rain, great hailstones, fire, and brimstone."

His pulse quickened. Since the end of the Cold War, the US had foolishly let down its guard with regard to Russia, the evil power that was quietly repositioning itself to regain its status as a world player. Christian's jowls quivered and his blood raced as the dust cleared from his brain.

1948 and the creation of the state of Israel had ushered in the second act of the biblical drama that was to culminate in the Rapture. Today, the continuous and overwhelming signs that Act Three had begun were impossible to ignore. The creation of the Euro foreshadowed a biblically prescribed international currency while the Zion-hating United Nations showed itself as the obvious precursor to the one-world government alluded to in Revelations 13:2-7, and now this—this crucial yet hardly trumpeted sign? Why, believers everywhere ought be joining hands in joyous anticipation of Christ's glorious return. The End was coming all right, and when it did, Christian would sit back, put his feet up and watch the show begin. A delicious shiver traveled down his spine as he popped the last chocolate éclair into his mouth.

❖

Having had his fill of melancholy, Christian switched the sound system over to video. While *Lesbian Lovers: Two Hot to Handle* booted up, he reached for the phone and dialed his most recent flirtation, Tandy Ghiz. Tandy, a saucy twenty-seven year old divorcée, had recently moved to San Antonio from Tuscaloosa. When she joined Male Headship as a tithing member she immediately made it clear to Christian that *his* male headship was precisely what she wanted. Though she "sought his counsel" on a regular basis, the sexual promise between them had yet to be fulfilled.

"Tandy, Pastor Hillcox here. Apologize for calling so late but it only jest came to me we don't have enough womenfolk to help out in the nursery durin' services tomorrow. I'm wondrin' if you might could give us a hand?"

Tandy purred, "Why Pastor, I'd like nothin' better 'n to give you a hand. *Any* kinda hand you want. You must know by now, I'll do whatever you ask."

From there, the conversation veered sharply downhill, and a few minutes later, thanks to the combination of dirty talk and the X-rated super-sized images flashing on the screen before him, they brought each other to climax, after which they made plans to physically consummate in the very near future.

Putting down the phone, a still dissatisfied Christian stared blankly at the two women on the screen while his mind wandered into the introspective territories he usually avoided. These anonymous women served a purpose—a sinful one at that—but he wouldn't even recognize them if he passed them on the streets of San Antonio. His mansion might be called Second Coming, and he *had* had two orgasms in the past hour or so, but, still and all, he had no one to talk to. It struck him suddenly and surprisingly—phone sex or real sex be damned, Yusuf had it right—what he really did need was someone to talk to. He looked back at the TV screen, where a third woman had entered the scene—small, dark, Latina—a timid, almost panicked look in her eyes. And the dead Mexican woman's face took over once again and would not go away.

❖

Unsettled, Christian shut down the theater and grabbed the keys to the convertible. Roaring down the interstate, the coupe was soon speeding along at 95 miles an hour. An hour later, when the first drops of a looming cloudburst splattered down on him, he took the next exit, pulled over, and secured the top. Back inside the car, he sat for several minutes in the dark when a bolt of lightning illuminated a still-open bar just ahead. He could have turned back but, desperate for company, he headed for the parking lot. He figured the risk of being recognized was minimal. The lighting would be dim and he was not at all dressed as he would be on television. Besides, he liked the bar's name—The Abyss. It was the perfect reflection of his current state of mind. Late as it was, the bar was very nearly empty. A few groups were scattered among tables and at the bar. It was impossible to ignore that the clientele was all male, but as lonely as he was, he pushed the thought aside and pulled up a barstool next to a lone, youngish looking man, "Okay if I sit here?"

The stranger gave him the once-over and mumbled, "By this time of night Sheriff, I'd say any stool in this joint's got your name on it." He held out his hand. "Name's Joss. What'll ya have? My treat."

Christian hesitated. "My friends call me, uh—Chris. An' I'll take a scotch if yer offrin', thank you very much. Straight up. Oh, an' make it a double."

For a man to whom small talk normally came easily, Christian's initial awkwardness seemed at first to be insurmountable. Looking around, he assured himself that no one in the bar recognized him and, before long the scotch worked its magic and he began to relax. As the conversation transitioned from the general to the personal, they relocated to a booth in the corner.

Joss told Christian that he was a long-distance trucker and that he really enjoyed his time on the road. His tone darkened when he revealed that his wife of ten years had recently kicked him out after discovering he'd been having an affair—he gestured vaguely—up north. Pain seemed to ooze from the sad man when he said she had gotten a court order to prevent him from spending unsupervised time with their three- and five-year-old boys. Christian, so steeped in his own self-pity, didn't give a thought as to what would compel a woman to deny her children their own father. Thanks to the drink in him, the warmth of companionship blasted past his usual defenses. Ever the pastor, he offered a willing ear, as much out of habit as from the shared solidarity of their mutual loneliness. Joss didn't ask what Christian did for a living, and Christian certainly didn't offer. All the trucker seemed to care about was that his portly drinking companion, this man who seemed to have a way with words, offered kindness and understanding.

When the bartender announced last call and Joss suggested they go back to his place for another drink, Christian readily agreed. Anything was better than the emptiness awaiting him at home. Besides, he had enough presence of mind to know that he was too drunk to drive safely. The two men clambered up into Joss's truck cab and drove a short way to the Windy Acres

Garden Apartments, a 1980s down-at-the-heels apartment complex next to the highway.

Stumbling inside, Joss fumbled for the light while Christian found his way to the nearest chair. Out came a bottle of Southern Comfort. It was two o'clock in the morning, an hour Christian hadn't seen in many a moon, thanks to the little blue pill. They talked and drank for a while longer. Whether it was the late hour or enjoyment of the company—or the fact that Christian was, by now, doing most of the talking—he slowed his consumption in a conscious desire to feel the emotional release of what seemed to be the beginnings of friendship.

When he put a hand over his glass to stop another pour, Joss asked, "Hey, you ever do any drugs?"

Christian shrugged, a non-answer. He sure as fuck did *legal* drugs. Besides, in his current state, he wouldn't object to much of anything.

"I got somethin' you're gonna love the fuck outta. Come with me. In here."

Christian heaved himself up from the chair.

In the next room, Joss pulled a small ampoule from the drawer of the bedside table. "Try this, Chris," chuckling to himself at his unintended rhyme.

"What is it?" Christian asked.

"Can't remember the name. Alls I know is it makes ya feel like you could fuck the entire world all at once. You wanna try?"

Christian shrugged indifferently, which Joss took for a go-ahead. He snapped open the capsule and held it beneath Christian's nose. Instantly Christian felt a rush like nothing he'd ever experienced, followed by a glorious sensation of being wildly alive.

Joss flipped on the stereo, the music filling Christian's head with the craggy, soulful voice of Jim Morrison. Familiar as it was, Morrison's crooning struck Christian as if he were hearing it for the first time. Rhythm pulsed through him, becoming part of him—or maybe he became part of *it*. Music is your only friend, dance on fire, until the end, until the end. Morrison owned him, animated him, brought him to life.

That was when Joss surprised him with a deeply searching kiss, and Christian offered no resistance. It was a kiss so searingly exciting that he felt *himself* to be on fire.

Hello, I love you.

Won't you tell me your name?

His heart throbbed wildly as he experienced, for the first time, the ecstasy of losing control.

Save us! Jesus!

Utterly liberated, he didn't notice his clothes drop from his body, didn't stop when Joss led him to the bed, didn't resist being guided onto his stomach.

Hey, Morrison. S'me. I'm your backdoor man, c'mon— yeah, c'mon—yeah, c'mon, I'm your backdoor man.

By this time Christian was out of his mind from the booze and whatever the fuck drug Joss had wafted under his nose— out of his mind but deliriously happy. Some might even call him "gay." One, in particular, would call him Chris*tine*.

The voice from the stereo growled, seduced, Cancel my subscription to the Resurrection.

What the fuck. Christian lay face down, and let the wild bronco ride, and then ride some more.

29

Let There Be Light

June 3, 2001

AS DAWN'S EARLY LIGHT made its way through water-stained curtains, Christian cracked open a sleep-encrusted eye. His head on fire, he turned cautiously, jerking upright when he saw a naked young man asleep in the bed beside him, the sheets wildly askew. Christian rocketed upward and rammed his fists against both sides of his head as if to crush his skull. What the fuck? What the freaking fuck? Fuck, fuck, fuck, fuck mother-fuck. He looked down at his nude flesh, felt a stickiness between his legs, a painful soreness in his rectum and a glimmer of the night's activities came back to him. He had lain with a man. Had been sodomized.

To his revulsion, a sensation of something vaguely erotic ran through the reptilian part of his brain and he recoiled at the involuntary hardening below. Jumping out of bed, he stumbled in search of a bathroom in the unfamiliar and seedy apartment, and when he found it, he hung his head over the toilet, remaining there until the entire contents of his stomach pooled brown inside the bowl. Rising to look in a cracked mirror, he expected to see, not himself, not even a man, but the Devil. Alas, the face that looked back was nothing more and nothing less than his own, lumpy and disheveled though it was. He pinched himself hard in the hope that this was merely another, albeit a wretchedly different, kind of nightmare. To his growing horror, he had to face the fact that this was not a dream from which he would blessedly awaken.

If there is a man who lies with a male as those who lie with a woman, both of them have committed a detestable act; they shall surely be put to death. Leviticus 20:13 screamed inside his head, echoing the innumerable times he had used this very verse to rail against the faggots and their satanic depravity.

At the moment he couldn't think of anything that would suit him better than death. Slumped against a grimy toilet bowl on a strange bathroom floor, he tried frantically to piece together the circumstances that could have led him to this Hell. The last things he remembered clearly were the sense of detachment he'd felt when he and Tandy Ghiz ended their call, and that he'd gone out for a not-so-joyful joyride, in search of company. Beyond that his memory was muddy. A flash of kindness here, a stab of excitement there, a fleeting sense of flying—these were the sensations that struck him. Then, other words juxtaposed themselves against those of Leviticus—I'm your backdoor man—where the fuck was that coming from? He glanced down at his finely manicured hands, seeing them as though they belonged to someone else. But they were his, wedding band and all. His watch read five-fifty and he searched his mind for what day it was.

Holy crap! Today's Sunday. Fuck me! I gotta get the flyin' fuck outta here before that sodomizing freak in the bedroom wakes up and sees me in the light of day.

Silently he searched for his clothes, the various droppings of which formed a trail, like Hansel and Gretel's bread crumbs, from living room to bedroom, and he very nearly chuckled at the notion of himself inside a house made of figgy-faggy candy. Following a "fairy-tail" witch into the oven didn't seem far-fetched at the moment.

Peering out the living room window, his heart sank. He didn't see his car anywhere. How in fuck's name could he flee if he didn't have a way out? And anyway, where the fuck was he? He crept back into the sex-sick bedroom to search for clues, anything. When his eyes fell again upon the passed-out, naked fruit, he froze, rooted in shame and disgust. From out of nowhere, the sodomizer's name came to him. It was Joss—that was it.

Joss, the ass-fuck, lay so still it looked as though he might be dead, and Christian realized that as bad as things were, they could always get worse. Screwing up his courage, he gave the comatose body a shake. Nada. Zip. Niente. Searching for signs of life, to his great relief, he detected a gentle rise and fall of the man's bare chest. At least the nightmare wouldn't further descend into tabloid headlines—"Renowned Mega-Pastor Murders Man in Homo-Erotic Frenzy."

On the floor next to the bed, he found a matchbook. Snatching it up, he read on the cover,

The Abyss
1634 Blandon Road

Graphic flames licked at the name and address on the matchbook. He flipped it open. Inside the match cover, it announced again "The Abyss," this time with the added slogan, "Where the Boys Come Out to Play." Fuck this! We ain't talking Abyss, we're talking gen-u-ine HELL. He opened the apartment door and spotted a slovenly woman, one who undoubtedly had secrets of her own, moving soundlessly into an apartment down the way.

"Psst. You down there. Pssssssst." Halfway inside, she stuck her head out to hush him.

"Quiet, wouldja? F'he larns I been out, he'll kill me."

Needing to keep the silence more desperately than she, he tiptoed her way. Whispering, he pointed to the matchbook asking if she could direct him to The Abyss. Looking at him like he was a half-wit, she sniggered, motioning to a darkened sign rising high above the road, less than six hundred yards away. It read: The Abyss.

Lady Luck was apparently on his side this morning, even if she'd come in the body of a filthy harlot sneaking into her own apartment. Christian was too ashamed to credit the Lord for help out of this mess, but if Lady Luck chose to offer a hand it would do him just fine.

❖

Two hours later Christian was back at Headship, safely locked inside his office. Hands trembling, he ran a razor across his face, donned the suit he kept on hand for emergencies, draped a fringed talit, given him by the Israeli ambassador, around his neck, and placed a beautifully hand-embroidered yarmulke upon his head. Shelving last night's transgression for another day, he went out to welcome the worshipers, looking more Rabbi than Pastor. Their faces glowed with the joy of community as he greeted his flock like it was any other Sunday. After the requisite time, he withdrew to a room off to the side from where he would make his grand entrance into the chapel.

There stood Darlene.

"My, my but aren't we the Nervous Nelly this fine morning," she sneered. "Calm yourself, *Pastor*. If you think for a moment I give a goddamn where you were all night, much less *who* you were with, then you're even more delusional than I imagine. Far as I'm concerned, you can slap that flesh a yours 'round with anyone you want so long's our son never finds out about it. Truth is, I pity any woman who'd have you."

If only it had been a woman, he thought.

"Preacher Man," she spat, "you mightn't a noticed, but I cringe every time you touch me, Which means there's little else in this world that'd give me more pleasure than to have you relieve yourself somewhere else—*anywhere* as far as I'm concerned." Christian smarted at the sting of the insult. "How 'bout this? You agree to renounce all conjugal rights from here on in an' I won't let on to your congregation what a sinnin' hypocrite their great pastor is. Oh, an' do me one more favor—whoever the poor fool is, give her my condolences *and* my thanks."

Preacher Man, the name he used to thrill to, now cut through him like a knife.

Darlene continued. "Thing is, I only come here to put on a show. That's it. At least I admit that's what we do here. We put on a show. Far as I'm concerned, the only thing left between you 'n me are the godforsaken roles we play every Sunday so how 'bout we drop the charade b'tween us?"

With that, she turned to go. "I-i-i-i-it's showtime," she announced, carnival-barker style. "See you in church, lover boy."

He shivered to think how much more accurate it would have been had she said "boy lover."

❖

Parading down the center aisle to the usual pomp and circumstance, Christian headed toward the stage where Darlene, his covenantal bride, awaited him. As he walked, his Joss-bruised lips gummed for moisture in a mouth dry as cotton, all the while his thoughts skittered downward into a dizzying vortex. This time, he *had* crossed the proverbial Rubicon. What had happened last night was as irrevocable as it was unforgivable, if not to God, then to himself. Wending his way down the endless aisle, the soreness in his hindquarters amplified his shame, while at the same time the congregation beamed its trust and love his way—their beloved pastor, the great giver of wisdom. The mask that was his face displayed more grimace than smile as his brain frantically processed the situation.

This was not my first nor my worst sin. I was reborn on the day I found Jesus. On that day, I repented and in that moment I was forgiven. But last night, last night, I chose buggery—chose, or at least failed to resist—buggery, unnatural, repugnant, entirely avoidable, just say no, buggery.

But what if I'm tempted to do it again? Tempted. Satan—the tempter. What if Satan tempts me again? Because last night I gave it up, not for Jesus, but for Satan.

But one lost battle does not make a defeat. This is not the final outcome—there is a war yet to fight, and I cannot be blamed for Satan's temporary victory.

And I have been forgiven, most certainly I have been forgiven, for JESUS DIED FOR MY SINS—for my sins.

With his world turned upside down, Christian jettisoned today's prepared sermon, ironically entitled "Marriage: God's Sacred Oath." It was to have been a dry run for next Wednesday when he was scheduled to preach in front of one of the largest television audiences in history. But the hypocrisy of a sermon that fiercely decried homosexuality as a *conscious choice* made him question if he could *ever* speak the words that now smoldered in his pocket.

In a voice as vacant as his soul, he began the service with the usual words, flat though they were, when, from out of nowhere, a different sermon materialized. Perhaps it was his shame speaking, or maybe it was God, but the uncharacteristically humble words that tumbled from his mouth turned into the most affecting sermon of his career.

"Lord, you are the source of all that is good. We stand before you in deep humility and ask your forgiveness. Each of us, we were all born sinners. You, my dear friends, know this, if only because I say it so often. What I don't usually say is that no matter how hard we try, no matter how strong our walk with Jesus, we each remain susceptible to temptation every step of the way. It is how the Devil works.

"Here's today's question. When, from time to time, a man slips, as we all do, does that mean that he forever falls from God's grace?" He paused, a long and pregnant pause. "If you answer *yes*, doesn't it follow that we may as well throw in the towel and live our lives in search of pleasure? Or, should we instead see each mistake as an opportunity to grow ever nearer to our Lord Jesus?

"If you take only one thing away from this morning's sermon, let it be this. Satan resides among us—everywhere and every day. If you lose one battle to him, you *mustn't* give up on the war. With each fall, you have to fight all the harder to find your way back to His forgiveness. For we are nothin', an' I mean NOTHIN', if not Soldiers—no, make that WARRIORS, FOR CHRIST in this, the WAR TO END ALL WARS.

"Y'see, it's easy to fall into the trap a thinkin' that since none of us can possibly measure up *all* the time, we may as well not try. Maybe you got a neighbor, someone you think is more righteous than you because he's got a cleaner house or a better-kept yard, or maybe his children look ta be better behaved 'n yers, an' comparin' yourself to him, you come up wantin'.

"What you don't know it that more often than not, them what have the most to hide *looks* the best—on the *outside*. They *look* more virtuous, more morally upright than you yourself feel, but the truth is, what's really goin' on is that they're hidin' behind a shield of false sanctity. It'd take a mere nick of the surface to uncover the most surprisin', if not shockin', transgressions perpetrated by those you see as holy."

Darlene reddened visibly, alarmed that Christian might be referring to her. Suddenly afraid that he had somehow learned about her and Mason—that his absence last night was not about another woman but about JJ—she sensed that these words were the beginning of the final dance between them. In the pews as well, the scene was a study in the groupthink of private guilt, guilt for transgressions large and small as each and every person gathered together at Headship considered his or her own failings.

"Contrary to what the godless masses out there want you to believe, it is *not our acts* that define us. We are judged, not by *what* we do but by the *strength* of our faith. More bluntly put—we are *never* judged by our failings, but *only* by whether or not we've taken Jesus into our lives."

Not a word of what he said was new, but the fervor with which he said it set the congregation's mind collectively afire. He continued, "We have all, every one of us, prayed over the words of Paul many times: *For by grace are ye saved through faith; and that not of yourselves; it is the gift of God; Not of works, lest any man should boast.* You ask, does this hand me the license to sin so long as, afterwards, I give myself to Jesus? Hmmmmmmm—I wonder. If it's not our actions that count, but only our faith, doesn't that make it all the more important we at least be as forgivin' as Jesus? That we forgive ourselves the way He has? How 'bout that question we're always askin'?" Christian held his hands out, waving them ever so slightly, in a gesture familiar to the worshipers.

The crowd roared as one, "*What would Jesus do?*"

"Like David said: Have mercy on me, O God, because of your unfailing love. Because of your great compassion, blot out the stain of my sins. Wash me clean from my guilt. Purify me from my sin. For I recognize my shameful deeds—they haunt me day and night."

He paused for a time, slowly searching the faces below, making each and every person there feel as if he were looking into his or her soul. There was something different in the air this morning—an electrifying current seemed to permeate the sanctuary. Pastor Hillcox had never seemed as authentic as he did today. No one could have imagined the genesis of this authenticity. Nonetheless, the congregation was more deeply moved by Christian's humility and sincerity than they had ever been by his usual histrionics.

Quietly he repeated the line of King David: "I recognize my shameful deeds, they haunt me day and night." Then he intoned, "*And Jesus said, Father, forgive them, for they do not know what they are doing.* Friends, when you see your neighbor falter, judge him not. Instead, be kind, tenderhearted even. For no man can know when his day of reckoning will be upon him. All he can do is to make sure he's ready. No matter what transpired yesterday, no matter how foul the deed, the sun rose in the sky this morning, bringing with it another day in which to praise Jesus."

Just as suddenly as the words had come to him, he ended the morning's worship quietly and without fanfare. "Let us rejoice, for if we know anything, it is that the end is near. Settle up with your enemies, get your houses in order, and know that, without Jesus, the worst is yet to come. As for me, I say, bring it on. I'm ready, I'm willin', an' I'm achin', truly achin', to meet my maker. I am ready to walk in His Kingdom an' I pray that those of you who still procrastinate will make the only decision there is and find your way to Jesus today."

Without the usual fire and brimstone and its consequent frenzy, the crowd filed out quietly, thoughtfully. Christian was not at the door to bid his usual good wishes. He had fled to his office where, once again, he locked himself safely inside.

❖

As cleansing as the sermon had been, Christian remained a broken man. His heart ached in the silence of his chambers, alone again with his thoughts, until the shrill ring of the telephone shattered the quiet. Ignoring its summons for as long as he could, he finally picked up to hear the sound of pure evil on the other end. And on today of all days.

"Christian, that you?" Luke asked, his customary bravado curiously absent. "This ain't no social call I'm makin'. You don't gotta worry." Luke's voice broke. "I'm wantin' to let you know your father passed last night. Of a sudden. Musta been his heart." Christian, stunned, remained silent.

"Didn't think you'd much care but figgered I oughta let you know. There ain't no arrangements to be made, far as I know, or anyone to call, less you know the whereabouts of yer sister. Thing is, Mason didn't have a pastor or nothin', so I'm wondrin', maybe you could find it in your heart to lead us in a farewell? Consider it payin' off a debt to the man who gave you life?"

Christian sat back in his chair and felt the tension of the last several hours melt away. *How 'bout that? Woke up this mornin' a pansy-boy an' now, barely past one, I learn the Devil himself is gone from my life forever.*

With Mason's death, so too died Pansy-Boy, so too died Chris*tine*. Slowly, deliberately, he answered. "Luke, ya know what? You might could be right the first time in your sorry-ass life. I think I *should* do this." As he spoke, a sudden relief replaced what, moments ago had been agony of the highest order. "It'll be the only time the fuckwad ever needed me. Tell me when and where an' I'll be there."

"Ten o'clock, Tuesday mornin' at Grace Be Thine." As Christian put the phone down, Luke could have sworn he heard him smiling.

❖

The news of Mason's death stunned Darlene as much as it had Christian. The moment he told her, they withdrew to their separate quarters, each to consider the new state of their transgressions.

What went on inside Second Coming that night was the stuff of psychiatrists' dreams. Christian's self-loathing melded with the realization that Mason would never again disparage his masculinity, and he couldn't quite believe his timing. In death, his father had given him what he never could in life—a sense of peace. It was a peace that was all the more remarkable given what had gone on only hours before. The Devil may have used Joss as his calling card, but the Good Lord had swept back in to rescue him. Temptation might be sweet, but redemption, ah, it was all that much sweeter.

As for Darlene, she'd thrown herself off the proverbial cliff the night she'd lain with Mason, and after that night, she'd fallen further and further into a dizzying hell of her own making. Now, with Mason's passing, she too received word that a lifeboat was headed her way. With his death, the world would never have to know JJ as anything but Christian's son, and so, in an odd but very real way his dying gave Darlene a second chance—a rebirth, if you will. She fell into bed and let the exquisite relief of it all wash over her. Since abandoning the Catholic Church those many years ago, she had never really pondered the existence of God. But now, how else could she explain falling to her knees where, wonder of wonders, she heard her lips praising Jesus—sincerely and with all her heart.

Then, for the first time in seven years, Darlene exited her room to walk down the long hallway and knock on Christian's door. She wanted—no, needed—to know if the divine feeling she was experiencing was real. He opened his door, and instead of disdain she saw only relief. In silence, they reached for each other and stood for a long time, not moving, just holding. Quietly and without passion, they went to the bed and lay down. Wary of shattering the fragile peace, neither one made a move. When finally, they made love, it was just that—love. What their joining lacked in intensity was more than made up for in tenderness. Having lived alongside Christian for nearly two decades, having seen the transformation from poor white trash into the powerful instrument of God he had shown himself to be today, she needed to believe as he did. In the moments of their lovemaking, she stunned herself by silently confessing her sins and asking His forgiveness. In those moments, what she felt was more honest than anything she'd known before. When she felt Christian's warmth flow into her, she opened wide her gates to let enter the Lord, and Darlene Steeger Hillcox was born again in the fluids of their love.

30

Paint It Black

June 5, 2001

MORNING, NOT MOURNING, comes to Pearsall. Ain't no sorrowin' goin' on 'round the likes of Mason. Today's lesson: Grief . . . or not. Should you chance to place your ear to the ground and listen carefully, you might make out the faint whisperings of Life. And what Life has to say might sound something like this:

Listen up, JJ, Life might say. Today's a red-letter day. You've come to witness the burial of a man who was different things to different people. To your father, he was more than his pappy, he was his lifelong tormentor. For your mama, he served as a mostly absent father-in-law turned lover-rapist. As for you, boy, the man you're soon to see lowered in the ground, well, he was more than your grand-pappy. Wonder of wonders, he was your real-as-rain pappy as well. The man who gave his seed for you. Don't believe it? Ask your mama. You see, your father/grandfather represented the worst there is in human nature. But he was not the Devil, as your pastor daddy would have you think. No, Mason Hillcox was not that grand—he was nothing other than your run-of-the-mill depraved human bein'. Like every one of us, he had the capacity to choose how to live his life. An' he chose poorly.

But good can come from bad. Look at yourself, for example. You, who were conceived in violence and hate, stand here today, a fine young boy with the opportunity to rise above the wretch who sired you. Flawed though your mother might be, she is a good woman. Her greatest fault is that she trusted the wrong men.

Except for you. JJ, your mother's love for you is as pure as it is real. Point of fact, it's a testament to her courage, because it shows her to be a woman who rose above a morally defensible hatred to see in you not Evil, but Love.

Then Life draws its remarks to a conclusion: John Jr., a Herculean task lies ahead of you. Yours will be the challenge to escape the clutches of a man who calls himself your father, a man who calls himself a Christian. He will offer you power and riches so vast and seductive they will be all but impossible to resist. But resist you must. Because the one thing this man can never give you is love, and that is to be your life's tragedy. If one day you can learn not to hate, but to pity him, you will free yourself from the darkness in the way he never could. The times ahead will try your soul. In the end, though, that is what Life is really about.

But JJ was young, and the whisperings were faint. Only time would tell if he would ultimately grow up to understand Life.

❖

Christian's return to Pearsall was more a royal homecoming than a funeral gathering. The town had turned out to have and to hold, to comfort and to embrace, to love and to cherish their Pastor Man, their Christian. Entering the church, a sweetness in the air enveloped Christian and Darlene, serving to reinforce their physical union of the night before. Though no one in Pearsall had cared for Mason, the fact remained that he had fathered their beloved pastor. To the congregants of Grace Be Thine, Christian would always be theirs.

Before he stepped up to the podium, Luke cornered him. "That your boy over there?" he asked, pointing to JJ. "Awful cute, ain't he? From the looks a him, I'd have to say he favors his grand-daddy more'n he does you, don't ya think?"

Christian put his hands together in a prayerful pose to keep from pummeling Luke, the only living creature that could remind him of his father. As much as he wanted to hurl Luke to the ground, it *was* a funeral, and his father's at that, so Christian turned away and made his way to the pulpit.

"We are gathered here today in the presence of the Lord." Then, as it had two mornings ago, a new sermon formed in his mind as it came to him that he had the power to rewrite history. Swiftly, skillfully, Christian changed the elegy he had come to give.

"My father, Mason Hillcox, has gone on to be with the Lord. The Lord, who speaks with thunderous spirit, has called him. Called him to that better place.

"Folks, I'm not gonna try 'n fool with you—you know my past better than any. Which means you know what a time I had growin' up with no mother an' Mason as my father. But let me tell you what happened only a coupla two weeks ago. I was sittin' out back in my garden, havin' myself a piece of pineapple upside-down cake and a long, tall glass of iced tea, when I heard a familiar—an' may I add, *unwelcome*—voice callin' out my name. Yessir, that's the God's honest truth. I never much liked bein' 'round my pappy. Anyways, I look up to see none other than Mason Hillcox, fit to bust, somethin' clearly on his mind. I'd never seen him like this. Fact is, I'd never seen him anything other than mean.

"He said somethin' strange was happenin' to him and that I was the only one he could turn to. So I'm thinking, this *is* different. He'd never come to me for anythin' 'less it was to tan my hide." An uncomfortable chuckle rose from the gathering below. "I don't think I can emphasize enough that, my whole life, he never came to me. So you can imagine my surprise. Here stood the man who had given me life but, to be completely honest, nothin' else.

"Now, for the first time ever, my pops is tellin' me he's gotten to thinkin' 'bout things bigger than him. There's no sayin' why, no explainin' it. An' then," Christian paused, "all of a sudden he's askin' how he can get right with the Lord." Christian stopped again. "I tell you, I was as near to faintin' as a man can be."

And in the telling, Christian's fantasy was becoming real to him.

"We talked for hours—till the sun left the sky and the moon rose overhead. He told me he knew he hadn't been a good man, that he hadn't never cared 'bout nothin' but hisself before. Here he was, all wound up, a glow on his face that near to outshined the moon. There was a transformation taking place in him, he said. Called it a miracle. I had ta pinch myself. Couldn't be sure if I dared trust what I was hearin'. I tell you, it was miracle enough jest to be sittin' together, him talkin' an' me listenin'. Y'see, this was our first ever connection, an' to think, it was born of the least likely of all things." He paused again, subtly building to the climax: "Mason Hillcox's hope for Salvation."

Christian looked down at Luke, who by now was seething, knowing full well that none of this had ever happened. But there Luke was, forced to sit by and listen to the man he most despised rob him of the only person he had ever loved.

"Before he left me that night, I said to him, 'Pops, I'll be prayin' for you, prayin' that you experience the true light of God and come to a savin' knowledge of His son, Jesus Christ.'

"We all know that the world today is full of sin and temptation. A world of Sodom and Gomorrah where truth lies flailin' in the streets while we sit back and watch our young succumb to the Devil through sex 'n drugs 'n violence 'n homosexuality." He didn't wince at the hypocrisy.

"Folks, it is two minutes till midnight, an' the Rapture Train is bearin' down on us at full speed. As the last generation to inhabit this world, we have been tasked with the overwhelmin' duty to bring salvation to as many souls as we can before the end comes, and believe you me—it's a-comin.'" He put his hand up to his ear as if to listen. "Don't you hear it?" he asked, using his best stage whisper. "Don't you hear its thunderous roar headed our way? I'll say it again—it's two till midnight. The last an' final chance to own up to the only spiritual authority there is, Jehovah God. An' oddly, over the past two weeks, I believe my pappy did jest that, even though neither of us knew then that it was to be only jest in time.

"In what little time the rest of us have on Earth, don't you think we owe it to our Lord and Savior to raise up the standards of physical purity, of moral integrity, an' of spiritual intensity? Lemme explain where I'm goin', on this, the day of my father's funeral." The congregation leaned forward as one, eager for more, completely enthralled by Christian the storyteller.

"Y'see, Mason Hillcox was far from perfect. Most would say he was not even a good man. But he was a man, and as such, a wretched sinner, as *are we all*, as is writ in Romans Chapter 3, Verse 23. *For all have sinned and fall short of the glory of God.* But then we turn to the ultimate escape hatch in Romans Chapter 5, Verse 8, *But God demonstrates his love for us, in this: while we were still sinners, Christ died for us.*

"All's I'm tryin' to say is that if Mason Hillcox could know God's love in the last days of his life, then *anyone* can. Because this man," pointing to the body lying in a gilded box far finer than any dwelling in which Mason had ever lived, "this man is us. He was born in sin, he lived in sin, but he died with God's forgiveness.

"The Lord gave a partin' gift to me and my father, bringing him to me a mere fortnight before his death so that *I* could show him the path towards redemption. PRAISE JESUS. An' together we wept as we witnessed the spirit of the Lord enter him."

The audience listened closely as Christian remembered the conversation that had never taken place. "The last time I saw my father, I saw the depth of his pain. Lookin' into his eyes, I wept for all that hadn't been. He wasn't much of a father to me, but still, he was *my* father and, at long last, he had come to *me* for spiritual guidance. My final words to him that day were words of forgiveness—that not only did I forgive him, but more important, so too did Jesus. He could not have heard my words before that day, but now he was ready to listen and, GLORY BE, it was with joy that he heard me.

"When I told him, blunt as I could say it, 'there is no way to approach the Holy God except through Jesus Christ,' he asked me, point blank, did I think there was any chance he could get to Heaven? He said, and I quote, 'I've led a cowardly, lust-filled life. I wasn't much of a husband to your mother and even less of a father to you and your sister. I'm a drunk, I've whored around with any woman who'd have me and I never prayed a day in my life. An' that's jest for starters. Tell me, why would your Lord want me after all that?'"

Christian paused and scanned the room, straining to meet the eyes of each and every person in attendance, finally resting on Luke. He continued, his voice full of vigor. "Good people of Pearsall, let my father be a shinin' example to all. Maybe he sensed his end was near, perhaps not. Who among us knows when our time will come? Very few. But God does, and in the knowin', he chose to send his lost son, Mason Hillcox, to me. Although we didn't see eye to eye in life, I praise Jesus for showin' my father the way before his death."

Touched by the fable he'd spun, tears of loss began to stream down his face. And after the yearning his own tale inspired in him, the tears were genuine. Gently, he wept for the beaten-down child he would always be, for the brutality and barbarism Mason had subjected him to all his life, and, perhaps most of all, for the mother who had been taken from him on account of this man. Hardest of all, though, was the realization that, in many ways, he and Mason might not be so very different.

These, his oldest and truest followers, jumped up, thronging the pulpit to reach this man they so dearly loved. Fondly grasping a shoulder here thumping a back there, he accepted their affection and dried his eyes. When everyone returned to their seats, he brought the funeral to its conclusion.

"Mason Ray Hillcox, you're goin' home to Jesus, Praise God. Your days on Earth have ended, for He has called you to Him, but know this: they have ended well. There is still much left for me to do here on this Earth, but when my time comes, Pops, I'll be joinin' you in Paradise where we will finally be Father and Son for Eternity, surrounded by His glory. In closin', I praise thee, Almighty Lord, for this man . . . my father . . . who though imperfect, sowed the seed that gave me life. I thank you for guidin' him to me, at the end of his life, so that I could be but an instrument in his Salvation from Damnation and instead, give my father, Eternity. Hallelujah and glory to the Lamb of God. Amen."

31

Glory Be

June 5, 2001

JJ BURIED HIS HEAD IN his mama's lap. It wasn't so much that death frightened him—being the pastor's boy, he knew pretty much all there was to know. Besides, his best friend Cree's gramps had passed a couple weeks ago. Since then all Cree talked about was how much he looked forward to the day he'd get to join him up in Heaven, where he'd also get to see his fifteen-year-old cousin Jimmy, who'd died suddenly last year on account a takin' too much drugs. To hear Cree, you'd think he couldn't wait to die himself, which JJ sort of understood being that most days, aside from Cree, he didn't have a friend to his name. The only things that made JJ happy were food and his mama, and from what he knew about Heaven, at least there he'd get to eat as much as he wanted and not have to endure his father's jeers about his weight—fat pig that he himself was. At age five, JJ, heading toward obesity, teetered on depression and was universally despised or ignored by his homeschooling peers.

No, it wasn't death that JJ feared. Growing up in church made the next world sound better than his life. It was just that, well, it was hard to sit there, smack-dab in front of his grandpap's dead body, all white and waxy looking with its sickening odor assaulting his nostrils, and ignore the sense of horror rising from within. It was so hard, in fact, that it took super-power strength to keep from bolting. Yet in spite of the revulsion he felt, a morbid fascination held him firmly in place until, surprisingly, curiosity got the better of him, urging him to take a peek. Unlike Cree, JJ had never met his grandfather. He'd heard about him, of course, and all of it bad. Having absorbed a piecemeal characterization of Mason as a lawless, godless ne'er-do-well, JJ, a diehard lover of old westerns, preferred to think of him as a dashing outlaw who lived life on his own terms. To hear his father up there saying that Mason found Jesus at the end seemed wrong. It was like his father was purposely trying to rob JJ of his real-life hero—to deny him his romance. Thanks to the fantasy that JJ and Cree had created, they'd derived a motto: *Live hard, die young.* After that, you get to go to Heaven an' eat all the pork rinds and Ding Dongs your heart desires.

When they were about to close the coffin, JJ glanced at the body one last time. Without knowing why or even how, he arose and stepped up to the casket to look at his grandfather face-to-face for the first and only time. To his great surprise, he leaned in and kissed Mason's brow. If it had been orchestrated, the gesture could not have been better staged or more poignant. The sight of this innocent child of God reaching out to kiss a man whom everyone had long ago condemned did more to make the worshippers rethink the idea of judgment than anything Christian said.

For JJ, however, this well-meaning gesture turned into one of horror. His grandfather's face was cold and rubbery and the combined smell of death and formaldehyde sent the chill of the Devil through him. He began to scream, whereupon Christian stepped down from on high to rescue him.

"Son," he said gently, but loudly enough for everyone to hear, "be not afraid," setting his hands on the boy. "There is nothing to fear in death, especially in a death as beautiful as your grandfather's. He is in a better place now, a place where one day, we'll all meet again." Ever the theatrical master, Christian kissed his son on the head. Shivering, JJ scurried back to his mother's side.

❖

The current of fear that passed through JJ was contagious and electric, splintering the air as he rushed toward Darlene. Her mind was reeling and she had heard little of what Christian said. It was curious that in the years since she'd sent her father-in-law packing, Mason never followed up on his threat to return, but the fear had never stopped haunting her. From the very beginning she had known it was Mason's baby she carried. Years earlier, long before Mason arrived on the scene, she had found test results in Christian's pants pocket from a clinic in Albuquerque declaring him to be infertile. She left the results in the pocket where she found them. Christian never shared the information with her. Through all the subsequent years of trying to conceive, years during which he so cruelly blamed her, she had never, in deference to his ego, confronted him with what she knew. It was by far the kindest thing she'd ever done, and oddly, in the end, it had worked to her advantage. When she'd told him of her pregnancy, she was surprised by his seemingly genuine enthusiasm, considering that he knew himself to be sterile. All she could figure was that he had convinced himself that God had worked a miracle and placed one fertile seed inside her womb, like he had done for Sarah in the Book of Genesis, thus making fool's work of doctors and their scientific methods. Come to think of it, it was about then that he'd started to become more vocal in his condemnation of science as a whole. Whatever it was that allowed him to believe that the child was his, she was as grateful for it then as she was now.

❖

The air in the church had grown frosty. When JJ stumbled back to his mother, she reached for his hand and found herself touching flesh so cold it hardly seemed human. Looking at him hard, she made a bargain with herself. No longer able to deny that one half of her son was derived from Evil, she made the conscious decision to accept the story of Mason's uncharacteristic conversion. To accept that he'd been saved was to believe that JJ needn't one day turn into a bad seed. And so, Darlene publicly threw in with the zeal of the newly converted. Rising to her feet, she waved her hands high in the air and cried out to the glory of God. She looked up at Christian, and, unbeknownst to each other, this time it was their individual sins, not their lust, that bound them together.

32

Home Again, Home Again

June 11, 2001

FROM THE ABYSS AND beyond, to Mason's death and all that was Freudian, Christian had indeed been to Hell and back. Mason's funeral provided only a short reprieve from the torment raging in his soul. Nights found him home with Darlene, terrified of where a ride in the car and his newly uncovered urges might lead. He gave up evening ministry duties and other church meetings, allowing Darlene to instead minister to him. Depleted in mind, body, and soul, there was no peace to be found—not in the shower or when dining or visiting Queen Esther in the barn, not even in the furied, frenzied sex he had with the newly revived Darlene. Chasing ghosts, he had her once, sometimes twice a day since the seminal event. Most ominous of all was the presence of disorientation during copulation: once he even caught himself fantasizing about Joss in order to see the act through. Work provided the only relief. Up at six, he was out of the house most days by seven, his office his refuge, its walls lined with priceless art, the mahogany shelves crammed to overflowing with books and photos, all attesting to the wealth, privilege, and power he had attained. A magnificent oil of Darlene, JJ, and himself, commissioned several months ago, hung directly across from his desk, serving as a constant reminder of how deeply he'd perverted the institution of marriage.

Finally, God spoke to him through the prophet Jeremiah.

The Lord said to his people: You are standing at the crossroads. So consider your path. Ask where the old, reliable paths are. Ask where the path is that leads to blessing and follow it. If you do, you will find rest for your souls.

Christian had a choice. He could either spend the rest of his life beating himself up, or he could free himself by acknowledging that what had happened with Joss had not been an act of free will—that it had been keenly choreographed by Satan. In his drunken and medicated state that night, the weakened Christian had had no defenses with which to fend off the Devil. Recognizing the value of bringing down someone as prominent in the Christian world as he, Satan had seen the opening and had struck. But if God had once absolved him for taking a human life—and there was no doubt in Christian's mind that He had—it stood to reason that He would forgive Christian a single act of sodomy, and that in God's forgiveness Christian should find the ability to forgive himself.

But forgiving himself this particular sin was a herculean task. Since finding Jesus he had fallen often and come up short, but before now, he'd never had a problem justifying his actions. Then again, he'd never gone down this particularly loathsome road. This wasn't like the many women with whom he'd strayed. It wasn't even like the ignominy of his time with Tiffany, a mere child. This was man on man—*a man who lies* *with a male as those who lie with a woman—a detestable act—*the very thing he railed against almost weekly. It sickened him so greatly that, try as he might, he still couldn't look at himself in the mirror. The only good to have come out of it was that he'd spent a week free of his Mexican nightmare. But the other thoughts that invaded his sleep—thoughts of cock, of Joss—made the memory of what he'd done impossible to suppress. A lifetime of female conquests should have been all he needed to prove himself a man. But one night with Joss and it was all gone. Stiffening his jaw, he lifted his eyes once more to the family portrait. After looking Darlene and JJ straight in the eye he made the decision to set to work.

In no time, Christian completed the paperwork to establish the most important ministry of his career: Straight On With God. The mission statement fairly flew off his pen.

Straight On With God—Our mission is to offer homosexuals the tools with which to make more godly choices. Recognizing that homosexuality is a choice and a condition that can be cured, we will minister to those in need as they find their way back to Christ. We will, through the love of Jesus, speak Truth to a fallen world that has been weakened by the temptations of the vast homosexual agenda.

Within a week, Christian held Straight On's inaugural meeting. Only two people came; a mother and her hostile teenaged son, Todd. Christian wasn't discouraged. It was a start. By most standards, the meeting was a complete failure. Todd was barely in the door when he turned to leave. He'd heard Bible-talk far too often, and most nights it was accompanied by brutal beatings courtesy of his father. He wasn't about to sit here and listen to this slime-ball of a pastor dictate to him whom and how he should love. Maybe his mother, whom he both adored and pitied, couldn't see that the pastor was nothing more than a snake oil salesman, but Todd could. If Todd wanted to talk morality, Pastor Slick here was the last person to whom he'd turn.

Christian called out to the fleeing boy, "Todd! Don't leave! None of this is your fault. It's all the Devil's work. He's blinded you. We have ways here—programs to cure you. May Jesus be with you in these trying times. I shall pray that you see the way to cleansing yourself of your filth."

As the door swung shut Todd muttered, "Don't do me any favors, phony-ass," just loud enough for Christian to hear.

For once, ironically, Christian had spoken from the heart. He had to admit that he was relieved by Todd's exit, uncomfortable with having the mirror held up so soon. He sat with Todd's mother, Lurleen, for upwards of an hour, spouting a kind of spiritual diarrhea that bubbled up from his tortured soul. Lurleen didn't notice his lack of composure or his failure to hear a word she said. She was oblivious to everything but her own pain. A godly woman, she thought of herself as a good mother. To wake up one day and learn that your only son has made the intentional choice to go against the Lord in such an unnatural way was difficult enough. But to remain silent as, night after night, Todd's father lit into him—*that* had become unbearable.

And even though Todd shunned his help, Christian decided to use the time with Lurleen as a practice session. If the ministerial sales pitch he had been working on could convince her that homosexuality could be managed then he might also have a chance of convincing himself.

"Lurleen, much as I'm not a great believer in science, preferrin' God's word to that of man, I believe there are exceptions, and that this unfortunate situation represents one of them. I have read several irrefutable scientific studies concluding that homosexuality is a choice, not a genetic predisposition, as the Left is so fond of saying. Science has proven, beyond a shadow of a doubt, that with behavioral modification and re-programmin', we *can* alter these deviant choices and return your son, or any like soul, to a normal life. Straight On is a brand new ministry, and as such, we are still exploring the methods that will best help Todd and any others, in and beyond our church family, who have succumbed to this particular tool of the Devil. Because I see this to be one of the greatest battlefields of all, we will spare no expense nor leave any stone unturned in makin' Straight On into our showcase ministry.

"As the Lord sayeth in Leviticus 18:22, 'You shall not lie with a male as one lies with a female; it is an abomination'; you can understand why curin' boys like Todd is so important to me.

"Y'see, homosexuality threatens all of us by makin' a mockery of marriage. And marriage, quite frankly, marriage is the stronghold, the very foundation of a moral society and therefore it demands our fullest protection. There is no single issue more important today because if we let down our guard on this one, the secular Left will have their way in promotin' man on man. Then what comes next? Man on boy? Man on dog? These perverts started back in the 60s makin' sexual freedom their key agenda an' they sure as Hell have come roarin' back. If we don't stand up for the family now, I promise, we'll live to regret it. If that means goin' head-to-head with Satan's emissaries, I'm more than ready. Make no mistake, Lurleen. This is war. But I can't tell you strongly enough that Todd is *not* to blame." He reached for her hands covering them with his. "No madam, he most certainly is not. Nor are you," and he noted with satisfaction the tears welling up in her eyes.

"The Evil One has reached deep into your son and is usin' every means available to bring him down. It's how he works, temptin' boys into unnatural acts. An' you, why you're as fine a mother as I've seen because you care enough to face the fact that Todd is at grave risk. I am saddened—not surprised, but saddened, that your son has ta go through this. If it helps at all, know that he is far from alone. But if we are to save him, you must first clear yourself—and him—of blame. God already has. When you see your way to doin' this, *then* we can set to work repairin' him. Remember, this is a Holy War we're fightin' an' Todd is a soldier for Christ, a soldier who's fightin' the battle of all battles against the most formidable of all enemies. Like any war, sometimes, in the midst of the fightin', enemy forces may appear to be gainin' ground. Do yourself a favor—when you leave here, go on home an' read your Bible. There you'll see that one battle does not a war make. I promise that, together, we'll find a way to put the final stake through Satan's heart. When we do, we'll strike a blow for your family, and for humanity, at the same time."

Lurleen wouldn't let go of Christian's hands. "Pastor, I cain't do this alone. I simply cain't. I gotta believe what you're saying. If not, how can I live with myself? I beg you, bring my God-fearin' boy back to me. Right now, you're the only hope I got. If he don't change his ways an' fast, I fear for his life. I can't speak for what his daddy might do. I seen such terrible things. Terrible." She shuddered. "My husband's a violent man an' when he says the only good fag is a dead fag," he means it. She stood up. "No one can know what I'm goin' through. I beg you Pastor, pray for our souls."

"Madam, I've already begun."

❖

First thing the next morning Christian was on the phone conferencing with several nationally prominent ex-gay church leaders. They perceived Texas as a state rife with cowboy-in-the-closet types and knowing Christian's stature, they were happy to advise and bring him up to speed about their work. Driven by a sense of urgency born of his night at The Abyss, Christian immediately engaged professionals from The Bible Way, an ex-gay reform organization based in Colorado Springs, to set up a temporary office in San Antonio the very next week. The Bible Way had name recognition and would bring instant legitimacy to Straight On. The program would begin on an outpatient basis, with an all-residence facility to be opened as soon as possible. Headship would fully subsidize the ministry, money never being an object. When Christian wanted something, thanks to the Lord's blessed income stream, it happened.

❖

Christian began to regain his sea legs. No longer fearful that temptation would send him back in the direction of The Abyss, he spent most evenings on the speaking circuit. It felt like a second rebirth. This time around, his goal was to be the most visible and rabid anti-gay crusader in the region, and he appeared more often than not with his loving, sexy wife at his side. Christian delegated the task of locating a residential facility to Darlene, and within days she struck a deal to purchase a nursing home that had recently gone out of business not far from the church. Christian used Headship's power of the purse and his personal and political connections to secure the permits they needed to open the facility. Darlene wheeled and dealed to get the needed furniture and beds. A load of Bibles, a carton of strong one-way locks and Straight On was in business.

Miraculously, the "clinic" was up and running far sooner than anyone could have dreamt. The day the residential facility opened its doors, all eighteen beds were spoken for, with a waiting list of twenty-two and counting. Christian hired two permanent staff members—the "Straight Militia"—from the Colorado Springs operations, both of whom were eager for the Texas challenge. They were immediately dubbed the "Straight Asses" by the inmates who, upon admittance, traded in their identities for a number. In both looks and demeanor the Straight Militia's resemblance to storm-troopers was startling. They were muscular, buzz-cut, Aryan-looking hulks, drunk on the power they wielded over the fragile inmates now under their authority. These tough, no-nonsense thugs were welcomed by the Christian community, which was very much in agreement with the importance of ridding itself of the grave homosexual threat to their children. Heralded by the Christian press for "taking a courageous stand against the pervasive homosexual agenda in Texas," the Hillcox star resumed its meteoric rise. Christian's personal fall from grace faded to little more than a memory he shared with no one.

With Mason's death having erased certain ghosts, Christian was free to retake the path of the True Prophet. He had regained the reins of power and what had so recently looked to be a gathering storm had mercifully retreated.

33

If You Build It, He Will Come

July 17, 2001

DWIGHT SESSIONS WAS THE designated CEO of Straight On, with Christian the unofficial, self-anointed leader. It quickly became clear that Texas had more rehab-seeking queers than it did beds, turning Straight On into that rare start-up success. The clinic received early and major publicity. Only weeks after opening, TRUE News did an in-depth, hour-long special on the ministry, with a focus on the remarkable number of "cures" they'd achieved in record time—Christian quickly learned that there was magic in numbers, as long as you were the one controlling them. This week, Straight On was the cover story for The Word, circulation two million, and he'd been approached by one of the cable networks to consult on a made-for-television docudrama called *Cured*. It was an exciting time for everyone at Male Headship, with Straight On quickly becoming the jewel in its crown. And when multimillionaire board member Borth Fuller died suddenly, single and childless, Christian learned that Fuller had altered his will, leaving his entire estate to Straight

On, on the very same day he had accepted the invitation to join the board. Christian let his mind wander only briefly into thoughts about the bachelor's own questionable sexuality before moving on to the business of spending the man's money.

One sunny afternoon, Christian and Dwight were feasting outdoors on a bucket of Beesun's Fried Chicken when Christian looked up to see none other than Joss himself, suitcase in hand, being reluctantly shepherded through Straight On's tall glass entrance doors. Instinctively, Christian leapt up and, without a word of explanation, bolted across the lawn. Dwight shrugged and continued eating, figuring Christian must have remembered a meeting back at the church. When Dwight polished off the last drumstick, he headed inside to greet Straight On's newest inmate.

❖

Out of breath, his heart racing, Christian reached the church, where he sequestered himself behind locked doors for the second time in six weeks. How could he not have seen this coming? He was a fool to have thought that he and Joss wouldn't cross paths one day. Early on, his greatest fear had been that Joss would see him on TV and come to the church to out him. Or more likely, as Luke had done those many years ago, Joss would show up to stake his claim in the blackmail line. When neither fear materialized, Christian dismissed his concerns, convincing himself that a godless sodomite like Joss most assuredly never watched Christian television. He had never imagined *this*.

Even now though, it was possible he was panicking for no reason. Joss had been so unresponsive on that shame-filled morning that it wasn't likely he'd even remember Christian.

Still and all, it would be prudent to stay out of sight until Joss "recovered" and moved on. He'd explain to Dwight that other responsibilities demanded his temporary absence and that he'd be back to counsel on a regular basis as soon as he possibly could.

One other issue remained. At the program's inception, Christian had instituted a formal Graduation Day for each inmate who successfully achieved a "cure." He believed that putting the graduates on show would increase the pressure for them to remain straight and thus reduce recidivism. He had insisted that graduations were to be led only by him—another tool that he felt upped the ante of commitment. As an added plus, every time he bestowed his blessings on a newly redeemed graduate, he imagined that he himself would move further away from his own "episode." Having insisted that he lead the ceremonies himself was a problem, at least when it came to Joss. But he could always concoct a trip to DC and let Dwight or even Darlene step in—there was always something credible that demanded his presence.

This slight relief notwithstanding, it felt like things were closing in again and once more, he felt the unraveling. In the space of a day he had gone from King of Kings to a weakened, pathetic man teetering on the brink. Hands shaking, he rummaged through the back of a file cabinet where he kept a flask of Wild Turkey and a bottle of pills. At this precise moment, it was either self-medication or sucking on the wrong end of a loaded gun. He didn't see any middle course. One long drink and two Xanax later, his anxiety abated. Immobile and in somewhat of a fog, he remained at his desk until dark. Neither loud knocking nor ringing telephone moved him. When at last he arose to leave, it was dark and the church was empty. After a few tentative steps he made his way to his car and somehow managed the short drive home to a frantic Darlene.

"Christian! Wherever have you been? I stood outside your office half the day, poundin' on the door. Why was it locked in the first place? Nobody's seen you since lunchtime. I came home at five and when Joretta Simmons phoned 'round six and said your car was still in the lot, I near to died. If you hadn't a walked in that door, I swear I'd a had the police over to the church to break down your door."

Another look his way and the old fear returned. She went to him, only to have him pull away. "Christian, what is it? You look like you just woke up from a nightmare." He didn't wince at the accuracy of her words, but only because he hadn't heard them. She led him to the kitchen table, much like Joss had been led into the clinic today. While she went to work warming the dinner the staff had prepared, he rose from the table and quietly shuffled away. When Darlene turned around, he was gone. He'd left home this morning his usual jubilant self, only to return a shadow of what he'd been. Staring at his empty chair, her thoughts naturally returned to Mason—that somehow Christian had learned the truth. Though dead and gone, it seemed the aura of Mason's presence would linger on forever. But Christian hadn't seemed angry, only defeated. She put the food away and headed upstairs to face the music, whatever it might be.

Christian was passed out on the floor outside their bedroom.

34

The Evangelicals Come A-Callin'

July 18, 2001

"DAMMIT TO HELL, WHERE'S my blue suit? I'm late. Goddam weak-assed Evangelicals are out for my ass as is. S'not like I can afford ta be late."

Darlene swept in, an anxious smile plastered onto her face, two suits in hand. "Which one you want, the light one or the dark?"

He moaned, "You choose. My head. It's killin' me." Putting a cool hand to his forehead, she led him to the window seat and sat him down. "Light blue it is," she chirped. Shifting his bulky legs around, she shimmied him first into his pants and then the jacket. "Now don't you worry about those men. You've handled far worse than a bunch of soft-bellied Evangelicals. Once they get a taste of Pastor Man, they'll be eatin' outta your hand. A little bit of Christian charm goes a long way, you know." Spinning him around, she tied his tie, kissed his cold, lifeless lips and sent him on his way.

❖

Stepping into the bright morning light, he settled himself inside the softly purring Lincoln all the while his mind screamed, "Caution! Dangerous Curves Ahead." He was headed for the lion's den to meet up with Dan Carmody's pride of weak-kneed Evangelicals. Instead of being on the same team, Christian's team, they were on their way to crucify him. With his attention having lately been focused almost exclusively on Israel and Straight On, Christian had failed to notice the cracks that were forming within the ranks of Evangelical Christians.

With none of his usual armor about him, he knew things wouldn't turn out well today. Carmody, the pastor of the rapidly growing Saddle Up to God Non-Denominational Church, seemed to be showing up everywhere of late and his complaints about Word of Faith preachers like Christian had started to attract attention. He assumed Carmody and his gang would be out for blood today. As his heart thudded wildly, his breath grew shallow and animal-like. If he knew anything, it was that they were sure to tape the meeting, which meant that anything he said could and would be used against him. He'd better find his game face and fast. Leaders from other white-bread churches had made a stink about his brand of Christianity before, both to his face and in their newspapers, but this was a first for the Non-Denominationals. Whatever they left with today was bound to have a powerful afterlife in the press. He reached into his pocket and retrieved a couple more pills. Just for today, he promised himself. He'd cut back once he got through this. With Joss still very much on his mind, the pressure of the looming confrontation was too much and he needed all the help he could get.

He cued up: Preacher Man was on.

❖

Twenty-two so-called Evangelicals were seated around a large conference table at Male Headship. Female church volunteers darted in and out to replenish coffee cups and trays of pastry that seemed to disappear as soon as they were set down. There was no problem with *these* peoples' appetites.

Dan Carmody began, "Pastor, we want to thank you for hosting this lovely spread. May I begin by saying that all of us here today greatly admire your work, praise Jesus, and are most impressed that you've tackled the problem of homosexuality so actively." Carmody's words didn't mask the steel in his voice and Christian wasn't taken in.

"You have set a standard which we can only hope to live up to in our own communities. Sadly, however, we have not come here to sing Caesar's praises. As you know, some of what you people are saying is being construed as un-Christian in the eyes of the greater world and thus is harmful to us all. It is one thing to dedicate your life to spreading the Good News. Fact is, everyone in this room takes the Great Commission seriously. We have not come to tell you what to believe or how to preach, but we *are* here to say how deeply troubled we are by the direction your preaching, and the preaching of those like you, has taken."

Christian's face was a mask of inscrutability but for the telltale beads of perspiration he furtively wiped away. He looked nothing if not intimidating. Carmody continued.

"Pastor, please enlighten us—when did taking money from the poor replace Jesus' call to care for those in need? And where is it writ in the Bible that famine, war, or the decimation of our planet be the preferred form of birth control? It seems, according to you and those sharing your beliefs that, when the last tree is felled, we should shout 'Hallelujah, the End has come!' As Evangelical Christians we have been taught to be stewards of God's Earth, not to facilitate its destruction. We're not blind. We see how greatly you've enriched yourself, how political you've become and how you run around impeding peace while seeding the ground for war. We're here to say that if you and your kind don't take a step back, we fear that your words and actions might actually bring about your longed-for prophecy, culminating in an unnecessary nuclear conflagration that just might be the equivalent of the world's end. If you know the Bible at all—and we know that you do—you are more than aware that there are none among us who can know when Jesus will return, just as is it not possible to hasten His coming. But you, you lie to yourself, you lie to your flock and, worst of all, you just might lie your way into bringing on a worldwide confrontation.

"It is abominable how you Prosperity Preachers run up and down the stage, ranting about abortion and the dangers of stem cell research, yet you say nothing to advocate for the human condition after birth. Poverty, disease, why, the very air we breathe—the list goes on—these hard realities do not seem to exist in your world except to serve as punishment for those who suffer them. Speaking for myself, I'm spittin' mad at how you've seen fit to bastardize the Word of God, all the while you line your bottomless pockets. And believe you me, I speak for the majority of good Christians in this country."

It was a well-paced and blistering attack, and with Christian in no shape to parry Carmody's words he fell back on the only techniques available to him—distract, deflect, and attack. Donning his fighting gloves, and with no desire to ameliorate, he readied himself for battle with these contemptible pretenders. Pussies masquerading as Men of God.

Leading with a feint, he began, "Pastor Carmody, I must say I am taken aback by the vitriol you bear me and the Word of Faith movement. *You*, sir, are no Christian." Directing his barely controlled anger toward the silent participants at the table, he continued, "An' you. You sit here, the bunch of quakin' cowards you are, an' you let this man accuse me of the most hideous of untruths. How dare you? It's easy, isn't it, bandin' together like a bunch of schoolboys? The classic bully's tactic. Your supposed concern for The Great Commission sickens me and *you* sicken me as well. So politically correct are you, so deeply have you drunk of the liberal Kool-Aid, that you hardly know what it is to follow the Word of God. No wonder our society is flounderin' in oceans of depravity never before witnessed in the history of mankind." Unable to rein in his fury any longer, he let his voice rise to a fevered pitch.

"If you think for one moment that you people reflect the views of our Christian brothers and sisters across the world, I am here to tell you, *you do not*. The world is changin' my friends, and it's doin' so at an ever-acceleratin' pace. Read your Bible the way it's meant to be read why don't you. If you sissified cowards did that, you'd know that none a what you say matters because we are nanoseconds away from the Rapture. While you limp-wristed phonies play patty-cake with the Antichrist, the world is spinnin' out of control in God's pre-ordained plan and guess what? There ain't a thing you can do about it."

The room was silent. Something big had just happened. Carmody and his associates had come today in hopes of beginning a dialogue but instead they found themselves in the presence of a far more crazed megalomaniac than they could have imagined Christian to be.

Dispelling any hope for reconciliation, Christian exploded. "*Get the fuck outta my church*. I will *not* sit here listenin' to *you* tell *me* about Christianity. Your heads are shoved so far up your asses, you holier-than-thou pieces of shit, that to hear you call yourselves Christians makes me wanna rip you to shreds. *So get the flyin' fuck outta my church, my house of prayer, and don't you ever darken my doorstep again.*"

With that, he stormed out, leaving behind a roomful of good Christians, mouths agape, tape recorders still running. He didn't give a fuck about their tapes, and only wished he had had the physical strength to upend the table before his grand exit.

35

It Ain't Over Till the Fat Man Sings

September 2, 2001

TIME PASSED AND WHEN Christian heard nothing more from Carmody, he put that particular worry away for another day. He could only speculate that his outburst had scared those knock-kneed Christians enough so that they didn't know how to react. Joss's continued presence at Straight On kept Christian in a heightened state of anxiety, compelling him to continue his daytime use of Xanax. He had taken the drug as a sleep aid for so long that he was able to function adequately when he used it to get him through the day. If Darlene knew he was using, she didn't let on.

Labor Day was a big day at Male Headship. The event had grown to the point that it was touted as one of the ten best fireworks displays in the country. Each year, it was a day for Headship to step onto the world stage and spread its name and brand far and wide. This year's event was to be the most spectacular yet. They'd moved it up to Sunday so that the revelers could stay late, dance the night away, and sleep in on Labor Day. It had been a rainy week and showers were predicted for early evening, but unless the heavens let loose, the show would go on. Announcements at church that morning encouraged everyone to pray for the best but prepare for the worst. Christian dispatched the grounds crew to lay down as many tarps as possible in an effort to keep the mud to a minimum. Too much work and planning had gone into the event to let the threat of bad weather wash out their parade.

Labor Day at Headship was also a big draw for the nation's largest Christian broadcasting network, where it, along with 1-800-LIVE-4-HIM, would be seen by millions of viewers. With the sizable audience in mind, Christian took extra care in dressing. He slipped into a black silk sateen shirt, fully appreciative of the sensuality of the fabric. As it slid across his fleshy surface, he noted that nothing felt quite so nice as fine silk on a man's skin. To emphasize that he remained a man of the people, he pulled on a pair of chubby-sized Levis, angled his feet into a pair of hand-tooled cowboy boots, and topped it all off with a ten-gallon Stetson hat. Scrutinizing himself in the mirror, he was pleased with the overall effect. He might be as wide as the side of a steer, but hot damn, he looked good. Slathering on an extra coat of deodorant, he spritzed his mouth with Dr. Earl's Halitosis-B-Gone and doused himself with Calvin Klein's Eternity. Primped and fragrant, he was ready to greet the world, weather be damned.

Darlene was captivating as well. The plunging neckline of her red, white, and blue halter exposed ample cleavage, while a hint of well-toned flesh peeked out between her halter and overly tight red pedal-pushers. She debated, but only for a moment, before throwing on the three-and-a-half-inch heels she'd bought for this day, mildly concerned about the rain-soaked earth. Sometimes, a woman had to take a chance for the sake of beauty. Besides, without the shoes, the outfit would fizzle. If she had to toss them after one wearing, so be it.

Christian, resilient as ever, had managed to regain his spirits after the evangelical sparring match with Carmody. Today was a day to celebrate His labor, and Praise Jesus, he would do just that.

Starting well before dawn, workers bustled about, setting up grills and the tables on which they'd cook and serve everything from burgers and hot dogs to deviled eggs, pickled tomatoes, Texas chili, corn on the cob, and anything else a picnicker could ask for. Sound system components were loaded onto the temporary stage that had been built the day before, and the Christian rock 'n rollers who would be performing later relaxed in and around their private luxury tour buses nearby. As families arrived a hodgepodge of blankets created a sort of crazy quilt over the tarped landscape. It was a picturesque and patriotic slice of Americana. The skies were threatening, but so far, the day remained dry. Camera crews set up shop on strategically placed platforms while the broadcast operation was directed from the church's own control room. American and Christian flags flapped in the breeze attesting to the holiness of America, a Christian nation.

The Holiday Committee had outdone itself, and the Christian broadcasters caught image after image of happy, celebratory citizens demonstrating how real Americans honor God and country. Christian and Darlene ambled about, the lord and lady of the manor. It was the kind of event Christian loved most, one filled with a sense of belonging, and the thrill of celebrity, both of which he never got enough. Yes, God was good and Christian was in his glory.

After a time of strolling about and greeting, glad-handing and shoulder slapping, Christian and Darlene directed JJ to the children's area, picked up their dinner plates, heaping as much food upon them as they could hold, and headed over to the VIP tent. Seated there were several members of the church board and Dwight Sessions from Straight On. Christian hadn't seen Dwight since having temporarily relinquished his duties there. Dwight had never questioned his absence, nor had he pushed back when Christian phoned to tell him he wouldn't officiate at graduation for the time being. No questions asked. No truths told.

As dusk fell, the still rainless skies filled with the roar of two U.S. Military F-16's, or Silver Demons, as he liked to call them, swooping down from out of the clouds with a deafening roar, followed by a thrilling demonstration of the Elite Strike Force Silver Wing Parachute Team. The jets inspired a feeling of reverence for the power they represented, the kind of power that, if properly directed, would help bring on the Second Coming.

Next came the music. Bercy Fremont and the Gospelettes, a traditional Christian quartet, opened the show. Christian put in an early request for "Oh Happy Day." Whenever he heard it, he couldn't help but cut loose and join in at full throttle, belting out for all he was worth, the King of Christian Soul himself. And *that* would make for great television. Next, while the stage was being reset, the show featured some local talent—for Christian, the real highlight of the pre-fireworks entertainment—the First Baptist Junior High School Dancing Queens. Though he no longer dipped his pen into any inkwell except Darlene's, there was nothing wrong with jump-starting his battery every now and again. If looking at the sweet young flesh of *female* virgins did it for him, then look he would.

The musical portion of the show closed with The Crucificators, the hottest group in Christian rock. The grounds teemed with youth, and although Christian was inwardly disgusted by the grungy gothic band, outwardly he played the fan. These mangy, unkempt creatures, whose every visible centimeter of skin was tattooed and whose bodies had piercings in every conceivable gathering of skin, reeked of immorality. No matter. These musicians and others like them did their gothic best at proclaiming their faith and they held a cult-like sway over Christian youth. He'd heard them described as "crossover artists" since their songs could be heard on non-Christian stations as well. To have the Crucificators here at all was a media coup that would attract huge numbers of television viewers, exponentially increasing ad revenues, not to mention, of course, the saving of more souls. If the gospel could be preached through punk rock, who was he to object? He'd be a fool to chase away the goose who laid the golden egg. And Christian was nobody's fool.

The Crucificators played like it was the last night on Earth, and when darkness fell, the final notes of their encore segued seamlessly into the opening lights and sounds of the fireworks extravaganza. The pyro-techies, or Master Blasters as they were dubbed, had been hard at work in a neighboring field since last Friday on the set-up for what promised to be a fireworks display like no other. The promise was fulfilled—the event would break its own records not only in viewership but also for the amount of money pledged to 1-800-LIV-4-HIM.

As the Master Blasters took over the sky, the crowd settled onto their blankets, couples snuggling together, youngsters asleep on their parents' laps. Christian, having gyrated and boogied the night away, fell onto his seat drenched in sweat and overcome by the sheer joy of what he had created. Darlene was off making the rounds when Christian looked up to see

Dwight's eyes trained on him. Figuring it was better to know if there was a bullet with his name on it, he turned a casual voice Dwight's way, Hey, podner. How's things goin' over at Straight On? Numbers holdin' steady?"

"Steady?" Dwight's eyes opened wide in awe. "Fuck, we could open a wing with a hunnerd more rooms an' still not fill the need out there. An' it's all thanks to you. You got yourself so much publicity, we get calls most days from all over the country. Sometimes from outside the country too. But I'm tellin' you, we miss you over there. Them little fruits could use the kinda ministerin' only *you* can give. One dude in particular been askin' why the pastor don't come by. Think you might could make it over every now an' then jest to say 'hey'?"

"Dwight, don't ask me that, not now. You of all people know what Straight On means to me. Why, I'm lucky to be here tonight, things bein' so crazy lately. I've hardly had a minute's rest what with my goin' back n forth to Washington, but mark my words, what I'm accomplishin' out there will change history. More and more legislators are findin' the courage, not only to speak out, but to vote the Bible as well, and our lobbyists are gainin' influence daily. I tell you Dwight, we're finally becomin' the force I knew we would. We're raisin' up an army for Christ an' aside from the godforsaken—and I mean that literally— liberal press, there ain't been much pushback. So please, for now, keep makin' my excuses over there. There's enough a you to straighten out 'the girls' without me. Anyways, hasn't Pastor Greg been goin' over there regular?"

"He has. T'ain't quite the same though. S'you they want. But I unnerstand. It'll have ta do for now."

Looking out over the crowd, Dwight suddenly exclaimed, "Well, lookee here, there's two a my boys headed our way. I told 'em to come on by for the fireworks. They been so good, I'd say they're our best inmates. I invited 'em over as a sorta pat on the back. A Good Behavior Award I like to call it. Hope that's okay with you. I'll vouch for 'em—they ain't here to play hide the salami."

Fuck. He hadn't seen this coming. Sure enough, it was Joss and his "pal" making a beeline for their table. Christian whirled around, scoping out his escape. There was no fucking way he'd sit here and let it all come undone. *He* was *Christian*—the Lord's representative and a far finer man than either of these sorry fucks could ever dream of being. He was also outta here.

"Shee-it," he said, looking at his watch. "I've got to run to the office—conference call I forgot about with Senator Mapes—he's in Israel right now an' it's mornin' over there— real hush hush political stuff. Be back soon's I can."

Melting into the darkness, he slipped away to the edge of the field where he positioned himself to watch. He saw Dwight get up to greet his "boys." Reduced to spying, Christian felt the noose tighten. He backed away, a thief in the night, poised to run at the first sign of danger. When he reached the church, he stayed in the shadows, inching along the building's perimeter so as not to be seen, taking the long way around to the parking lot and his car. As he climbed inside, the sky filled, from horizon to horizon, with red, white, and blue crosses, small and large, bursting by the thousands, proclaiming His Glory.

Won't be no more singin' from this fat man tonight, he thought, and quaking, he slammed shut his car door, gunned the engine, and headed north.

❖

Moments later, Darlene returned to the table to find Christian gone. Her gut told her something was not right, but she stayed put for fifteen minutes or so, making pleasant small talk with Dwight and the two gay men from Straight On. She was mystified—Christian was the last person on Earth to miss the evening's climax, as much as he loved his glorious fireworks. She finally asked Dwight if he knew where Christian had gone, and when he told her what Christian said before abruptly leaving, she excused herself. Pulling off her shoes, she sprinted through the spongy field toward the church. Small stones and twigs tore at the soles of her feet, making her cry out in pain. When she reached the parking lot and saw that Christian's car was gone, she jumped into her own and took off, with no destination in mind. She drove and drove, a fool's errand, only to return home hours later, alone, demoralized, and frightened.

An ominous sense of dread filled the house. It was as if she was strapped to a railroad track with a twenty-car locomotive bearing down on her at full speed. She had no one to blame but herself, what with the empty bottles of liquor and pills she'd continued to find stashed but not quite hidden—an unanswered cry for help. Whatever was happening, whether it was in his head or reality-based, he had not invited her in. But then, she hadn't pushed either. With Mason's death, she had wanted to believe their problems were behind them. Finally, the two-ton elephant that had parked on her chest these last eight years had gotten up and lumbered off, presumably to Hell, despite Christian's tale. Having looked evil squarely in the face, having paid the steepest price imaginable, Darlene had somehow come out the other side. That Christian had survived a childhood ruled by Mason's cruelty was all the proof she needed to appreciate the enormity of what he had overcome. The truth was, he had done much more than survive. He had thrived. Since forming her own relationship with Jesus, Darlene had come to know there was nothing Christian could ever do again that would make her turn from him. Wedded at long last to the Father, the Son, and to Christian, she had to find him and make him safe.

It was four in the morning. Leery of police involvement but just as frightened not to ask for help, she climbed the stairs to their room. Suddenly she understood she was not to call anyone. Christian must have fled for a reason and, whatever that reason was, he meant to keep it private. So she waited.

Early the next morning, with still no word from him, Darlene stepped into the shower hoping to clear her mind. After suffering water so hot it verged on scalding, she wrapped a plush, oversized towel over her lobster-red body and emerged from the bathroom to be met by the answering machine's blinking light. Angry at herself for having missed the call, she prayed aloud it would be Christian's voice on the tape. With great trepidation she pressed PLAY.

From faraway, his drug-slurred voice spoke to her through the machine.

"Darleeeeeen. S'me . . . I need you. I'm lost." There was a clattering sound and then nothing. Darlene shrieked at the heartless machine, "Christian, Christian! Where in hell's name are you?" After what seemed an eternity his voice came back to her. "Hullo? Musta dropped the phone . . . Hullo? Anyone there? H'lo?" Again, nothing, save for the sound of his slow, labored breathing. She stood frozen until the recorder cut off. Praise Jesus for Caller ID. Scrolling down, she gasped when she saw that the call had come from Bartlesville, Oklahoma.

What could have happened in the few minutes of her absence last night that would have taken him all the way to Oklahoma? She called the number on the ID only to be scolded by an angry busy signal. *Sleep-ing, sleep-ing, drugged and sleep-ing*, the phone chided. Think. She must think. Clasping her hands, she let the towel fall to the ground and paced the four corners of the room.

Noise from downstairs filtered up along with the everyday smells of bacon and coffee. The clock read eight-thirty, which meant there'd soon be a knock at the door—Maria, announcing breakfast. Throwing herself back into bed, she burrowed deeply under the covers, crying out to her new savior, Jehovah God, pleading for a sign, any sign.

Pushing TALK on the intercom, she heard Maria's voice, "Señora? How I can help you?"

Darlene responded in a polite if indifferent voice. "Maria. I will not be down this morning. Nor will Pastor Christian. We're both a bit under the weather—we had a late night—and we don't wish to be disturbed."

"Si Señora Hillcox."

With a curt "Gracias," she disconnected, dressed, and waited some more.

❖

For the second time in only three months, Christian awakened to find himself in a strange room with no idea of how he'd gotten there. Terror coursed through him as he fell through a haze, back to the time when he was small, anticipating his father's drunken footsteps heading his way, belt in hand. He bolted upright, his head gripped by searing pain, pulling him back to another bed, another day. The clock read three, but was that day or night? He stumbled to the window and peeked through stiff curtains into the sunlight and a strange parking lot. Had he returned to Joss's? He spun back around to the bed, and to his great relief, found it empty with no evidence of cohabitation. The Statement of Rates on the metal door told him he was in a motel, specifically the "Moonlight Motel, Bartlesville, Oklahoma. Payment Due Daily. No Exceptions." He fell back into bed, after first replacing the dangling telephone receiver. Searching for his pills, he found the empty bottle on the floor beside the bed, and the need for Xanax suddenly overwhelmed him. Unable to stop trembling, a sense of doom erased all hope. Not knowing how he'd gotten where he was, he curled up into a round fleshy ball and sobbed. From despair to fear and back again, he saw no way out—no escape from the memory of Joss, no escape from the drugs and alcohol. As he wailed the plaintive cry of the damned, the telephone rang. He picked up, tentatively, praying there'd be help on the other end. That was when a voice from heaven spoke to him through the wires,

"Christian?"

"Darlene? That you?" he sobbed.

"Christian. What's happened? Why are you in Oklahoma? Talk to me. No, don't. Just tell me where you are and I'll come get you. Just tell me you're okay. Please."

So many questions. How could he speak when he didn't know the answers? Still, he held onto the voice, the voice of an angel, his angel.

"Darlene, I'm lost—so lost."

"I know you are, my love. But I'll find you if you tell me exactly where you are."

He stumbled to the door and read from the rate card. "It appears I'm at the Moonlight Motel on Highway 60 in Bartlesville, Oklahoma." By now he was sobbing. "Can you come? Now? Please?"

"Baby, I'll be there fast as I can. But you have to promise me you won't leave the room. If you do, then I'll never find you. Turn on the television or go back to sleep. Jest don't leave the room. Do you promise?"

He muttered, "I'm so tired," and the receiver fell to the ground.

❖

The next thing Christian knew, he was inside Headship's private jet. Darlene stayed by his side throughout the flight, soothing him when he cried out, plying him with liquids and gently stroking his hair. Only twenty-four hours had passed, but for Christian and Darlene, it had been an eternity.

Once home, Darlene summoned her own doctor, a discreet, kindly man, and when he arrived she whisked him up the back stairs. After explaining drug withdrawal and what to expect, he left Darlene with a small bottle of pills and a tapering-off regimen. The days passed with Christian flying in and out of consciousness, his guts tearing at him from deep within his belly. Christian's palsied body continued to shake, his head was gripped with searing pain, and Darlene changed drenched sheets on the hour. Unaware that he was experiencing the sudden withdrawal from Xanax, his paranoid mind told him he was at war with the Devil, and the Devil was winning. At the moment, he didn't much care.

Time dragged on with Darlene running interference with the staff, fielding calls and visits from churchgoers, telling any and all who asked that, thanks to God's grace, Christian was recovering from a virulent flu. Beyond their prayers, she explained, what he needed most was bed rest. These were difficult days for Darlene, as alone, she saw him through the worst. At times he'd return to her, only to quickly retreat back into a world of his own. When he spoke, the things he said made little sense and Darlene didn't push, wary of triggering whatever it was that had sent him over the edge. Ornate flower arrangements covered Second Coming's every available surface, giving it the feel and smell of a funeral parlor. A daily parade of food offerings, all of it homemade and much of it his favorite things, poured in.

It was food, in fact, that brought him back to the living. Ambrosia, to be precise. His dependence on Xanax, while serious, had been of relatively short duration, making him one of the fortunate ones. When, finally, the worst symptoms began to recede, a great restlessness set in. On the day Christian exchanged his bedclothes for ranch-wear, Darlene knew he'd be okay. Though it would take time for the anxiety and insomnia to abate, when he first stepped outside the house and felt the hot September sun on his creaky, weakened body, it was with a renewed spirit that he headed for the pasture to visit with the newest member of the "Red Heifer Brigade." As the young cow nuzzled his hand, he felt the stirrings of hope return. Time passed, his memory cleared, and the terror of Labor Day began to recede.

Meanwhile, life had continued as usual at Male Headship and Straight On, with no one the wiser about his physical and mental flight. Calls and messages of support continued to reach Darlene, reminding them of what a great and lucky man he was.

One week later, Christian returned to work. He awakened at six thirty, dressed for work, kissed his wife goodbye and climbed into the limo. In the space of seven days, he had visited the depths of Hell, only to pass through the gates of Redemption once again.

36

Begin the End

September 10, 2001

MALE HEADSHIP, LIKE MOST businesses of its size, was a well-oiled machine and Christian's brief absence was of little consequence. Only a couple of hours back at the job and he was up to speed. Re-energized, it didn't phase him that Dan Carmody and the Hostile Evangelicals had resurfaced while he'd been out. This was a job for Super-Pastor and this time around, Carmody, that anemic dickwad, wouldn't know what hit him when the rehabilitated Christian came at him. Christian would never let anyone catch him in a weakened state again. When he left a message for Carmody, he salivated at the opportunity for a rematch.

Determined to face his real ghost, he called Dwight. On the pretense of checking in, they had a routine conversation. Christian's last memory of Labor Day was the explosion of crosses in his rear view mirror. He didn't even remember that, as he drove off, the heavens had let loose a torrential downpour, scattering the crowd and banishing any questions about where Christian had gone. Talk about Divine Intervention. Emboldened, he asked after the two young men Dwight had invited that night.

He heard the joy in Dwight's response. "Christian, those boys, what kin I say? They're good as new—cured I venture ta say, an' it's all thanks to us. 'Specially the good lookin' one, Number 77." Christian felt the floor drop out from under him. "I tell you, they come 'round so completely, I say, why not use 'em as poster boys for Reparative Therapy? I promise you this; they'll never look at a man *that* way agin. Even better, it's lookin' like Number 77 might even reconcile with his wife and get to see his kids agin. As for 82, he'll make some lucky gal a mighty fine husband one a these days. They're leavin' at week's end so if you git the chance, stop on by an' say hey. What with no graduation ceremony, I'm sure it'd be much appreciated."

"Sure thing Dwight. I'll do my best." *In my next life*, he thought, making a mental note to wait a full seven days before returning to Straight On. The amount of time it took for God to create the world, which was exactly what Christian was doing—recreating *his* world.

"Oh, an' Dwight. Soon's I'm squared away here, I'll be back full time at Straight On. I don't expect to be travelin' near as much, what with my recent illness an' all." Christian dare not risk being away too long from what he viewed as his own homo-cure. Hangin' with the faggots was the only way to assure he stay mounted in the rightful saddle.

"Take as much time you need, Pastor. With what you passed through, I don't want it on my conscience that you overdid yourself none. That an' Darlene'd have me fer lunch if I let you come back afore yer ready."

In the end, Christian's flight from reality had served a purpose. It had shown him his worth—as husband, pastor, and father. And in a psyche suffused with as much primal loneliness as his, there could be no greater currency. He'd had a narrow escape, but he had returned from the darkness, determined never to go there again.

It was then that the most affirming event of his life occurred. His secretary burst through the door, so overcome she could barely speak. Her arms flailed up and down as if to take flight, all the while she shrieked.

"Bless me Jesus. Oh Lord—Pastor C— the phone—he's on the phone!" She ran to him, pounding away on his shoulder till he could take no more.

"Tammy! Calm yourself. I don't have a clue what you're tryin' to tell me. *Who's* on the phone?"

"Pastor, I know you won't believe this but it's *him*! The honest to God President of the U-nited States!" He looked down to see line one blinking away.

John Christian Hillcox, kingmaker and rock star of the Christian Right, a man who dined with Congressmen and Senators, met with royalty and convened regularly with Israeli Prime Ministers, had never had a conversation with his own president. Over the years, the frequent calls emanating from the White House never came from the Oval Office. Not once had this wayward soul from Pearsall received a call from this far on high. He dismissed Tammy, took a deep breath and picked up the phone.

"Mr. President, Sir, this is Pastor John Christian Hillcox reporting for duty."

Damned fool, he thought. *Reporting for duty?* What a yokel he must sound. But in a way, he was indeed doing just that.

Yes indeed, for if he was anything he was Field General of the Warriors for Christ, present and accounted for, at the ready to take back the nation for Jesus Christ, thank you very much.'

A crisp voice at the end of the line replied, "Hold please for the President."

As if in a dream, the slow, familiar Texas drawl came on the line.

"Pastor! How ya doin'? I been hearin' an awful lot of good things 'bout you out here in Washington. You've made yourself some mighty powerful friends.

"I'll be brief here. I got a world to run, ya know?" The President chuckled. "Which brings me to the point. You know better than anyone these are unprecedented times we live in an' I sure could use your input on certain issues in the Middle East. Knowing millions of *real* Christians share your theological worldview, I believe it's time we meet. Unofficially, that is."

"Yes Sir, I would be honored, Sir." No stumbling there. "You've only to ask. I've a plane at the ready and am at your disposal, ready for duty."

The president chuckled again. "That's great. The decisions we make together will be among the most important in modern history, if you get ma drift. Would the twentieth of this month work for you? In the Oval Office. Say, two-thirty?"

"That will be perfect, Mr. President. Can I say again how deeply honored I am?"

"As am I, Pastor. I can already tell we're gonna be fast friends, you and me. See you on the twentieth then. Stay on the line so my secretary can give you the necessary information. And Pastor, for the record, I want to say that I think yours is the most important work there is, more important than even my own. May God bless you."

"Thank you most kindly, Mr. President."

❖

An hour later, Christian, still at his desk, was a bloated vision of redemption in the flesh. No matter what had happened before in his life, no matter how far he'd gone off the tracks, his worth had been validated today as never before. Indeed, he was Chosen. He could have stayed in his chair the rest of the day, glorying in the turnaround his life had taken, but for the aroma of fried food wafting toward his office. Following his nose to the boardroom, he found his staff laying out a sumptuous banquet in honor of his recovery. With difficulty, he kept the big news to himself, but not his joy.

What a homecoming today had been. In the space of a week he'd gone from physical and emotional distress of the deepest degree to receiving an invitation from the President of the United States. That, and the best fried chicken this side of heaven. Yes indeed, he was a cherished and important man. *Fuck my father, fuck the world, I am John Christian Hillcox*, he thought. Then he gorged himself on more food than ought to be legal, pled fatigue, and went home to "rest."

Darlene was upstairs in front of the mirror admiring the new bustier she had ordered during his recovery, in the event he needed a jump-start. She was so absorbed in her image that she didn't notice him until he came upon her from behind, grabbing her firmly by the buttocks. With a startled yelp, she let rip a lusty howl.

"Didn't mean to scare you!" he grinned. "I'm in the mood to celebrate. Where's JJ?"

"He's over to the Brayton's. Teresa's workin' with a coupla the boys on a Young Earth project. She'll bring him by 'round four. What're we celebratin', anyhoo?"

"How 'bout I say it's Top Secret, then you see if you can get it outta me. Maybe we start with a skinny dip so's you can work me over poolside?" he leered, sliding the palm of his hand between her legs.

"Y'ole rascal, you! Ya got it back, that's for sure. Tell ya what. Gimme a coupla two minutes to send the staff packin' an' I'll see you—and that means all of you—down by the pool." *Damn*, she thought. *Whatever had happened to make him run all the way to Oklahoma, she didn't much care if it brought him back to her like this.*

❖

His naked flesh jiggling on the way out the back door, Christian was stopped short by the sound of the doorbell. In an effort to shield himself, he grabbed an apron so scanty it hardly covered his front end, so he slipped inside the pantry to listen for the all-clear. The front door slammed and, snatching a Moon Pie off the shelf, he was quite the sight when Darlene returned. There he stood, buck-naked but for the skimpy apron, his hind quarters fully exposed and a Moon Pie oozing marshmallow from his mouth.

"U.P.S.?" he asked thickly.

Peals of laughter emanated from Darlene as she handed over a small package. He tossed it aside, popped the remaining half-pie between her melon breasts, and dove in after it, head first. It was clear they'd never make it to the pool. Never having done the deed in the kitchen, much less with Moon Pies as foreplay, they christened the Formica table with their renewed love.

"Well, my virile buck of a husband, I believe we got ourselves a marriage," Darlene gasped. "Now how 'bout you share that news we been celebratin'?"

He guffawed, "All in good time, all in good time." In a more serious tone, he added, "Ya know, I been pinchin' myself all day, things been goin' so well. But the best part is the two of us. I don't know what I did to deserve it, since I know I messed up plenty. I thank Jesus for bringing you back ta me. Seems ever since Mason moved on to the next world, you an' I got a fresh start."

An imperceptible shudder travelled through her at the mention of Mason's name. "Oh my, look at the time! We better make ourselves presentable before JJ and Teresa catch us in the buff!"

Darlene had only just thrown her clothes on when the doorbell rang for the second time that afternoon. "Fuckin' A! What are you, some kinda witch?" he hooted as he disappeared up the back stairs.

"Christian!" she cackled, hurriedly buttoning and zipping, running her fingers through her tousled hair.

❖

A couple of hours later, Christian, Darlene, and JJ were together, back in the kitchen. With the staff gone they were preparing dinner as a family, something they had never done before. Rooting around like the domestic strangers they were, they rummaged through pantry and fridge, hollering out when one of them discovered treasure—a can of beans and franks here, tins of corned beef hash there, all of which must have been there for the help. Upon seeing so many of his childhood favorites, Christian realized how much he missed *real* food. And when the lard hit the skillet and Darlene slung in the hash, the aroma of fatty pork transported Christian into hog heaven.

For the first time, JJ was witnessing his father and his mother as other children saw their parents. What should have been an ordinary weeknight dinner was extraordinary to him. As with all children, because he knew of nothing other than the family he had, the display in front of him was all the more unique and thrilling for its novelty.

Darlene broke several eggs into another sizzling skillet, singing all the while,

Jesus calls the children dear,
"Come to Me and never fear,
For I love the little children of the world;
I will take you by the hand, lead you to the better land,
For I love the little children of the world."
I am coming, Lord, to Thee, and Your soldier I will be,
For You love the little children of the world.
And Your cross I'll always bear, and for You I'll do
and dare,
For You love the little children of the world.

Keeping an eye on the food, she tossed in more lard in the quest for a crispy exterior. Popping JJ's beans 'n weenies into the microwave, she timed it all to hit the table piping hot at precisely the same moment. With sizzling sounds and fragrant smells jollying them along the boys ran about, hunting up plates and cutlery to set the table and filling glasses with syrupy sweet liquids.

It was a dinner so ordinary and intimate that Christian nearly wept. As they chattered away, excitedly interrupting each other, he was as surprised by how much JJ had to say as he was gripped by the sadness of how small of a role he had played in the boy's life. Truth be told, other than "Bible Hour," Christian had left JJ's upbringing entirely to Darlene and, sitting there with them tonight, he was awed by their closeness. Instead of the envy this observation would previously have caused, he thought about what it would be like to get to know this piece of his DNA. In perhaps the most human moment of John Christian Hillcox's life, he realized that what was happening in this room tonight was far more important than even today's phone call. Christian had achieved remarkable success in this lifetime. Funny how all it took was a simple dinner to make him see what really mattered.

❖

After dinner and clean-up, Christian, Darlene, and JJ set up the board for a rousing game of Genesis: The First Seven Days. Midway through Day Three, Christian went off to relieve himself and returned with the package that had arrived prior to their afternoon romp in the kitchen. Noting that it came from Pearsall, he slashed through the tape with his pocketknife. Darlene, distracted by Genesis, noticed neither the package nor the look of horror that spread over Christian's face when he looked inside.

A note, in Luke's raggedy, childlike scrawl, read:

Christian,
I figgered you might want these trinkets from your loving pappy.

Luke

Inside, coiled like a snake primed to strike, lay the well-worn instrument of Christian's torture: Mason's ancient, brown belt. Its leather crackled with age but the heavy silver buckle, the one Mason used to save for "special occasions," still rested at the end. If he looked closely enough, he knew he'd find stains of his own blood. It was difficult to breathe as he felt the long finger of evil rise up from the grave.

Beneath the belt, Christian shuddered to see the same small box that used to sit atop his father's dresser. With grave apprehension, he opened it for the second time in his life, knowing in his heart that nothing good could come of this. Despite the dread he imagined, what he saw inside was far, far worse. Incredulous, he picked up a small bottle of perfume, and before even opening the lid he knew it contained a scent as familiar to him as the woman in this room. It would be gardenia. The same gardenia that had perfumed his life from the day he and Darlene first met at Ina's Beauty Nook. For a split second, he hesitated, knowing he should look no further. For a monster lived inside this box. But he kept on, just as the dead man had known he would. And there, sitting upon a piece of red velvet, was the four and a half carat diamond Darlene had "lost." The one she had accused Consuelo of stealing.

Underneath the piece of velvet was a black lace garter, the initials DSH screaming up at him.

Darlene looked up and his face told her everything. He saw terror bloom in her eyes as it became clear to her that he finally knew the Oedipal depth of her deception. Covering her face with her hands, she began to wail.

Hands, the all-important hands. Hands, that had done double-time with the Devil, *Christian's* Devil. It was then that the words Luke had spoken on the day of Mason's funeral slammed into him. *That your boy? I declare, he favors his grand-daddy more'n he does you, don't ya think?*

Christian quickly did the math, calculating the months between Mason's visit and the birth of what he now knew to be his bastard son. Or rather he should say, his bastard brother. When he looked back at Darlene, he no longer saw her, no longer saw his wife. What he saw was the living, breathing incarnation of evil.

And he went after that evil with everything he had. He went after it with the rage, the hurt, the helpless hopelessness that had plagued him his entire life. Without thinking, Christian, a man possessed, reached for his father's belt, paying no heed to Darlene's cries.

"Christian, please," she begged, "You don't have to do this. Can't you see we've gotten past it? You don't have to let him continue to destroy us like he destroyed me. He *raped* me," she began to wail. "B'cause that's what he did. Raped me. There. Now you know," she continued to wail. "You can't punish me for what *he* did. But even as she pleaded he lifted the belt to strike her and when he struck he struck with fury. Looping round and round in his mind's eye was the image of his dirty, filthy father with his hands and mouth and organ all over and inside the woman he'd thought to be his angel, and Christian saw nothing. Nothing but the color red. The red of his rage mixed with the red of her blood.

JJ cowered in the corner, whimpering in terror as he watched his mother and father, so happy only moments before—two supposed people of God—dance their Satanic dance, and he knew there was nothing he could do.

37

Being Christian

September 10, 2001

HE BEAT DARLENE MERCILESSLY until, surprisingly, something in him made him pull back. Turning away, he slammed his hand into the glass window of the china cabinet, shattering it into a thousand pieces. Feeling no pain, he stared with wonder at his mangled, manicured hand.

Yes, you can tell a lot about a person by his hands. And Christian's hands spoke of strength and power, but most importantly, of restraint. He would not go down this genetic road again. If God had seen fit to send Mason to an early grave in order to advance Christian's mission on Earth, didn't that bind Christian to live up to His will? No, he would not allow the sins of the father to destroy his place in God's plan by turning himself into the common instrument of Darlene's physical death. Besides, death was too good for her. He would instead inflict a far more torturous, permanent, and deeply psychological death.

Call it Death by Shame, Death by Shun. Death by Blame, Death by Son.

Christian had already survived so much in his life—he would survive this too, and like Jesus, he would rise again.

Darlene lay still, her legs striped up and down with red, stinging welts from Mason's—no, Christian's—belt. JJ was at her side, a quivering mess. He managed to square his shoulders like a man and help her up. Christian's spittle flew across the room and landed upon the bastard's pudgy cheek as he roared the roar of a wounded animal.

"Get outta my sight, you father-fucking whore. An' take your filthy bastard son with you. *Leave my sight*—NOW!"

How he longed to kill her, to squeeze the life from her body, to watch the light in her eyes flicker and fade like the Mexican woman's had done so long ago. The difference was that this time, *this* one deserved it. But no, he wasn't about to let this father-fucking whore ruin him.

Because HE WAS CHRISTIAN. CHRISTIAN for a world that loved and needed him. And rather than be another headline, another pastor fallen from grace, he *chose* instead to play Judge and Jury. He, CHRISTIAN, would mete out her punishment as *he* saw fit. But without crossing the line of ruin.

Thoughts of revenge played a tune in his soul.

Banish the bastard, punish the whore.

Yes, that's what he would do. Send his brother-not-son to a place where Darlene could never find him, while keeping her close to him, always here—at his side. She would never leave. For if she did, he would tell the world what she had done to the good and beloved pastor, and there would be no place on Earth for her to hide. Such would be the living hell of her life.

Judge, jury, and jailer. For now, it would have to suffice.

Epilogue

One Year Later

HAVING ENJOYED TWO-AND-A-QUARTER centuries of invincibility, the nation had shed its communal virginity and, like Christian, was transformed. Soldiers trained for war, parents and lovers bid farewell and Christian subsisted on a daily brew of rage and deception.

Simply put, September 11, 2001 had saved Christian. Occurring when it did, only hours after learning the truth about Mason and Darlene, he chose to see the outrage as fit punishment from a just God. Additionally, the unprecedented act of jihad against a Christian America served to redirect his rage and searing pain. Not only did the horror of planes turned into bombs—bombs that struck at the very heart of American defense and capitalism—distract him from his own private hell, it set him immediately back on his self-affirming Rapture track. Underlying the national spectacle of the 24/7 media fear-a-thon was a Christian-style silver lining: The shock and awe of all that happened made the defense of Israel a clear military and political necessity. With Zion in mind, true Christians could rejoice at the speed of His coming. The great clash of civilizations had begun, enabling Christian to shunt September 10th as far back into his mind's cellar as the human psyche allowed.

To the onlooker it appeared that little about the pastor had changed. Questions about why JJ had been sent away were answered with curt explanations that the boy needed discipline. If Pastor Christian said JJ needed discipline, then he needed discipline.

But there had been an outward change in Darlene. While publicly she remained the doting wife, she did so as if on autopilot. She might have healed physically from last year's brutal beating, but the same could not be said for her soul. The ache of missing her son conflicted directly with the part of her that couldn't help but fear the inevitability of his "turning," and rather than confront such ambivalence, she let herself be emptied from the inside out. In ways not that different from the decline of Christian's mother, Darlene was headed off the rails. The simultaneous loss of her husband's favor and her role as a mother commingled with an inescapable sense of shame, plunging her into the places that presaged madness.

Away from the public eye, things were not quite right with Christian either. Dissemble and sublimate as he might, the old demons had resurfaced, and often at the oddest times. He had hoped that, in denying Darlene her son, in seeing her misery up close and on a daily basis, his thirst for revenge would be quenched. Instead, it was all he could do to stop himself from wrapping his hands around her neck and squeezing the life out of her. *Seems it always comes down to hands. Maybe though, it really comes down to murder.*

Except for Sunday mornings, Christian and Darlene lived separate lives. Free to stray, he did so with discretion, the ache in him never diminishing. Against all odds, he stayed away from pills, booze, and men—knowing full well that were he to slip again, this time all bets were off.

This year, with the first anniversary of September 11 falling on a Wednesday, Christian announced that Headship would commemorate the anniversary on the following Sunday. While most Americans had spent the past year in varying degrees of contemplation, 9/11 had fully liberated Christian to exploit his ingrained racism under biblical cover. Never-ending images of hate-filled radicalized Muslims blanketed the airwaves in a perpetual national discussion that sanctioned race-baiting and fear mongering not seen since the Japanese-American interment during World War II. Out of duty, he participated in the requisite pastoral summits—conferences that ran the gamut from spineless ass-kissing tripe like "Compassion and Forgiveness—Moving Forward As One" to the more meaningful seminars encouraging active engagement like "Why *They* Want to Destroy Us and How We Can Get Them First."

Long ago, at the beginning of his religious journey, the world was black and white. Devastated as he'd been by Darlene's Freudian betrayal, he'd somehow controlled his fury with the belief that the arc of his life still pointed toward Salvation and Resurrection. At least he *hoped* it did. He spent the early months after the "twin tragedies"—his and the nation's—engaged in virulent pronouncements about the danger Christian America now so clearly faced. But truth be told, the fact that he'd successfully bred no red heifer nor fathered a child—those were the "twin thoughts" that hovered over *him* in ways psychic as well as prophetic. Which was why, on the dual anniversary of the tragedies, he stepped onto the stage at Headship, outwardly belligerent yet inwardly drowning in uncertainty.

"Fellow Christians," he began from atop the Headship mount. "We gather today not only to mourn the two thousand, eight hundred and nineteen souls ripped so cruelly from this Earth at the hands of Islamic evil-doers one year ago, but also to talk about the grave risks we face, as Christians and as Americans, from this greatest of all conspiracies.

"More than thirteen hundred years ago, Mohammed *declared* himself the Prophet and Messenger of his *newly invented* God, Allah. Like charlatans before and yet to come, the mere presumption that any one *man* would dare to name himself *Prophet* is only the beginning of what I see as the most self-aggrandizing power play in history. After all, who *was* he, this common man, this A-rab? Born a lowly orphan, he was a man who in many ways was little different from our own new-age religion-maker, the Mormons' Joseph Smith. Both men, in granting themselves a kind of superhuman status, dared to profess into being a replacement for the one and only true God, Jehovah Lord.

"But religion cannot be created at will. Man cannot, on a whim, pluck a new god out of thin air and declare him into being. If he could, there'd be no limit to mythological gods and goddesses, nor even to Creation—to *anything* at all.

"Over the past year, a year of the most grievous mourning in America, you've undoubtedly witnessed the usual cast of liberal sissies bendin' over backwards to defend this, their latest 'cause.' This time their mantra goes, 'Islam is a religion of peace!' Well to these self-righteous defenders of evil, if you'll pardon my French, I say, PEACE, MY ASS! I ask you, where was the peace in sending jetliners into Wall Street and the Pentagon, the greatest symbols of American civilization and might?

"Fact is, Allah issued the first salvo in this *book*," slamming a fist down hard on the Koran that sat on the dais before him, "when he threatened, DEATH TO THE INFIDEL." With exaggerated disgust, he picked it up and read from it.

"Verily Allah has cursed the Unbelievers and has prepared for them a Blazing Fire to dwell in forever. No protector will they find, no savior. That Day their faces will be turned upside down in the Fire. They will say: 'Woe to us! We should have obeyed Allah and obeyed the Messenger!' 'Our Lord! Give them double torment and curse them with a very great Curse!'

"An' when Mohammed spoke of double torment you better believe he wasn't talkin' 'bout a walk in Central Park on a spring day. No-siree-bob. Even then, he was foreshadowin' showerin' death down upon us—spell that U-S—in ways more warlike and grievous than anything imaginable. Seems to me, all those millennia ago, the only thing this mortal man named Mohammed did was to *steal* from *us* the idea of *our* Rapture so's to turn it on its head, claimin' we *Christians* would be the ones to burn in Eternity. I'm sorry, but that's messed up. All of which leaves us with the question—ought we despair or ought we *rejoice* in what *Jesus* foretold about planes turned into bombs turned into heralds?

"As ever and always, the answer is found *here*," and he cast aside the Koran to pick up his well-worn Bible.

"*When you see these signs, lift up your head and rejoice. Your redemption draweth nigh.* Talk about foresight. To think our Lord and Savior, Jehovah God, saw September 11th comin' thousands of years ago. That, folks, is a GOD.

"Now I'm gonna talk straight here—no sugar coatin'. Islam is *not* a religion, an' you can take *that* to the bank. It's nothin' but a power grab atop a seismic cult atop a steaming pile a you-know-what. Last September, they thought we'd crumple with fear, after which they'd waltz on in an' take over our God-given land. Well, we showed 'em, didn't we?

"People, I know what I know an' what I know is that a year ago, Satan hisself—in the body of a man who goes by the name Osama bin Laden but who looks more like the Devil than the Devil himself—set up camp in a cave somewhere in Afghanistan. Believe you me, Mr. Bin Laden mighta been the one pulled the trigger on that black day, but it was none other than Lucifer himself that gave him the go-ahead. He said to his buddy, 'Osama my man—you been so kind as to let me take up residence in your mortal soul. How's about I return the favor an' help you destroy America—an' by that I mean those holier-than-thou Christ worshippers with their highfalutin American superiority?' Bin Laden, Osama, Hussein, Mohammed, Saddam—make no mistake. They're one an' the same—all of 'em agents of Satan.

"Today, there are more than 1.3 *billion* Muslims in the world. You heard me. 1.3 *billion*. Let's say jest ten percent of 'em—and I assure you, I'm low-ballin' it here—say ten percent have it in their DNA to take out Christianity an' all that's American, that alone means we're up against an army of 130 million jihadists—that's before our boots even hit the ground." By now, Christian was frenetically pacing the stage when, of a sudden, he stopped cold to look hard at the congregation. "Do you remember, what our Lord and Savior says in Matthew twenty-four? *When you see all these things, know that it is near—at the doors!*

"Did you hear that ? I hope so because what I'm sayin' is that the heathens are *at our doors*—an army 130 million strong *at our doors*. An army what plans to make Shariah the law of *our* land. Steal a loaf a bread? Off with your hand. Let your wife walk down the street not wearin' full-combat burkha, you might as well send out invitations to the stoning.

"An' then there's Israel." He paused for emphasis. "You been with me long enough to know how an' why Israel is *critical* to our—to God's—plan. Critical. An' you also know full well that the enemy'll do whatever it takes to obliterate *our* holy land, the very land on which the Second Temple *must* be resurrected— the land where *our* Prince of Peace will return astride his magnificent white stallion. Well, the truth is, as much as we *love* Israel, that's how intent *they* are on *destroyin'* it. If that means nukin' it outta existence, you better believe they'll do it.

"Which is why, last September 11th, you didn't find me weepin' an' wringin' my hands. Those a you saw me, saw a man who REJOICED!" A certain discomfort from below reached him, serving only to further ramp up his rhetoric. "What? You think that's not a Christian thing ta say ? Well, I *beg to differ.* On the contrary—to rejoice at biblical prophecy—to see His word play itself out—why that's the most Christian thing a man can do. When those A-rabs took it upon themselves to turn planes into missiles, I saw *opportunity.* I saw *signs.* An' I REJOICED!

"Fellow Christians, the greatest show on Earth was set in motion one year ago. A lot has happened since then and if you've been smart, you realize it's time for true believers ta pack our bags, gather up our mamas an' our papas an' all our lil children, bless their souls, an' REJOICE!

"Because while the Antichrist and his New World Order are revelin' in our nation's pain, while they lick away at their bearded chops, WE, who follow the *only* Lord, Jehovah God, *we're* the ones who'll be ready. If you don't happen to be in the camp what thinks bin Laden's the Antichrist, why there are plenty a others. How about Ak-madinejad over there in I-ran plottin' away for Zion's destruction? If you don't think it's either a them two, who knows, you might be right. Because we can't know for sure. For all we know, it could be one a our own here in these dis-U-nited States. Could be some as yet unheard-of, glad-handing politician, one who'll appear from outta the blue with promises to save the world. 'THE ONE,' they'll call him. To him I say, whoever YOU are, we're ready. We know you're comin' an' I hate to tell you but, *we're* the ones in charge."

It was then that the glaring sounds of dissonance clanged loudly in Christian's head, a bell that had been sounding with increasing regularity over the past year. Never an inward thinker, he didn't stop to examine the increasing disconnect between faith and reality that had broken through from time to time during the past year. Willing himself to subdue the turmoil that ravaged him today on the pulpit, he continued on.

"If Islam is the religion of peace the liberal sissies say it is, then why is all we hear 'bout is their fatwas," practically spitting out the word, "their lust for turnin' men into martyrs? An' every single day our limp-wristed politicians dally, the jihadists are busy fillin' the heads of tens of millions of their young, seducin' 'em with promises of martyrdom in an Eternity replete with seventy-two eager virgins."

Christian's sermons had always been filled with darkness, but this one went far beyond. Coincidentally, while preparing, he had uncovered an uncomfortable truth about Mohammed that turned his hatred for the false prophet into something much more personal. Evil is evil, no matter what form it takes, and, of all men, he knew it didn't always come in the body of Satan. Sometimes it came in the form of one's own father. Which is why, unbeknownst to everyone but himself, John Christian Hillcox set to baring his soul before a national television audience.

"I'm gonna share with you a little known fact. You know how we're hearin' all the time that the Muslims hate us for our freedom, *our* lack of morals? Well, listen to this. In studyin' the great Mohammed, I learned that not only did he satisfy his unnatural carnal urges and perversities with *thirteen* wives, but that he also fornicated with any slave girl that tickled his fancy. Far, far worse, though" and his voice darkened noticeably, "far more craven—in fact, in what I consider to be the sin of all sins—this supposed prophet betrayed his *own* son in the most despicable and unforgiveable of ways. He fornicated with the boy's wife. You heard me—the holy man lay with his own daughter-in-law. His son's wife."

Christian's words and the bile with which he'd delivered them shimmered dangerously in the air. Some squirmed in their seats, unsure of where to look or what to do with the vitriol coming from this seemingly out of context segue, while others, as always mesmerized by their pastor, reflected a mirror image of his outrage.

Seated behind him on the pulpit, Darlene's face morphed into a portrait of pain.

As quickly as Christian had broached the only subject that really mattered to him, he backed away to the safer land of bile and vitriol in which he felt at home. By this time he was practically howling. "They say Muslims want peace? I say, SHOW ME THE MONEY!" He held up the Koran again and spat out: "*I will cast terror into the hearts of those who disbelieve. Therefore strike off their heads and strike off every fingertip of them.*

"Does *that* sound like PEACE to *you*?"

The audience, at least those who were still with him, let out a deafening roar.

"Fellow warriors, lest you be deceived by the faggot-loving lefty Commies, hear me now—Islam is *not* now, nor will it *ever* be, a religion of peace. It *is* a demonic warrior cult with plans to overrun the world. America has so far chosen to keep its head in the sand about the fact that Islam plans nothing less than WORLD DOMINION. Like I said, while our pansy-faced politicians play footsie with their toothless laws an' limp-wristed Geneva Conventions, Muslim warriors are massing worldwide with the singular goal of establishing an international caliphate.

"An' you were worried that the Yids were the ones out to rule the world? Folks, you ain't seen nothin' yet.

"MAKE NO MISTAKE—ARMAGEDDON IS UPON US. Whoever pulls the trigger first determines who's goin' DOWN. It's that simple. Who'll it be? Will we let *them* take over our land, or do *we* have the balls to fight for JESUS?"

The roar in the room built to a sudden and satisfying crescendo as the congregation came back together, their cries of hatred filling the space with the force of a lynch mob.

"JEE-SUS! JEE-SUS! JEE-SUS!"

When the din died down he resumed. "I've a dear friend—a man who preaches the Word a little west a here—who says it best: 'One of America's *foundin'* principles was to see the very face of Islam destroyed.' So I say, let's destroy it! September 11, 2001 was a generational call-to-arms that WE CAN NO LONGER IGNORE! I, for one, WILL NOT IGNORE this historic call to battle. How 'bout you?" he bellowed. "WILL YOU FIGHT FOR JESUS?"

The crowd was in a frenzy. "YES WE WILL! YES WE WILL!" Jumping up and down, they thrust their arms to the sky in a gesture resembling a Nazi salute, while some muttered crazily in tongues, their eyes rolling madly round in their sockets.

"WORLD WAR THREE HAS BEGUN an' this is the one, folks—the big kahuna—the one I been preachin' on all these years. We stand today at an historic crossroads, you an' I, an' I say to one an' all," looking directly at the SWBN cameras, "YOU'RE EITHER WITH JESUS, OR YOU'RE AGIN HIM."

At the top of their lungs, the crowd below chanted, "JEE-SUS! JEE-SUS! JEE-SUS!"

He knew it had been a rip-roaringly good sermon—passionate, patriotic, and as always, permeated with just the right dose of fear. Solid stuff. Absolutes. Since starting out as a pastor to lost souls, Christian had inhabited a world of absolutes, and no matter how far he'd strayed those absolutes had always been there to pull him back in. That is, until the night he'd learned the genesis of his "son." The night the desire to commit that dodgy old Sixth Commandment returned in full force to muddy the waters of right and wrong. Slave to ambition that he'd become, he'd exhibited an almost super-human control, forcing his blood to cool, pushing the animal in him aside, always certain that faith would sustain. And in the times when uncertainty reared its ugly, heretical head, he'd resigned himself to playing the role of Believer—just as Darlene had done, yea these many, many years—until faith returned to reclaim him.

In that moment, he looked over at her, his long-ago, once upon a time savior, and he couldn't help but regret the ways in which it had all gone so wrong. Here he was, a man in the prime of his life and power, yet a man without love and, inwardly, without certainty. Adrift on the pulpit, before a cast of thousands, he no longer felt sure of who he was or what he should do.

Down below, the crowd continued its furious gyrations, their hatred mounting into a fury he no longer had the power to stop. He had unleashed a monster, all right, and having done so, knew there was no turning back.

Just then, the words of Jesus on the cross exploded in his head.

My God, My God, why have you forsaken me?

Soundlessly, Christian turned and walked off the stage.

The End

About the Author

K. C. BOYD, grew up in Ohio back in the day when religion was a personal thing. Decades later, Boyd awakened to a world where a growing number of radical right-wing Christians were quietly praying for the world to end so that Jesus Christ would return.

After the 2004 election demonstrated too much acceptance for this extreme Christian worldview among the right-wing, Boyd embarked on a strange and often frightening exploration of the far-right; attending evangelical services and conferences across the United States. Concerned about the increasing danger from mixing politics with end-times Christianity, she realized it was time to expose what she saw using fiction to convey her warnings. The result, born of close observation of key personalities, is *Being Christian*.

www.ingramcontent.com/pod-product-compliance
Lightning Source LLC
Chambersburg PA
CBHW031139020426
42333CB00013B/443